Pocket Guide to

Dogs

Pocket Guide to

Dogs

ANDERSON
MERCHANDISERS

A QUANTUM BOOK

Published by Anderson Merchandisers
P.O. Box 32270 79120
421 S.E. 34th Avenue
Amarillo, TX 79103
www.amerch.com

ISBN: 978-1-59027-131-5

This book was produced by
Quantum Publishing Ltd
6 Blundell Street
London N7 9BH

QUMPGTD

Printed in Singapore by
Star Standard Industries (Pte) Ltd

PICTURE CREDITS
Cover
Getty Images: front cover

Insides
iStockphoto.com: Page 6/jimkruger; Page 7, bottom/majorosl; Page 81/
HannamariaH; Page 83/LeggNet; Page 96/Dixi_; Page 97/Juanmonino; Page 100/
Thomas_EyeDesign; Page 101/Crazace2006; Page 134/jtyler; Page 134, bottom/
jtyler; Page 135/jeffdalt; Page 162, top/PK-Photos; Page 162, centre/Gordo25;
Page 162, bottom/renaschild; Page 163/silverlining56; Page 166, top/kkgas;
Page 166, bottom/ Thomas_EyeDesign; Page 167, top/meltonmedia; Page 167,
bottom/ Thomas_EyeDesign

All other images are the copyright of Quarto Publishing PLC.

Every effort has been made to trace the copyright holders of images that
feature in this book. The publisher would welcome any omissions being
brought to their attention.

CONTENTS

INTRODUCTION

ABOVE Of the nearly 40 races of wolf recognized around the world, four — *Canis lycaon, Canis lupus, Canis pallipes* and *Canis lupus chanco* are thought to be the most likely ancestors of the domestic dog.

Human contact with dogs as companion animals began at least 12,000 years ago. Scientific studies suggest that all of today's breeds have descended from gray wolves (*Canis lupus*), and bearing in mind that this species of wolf was formerly the most widely distributed of all mammals in the northern hemisphere, it seems likely that domestication began in several places, rather than at one single locality.

These early ancestors of today's dogs were probably used for herding purposes once it was realized that they could be trained for this task. In appearance, they would certainly have been similar to the wolf but, as a result of selective breeding, differences in size soon became apparent. The gray wolf itself varies greatly in size across its wide range. Large individuals from Alaska may weigh 177 lb (80 kg), whereas the race that lives in the Asiatic steppes can be as small as 27 lb (12 kg).

By 9,000 years ago, in what is now the United States of America, a clear divergence in the size of dogs was already evident. Remains uncovered in the Beaverhead Mountains of eastern-central Idaho have revealed both a dog similar in size to today's retrievers, and a smaller version, which probably resembled a Beagle.

This trend was to continue, and as society became more stable, so dogs of different sizes were developed for specific purposes. The larger forms were used as guardians of property, while other, smaller types continued in their traditional role of herding livestock. In the Orient these distinctions arose at an early stage in Tibet. Ultimately, the descendants of these dogs, such as the Tibetan Mastiff and Tibetan Spaniel, have become known in the West within the last century or so, although they have a much older ancestry, possibly dating back a thousand years or more.

The Development of the Pure-Bred Dog

Localized forms obviously tended to evolve into dogs of recognizable type, although they were not breeds in the sense that we understand the term today. These dogs were bred for particular purposes rather than to conform as closely as possible to a prescribed ideal form in terms of their appearance, as pure-bred dogs are today. Interest in this field arose largely during Victorian times, when "fancying", or the selective breeding of livestock for particular features, became highly fashionable. This was coupled with the rise of dog shows, where the various breeds were paraded and judged, with prizes being given to the winners in each category.

The most famous dog show in the world, organized by Charles Cruft, began in 1890. Originally, this had started as a show for the terrier breeds, which were extremely popular in Victorian England, but soon it began to cater to other breeds as well. Indeed, Queen Victoria herself entered some of her Pomeranians in 1891, and this royal link with dogs has continued right through to the present day.

The foundation of the Kennel Club in Great Britain, which became the governing body in the canine world, took place in 1873. This was to prove the major influence in the development of pure-bred dogs: from its inception, it began to establish stud books for the various breeds. The Kennel Club was also instrumental in establishing the standards against which the various breeds are judged. Once the Kennel Club had defined the required characteristics of the different breeds, it became possible for breeders to assess their dogs against the "ideal" for their breed, as laid down in the standards.

Since those early years, various modifications to the individual standards have been made, and dog breeding has become much more international. As a result, many new breeds have become available, and the Kennel Club has helped to nurture their development in Britain, in conjunction with the breed societies and the breeders themselves .

The influence of the Kennel Club has spread far and wide. In the United States, the American Kennel Club was established during 1884, on similar lines to its British equivalent, and a Canadian counterpart was set up four years later. Today, similar organizations are to be found in many countries throughout the world where dog showing is popular.

TOP LEFT Obedience trials at Cruft's.

BELOW Judges assess dogs on a variety of criteria, including proportions, condition, and coloration.

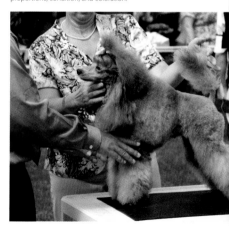

CHOOSING A BREED

During recent years, there has been growing concern about the temperament of some of the breeds, with Rottweilers in particular gaining a bad reputation in the media for their ferocity. When selecting a pure-bred dog, you must always consider its ancestry. Inherited traits established over many generations will still influence the behavior of the breed today. The Rottweiler has a long history as a brave and powerful guard dog, and has obviously retained some potentially aggressive traits within its personality.

Aside from providing us with companionship, dogs are still used for various working purposes. The Rottweiler is sometimes employed as a police dog, emphasizing the responsive and intelligent side of its nature. Other dogs, bred primarily for hunting purposes, are much harder to train successfully. Hounds such as the Afghan will prove far less amenable in this regard when compared to other sporting dogs, such as members of the retriever group. Throughout their existence, the retriever breeds have worked closely alongside their owners. It is no coincidence that while fulfilling their traditional role as gundogs, retrievers are also now used as guide dogs for the blind and for people who are hard of hearing. They can also be trained successfully to detect drugs and explosives.

Working sheepdogs can still be found throughout the world and they make popular companions, although these dogs may sometimes become rather bored and frustrated in urban surroundings. It is important to consider the individual needs of the breed, together with your own personal surroundings, before making any decision about obtaining a dog.

ABOVE LEFT Aggression can be a serious problem with powerful guard dogs like the Rottweiler, so it is essential that such a breed be trained responsibly from the start.

BELOW Afghans require considerable exercise, but few breeds can rival them for elegance and individuality.

While it is obvious that a large dog requires more space, and will prove more costly to feed than a smaller breed, other factors, such as the dog's temperament and ease of training are likely to be more relevant to the relationship between dog and owner. Other factors to consider when choosing a breed are the coat care required — the smooth-coated breeds such as the Grayhound being the least demanding in this regard — and, possibly, its life-span. As a rough guide, the large breeds, may live for less than a decade, whereas many of the smaller dogs will remain active well into their teens.

The cost of a pedigree dog is influenced by several factors. The relative scarcity of a breed will have a direct impact on its price, as under these circumstances demand will probably outstrip supply. The quality of both the bloodline, measured in terms of show performance, and the potential of the individual puppies themselves will also influence the price asked by the breeder. If you are looking simply for a pet dog, the cost should be correspondingly lower.

Breeders invariably have some surplus puppies that, possibly because of faults, will not do well in the show ring. Such dogs will invariably settle down and give great pleasure as pets, but beware of any individuals with a known physical deformity.

ABOVE Poodle puppies at 2 days old.

These could prove a source of worry, not to mention veterinary expense, in later life.

Although it is claimed that cross-bred puppies are healthier than their pure-bred counterparts, there is no real truth in this assertion. They are equally susceptible to diseases such as distemper and the various parasites that may afflict dogs. There is possibly a greater risk, however, that pure-bred dogs may suffer from certain congenital weaknesses such as hip dysplasia (HD) or progressive retinal atrophy (PRA). Responsible breeders will have their breeding stock screened for these particular conditions.

BELOW Guide dogs for the blind, or 'seeing eyes' as they are called in the United States, must rank as the most valuable group of trained dogs.

CHOOSING AN INDIVIDUAL DOG

ABOVE Many infectious diseases may cause severe dehydration owing to persistent vomiting and diarrhea. To replace the fluid an intravenous drip is required.

Having decided on a particular breed, you can then track down puppies without too much difficulty in most cases. Your veterinarian may be able to suggest a breeder within your locality, and there are also directories which list breeders of pedigree dogs, often on a regional basis. The various dog magazines and newspapers may also be a useful source of reference. It will obviously make life easier if you obtain your puppy as close to home as possible, although, particularly if you are looking for a potential show dog, you may want to see several litters before taking any decision, and this may entail traveling further afield. In the United States especially, a good range of pedigree puppies are available from pet stores, although you will obviously not have the advantage of seeing their parents or home surroundings if you buy from such a source.

BELOW A careful veterinary examination is essential before vaccinating a young puppy.

It is obviously vital to select a healthy puppy, and if you are at all concerned, especially when considering a puppy in a pet store, it would be best to delay your purchase. Puppies are normally lively, but remember that they will sleep for longer than adult dogs. Always watch them running about, as this will reveal any trace of lameness. The puppy's skin should feel quite loose when you handle it, and, over all, it ought to be relatively plump.

There should be no trace of either fleas or lice on the coat. If the pup is distinctly pot-bellied, this tends to be indicative of a heavy burden of intestinal parasites. When you are feeling around in this area, locate the remains of the umbilicus, in the mid-line of the body. In a few cases, a hernia may have occurred during the birth process, creating a swelling that might need to be corrected by surgery later.

ABOVE A Cavalier King Charles Spaniel bitch suckles her three puppies.

The puppy's motions should appear firm, although occasionally, following deworming, an outbreak of diarrhea may result. Even so, view any puppies with diarrhea cautiously, as this could be evidence of a more serious affliction. In any event, always make an appointment to take a newly acquired puppy to a veterinarian at an early opportunity, both for a health check and to discuss the necessary schedule of vaccinations. You must also sort out the paperwork regarding the transfer of ownership of the puppy to you, which will mean notifying the registration authority in the country concerned. The breeder should be able to advise you if you have any doubts about this procedure.

DOGS:
FROM THE WILD

The domestic dog still displays many of the behavioral traits of its ancestor, the gray wolf, in spite of a domestication process that occurred over many thousands of years. It is ironic that since dogs have become popular as household companions as well as working animals, the gray wolf itself has been eliminated from much of its former range by human persecution. The adaptability of wild canids is aptly demonstrated by the red fox, which is now commonly found living in cities, not just in the northern hemisphere, but also in Australia, where it has been introduced.

WILD COUSINS

Although, in some cases, the appearance of the domestic dog has diverged significantly from that of its ancestor, the gray wolf, all dogs still retain many features — both anatomical and behavioral — in common with their wild relatives. There are thirty-three different species grouped in their family, Canidae, ranging from the far north down to the tip of South America. The only inhabited continent without a native population of wild dogs is Australia. The red fox was introduced there in the mid-eighteenth century, while the dingo was brought to Australia by early human settlers.

Arctic fox (*Alopex lagopus*)
Circumpolar Ranging over the frozen north, the Arctic fox wanders from the former Soviet Union to Alaska. It is well adapted to survive in this terrain, with hair on the soles of its feet as protection against frostbite. Its ears are small for the same reason, while its coat is thick, providing insulation against the cold. There are two different color forms of the Arctic fox. Some are pure white, whereas others have blue fur with a grayish tinge. In summer these two forms become brownish and a dark chocolate shade respectively, which gives better camouflage. Rodents, especially lemmings, feature in their diet, but Arctic foxes will scavenge and even eat berries.

Coyote (*Canis latrans*)
North and Central America. There is a wide range in size among these wild dogs. Coyotes from northern areas, weighing up to 75 lb (34 kg), may be three times heavier than those at the southern end of their range, in Mexico. Its name comes from the Aztec word coyotl, meaning "barking dog." Smaller and more adaptable than wolves, the coyote has expanded its range from the western plains of North America, as the wolf population has declined in spite of heavy persecution from farmers. The coyote feeds on rabbits, carrion and rodents, as well as on lambs and goats.

Gray wolf (*Canis lupus*)
North America, Europe and Asia. The largest member of the family, the gray wolf used to range across most of the northern hemisphere. Today its distribution has been greatly reduced by human persecution and increasing urbanization. Living in packs, this wolf needs large areas where it can hunt prey such as deer. Recently, more enlightened attitudes have led to this wolf being successfully reintroduced to areas where it had been eliminated.

Red wolf (*Canis rufus*)
North America. Saved from extinction by a captive breeding program, the future of the red wolf is still uncertain. It used to occur widely through the southeastern United States, from central Texas to Florida. Loss of habitat and hunting pressures added to its decline. The first captive-bred red wolves were released into the wild in 1988, eight years after the species had vanished, and some have bred there successfully. Hybridization with the coyote, which has colonized the former territory of the red wolf, remains an on-going threat.

NEW WORLD CANIDS

The majority of wild canids are found in the Americas, but there is a clear split in their distribution here. The range of those found in the north, such as the coyotes, does not extend into South America. Smaller foxes are predominant on the southern continent. They are often described as zorros.

1 Red wolf
2 Coyote
3 Maned wolf
4 Gray fox
5 Swift fox
6 Culpeo
7 Gray Zorro
8 Crab-eating Zorro
9 Small-eared Zorro
10 Island gray fox
11 Hoary Zorro
12 Bush dog
13 Sechuran zorro
14 Azara's zorro

Gray fox *(Urocyon cinereoargenteus)*
North, Central and South America
Also known as the tree-climbing fox, this species with its short legs, is an agile climber, unlike other wild dogs. The dens of the gray fox can be located in trees as high as 30 ft (9 m), although this fox may prefer to live underground, especially in the northern part of its range, which extends up to the Canadian border. Its diet varies from small mammals and birds to invertebrates and fruit. The young are born with black coats.

Island gray fox *(Urocyon littoralis)*
North America
This fox is confined to six of the eight Channel Islands found off the coast of southern California. Similar in appearance to the gray fox, it has descended from the same ancestral stock. The island gray fox is smaller than its mainland relative and distinguishable by a shorter tail.

Swift fox *(Vulpes velox)*
North America
Occurring in the western areas of the United States, the swift fox has been recently reintroduced in Canada, where it had become extinct. Poisoned baits left for coyotes have been a major cause in its decline. Coyotes will also kill this fox, making it vulnerable in areas where coyote numbers remain largely unchecked.

Red fox *(Vulpes vulpes)*
North America, Europe, Africa and Asia
More adaptable than the gray wolf, the red fox has spread over a wider area in recent years. It is now a common sight in cities, where it has adapted to living by scavenging in garbage bags and on the streets for food, as well as hunting birds and rodents. Its distribution in Africa is presently restricted to northern areas. Red foxes taken from Europe to Australia for fox-hunting from 1845 onward have now overrun that continent. There they benefitted from the introduction of rabbits.

Golden jackal *(Canis aureus)*
Africa, Europe and Asia
This jackal occurs right across northern Africa and the Middle East, with its Asiatic range currently extending eastward to Thailand. Its range also extends further north than that of other jackals, into southeastern parts of Europe. It has a reputation for scavenging, but will also hunt, depending on the availability of prey. In Israel, snakes are hunted, as was shown after a poisoning campaign led to a decline in the number of jackals but an increase in snakebites among the people in these areas.

Side-striped jackal *(Canis adustus)*
Africa
This species occurs in the tropical areas of Africa, typically in forested areas. It has distinctive lines of pale hairs running down each side of its body, and a stronger, more powerful muzzle than other jackals. In agricultural areas it often steals vegetables, and feeds on carrion and rodents. This jackal is hunted in some areas for its body parts — the skin and claws are reputed to ward off evil spirits.

Black-backed jackal *(Canis mesomelas)*
Africa
There are two populations of this jackal. The southern group ranges across Africa from Angola and Zimbabwe to the Cape, and the northern is centered on East Africa. They are also known as the silver-backed jackal, because of the coloration. The young are grayish in color, acquiring their adult coloration after three months.

Ethiopian jackal *(Canis simensis)*
Africa
Also known as the Simien fox, this rare species is mainly confined to the Balé Mountains National Park in Ethiopia. Population estimates suggest there are

AFRICAN CANIDS
While the majority of the African species are solitary by nature, the African wild dog lives in packs. It is therefore a formidable hunter, compared with most other canids which depend on smaller quarry such as rodents as a major part of their diet.

1 Black-backed jackal
2 African hunting dog
3 Cape fox
4 Side-striped jackal
5 Pale fox
6 Ethiopian jackal
7 Bat-eared fox
8 Fennec fox

around 700 of them living there. It often proves quite tame, remaining as close as 10 ft (3 m) to people, making it vulnerable to hunters.

African hunting dog (*Lycaon pictus*)
Africa
Their distribution has greatly reduced, for reasons similar to those of the gray wolf. Both live in packs and hunt large prey, including wildebeast. The size of the pack has also fallen — today, groups of more than thirty are rare, while formerly, groups of a hundred or more were common. The African hunting dog packs comprise predominantly of males.

Cape fox (*Vulpes chama*)
Africa
Confined to the southern part of the African continent, this is the only Vulpes species found south of the equator. The Cape fox inhabits open areas of country and hides during the day. It frequents arid areas and hunts a variety of small prey, plants and berries. Solitary by nature, this fox also scavenges on

human refuse and has been blamed for killing lambs, although it is more likely to feed on carcasses.

Fennec fox (*Fennecus zerda*)
Africa
This species is the smallest of all the wild dogs, being roughly the size of a small lapdog and weighing just 2-3 lb (1-1.5 kg). Large ears help the fennec fox locate its prey, which consists mainly of rodents. But this fox can also kill creatures larger than itself, such as rabbits. The fennec fox lives in an underground den, where it retreats in the heat. It communicates by barking, and a sound similar to purring.

Pale fox (*Vulpes pallida*)
Africa
Also known as the African sand fox, this species is found in a broad band across northern Africa, in the Sahel region bordering the Sahara Desert. It is heavier than the fennec fox, weighing as much as 6 lb (3 kg) and measuring 10 in (25 cm) at the shoulder. Coloration varies from pale red to sandy buff.

Rüppell's fox *(Vulpes rueppelli)*
Africa, Middle East and Asia
This fox occurs further north than the pale fox. They are similar in size, but Rüppell's fox has larger ears, while coloration ranges from buff to grayish shades.

Blanford's fox *(Vulpes cana)*
Middle East and Asia
The range of Blanford's fox is now greater than previously thought and may extend into parts of the Middle East. This fox has a slender snout, suggesting that insects and fruit feature in its diet. It has been recorded eating fruit and also hunting small rodents.

Bat-eared fox *(Otocyon megalotis)*
Africa
There are two distinctive populations of this fox, located in eastern and southern Africa. It has large ears, with black tips, which is why it is also known as the black-eared fox. It is primarily insectivorous.

Bengal fox *(Vulpes bengalensis)*
Asia
This fox is distributed across the Indian subcontinent, more commonly in open countryside. Pairs appear to live together for most of the year, but may hunt separately. The Bengal fox lives in a den, which may take the form of either a simple tunnel or a complex network of interconnecting chambers.

Corsac fox *(Vulpes corsac)*
Asia
Present in central Asia, this fox lives at relatively high densities, occupying neighboring burrows, hence the description "corsac cities." Heavily hunted for fur, it has become scarce in some areas. Plowing has also lead to its decline, destroying traditional den sites.

Tibetan fox *(Vulpes ferrilata)*
Asia
Confined to Tibet and nearby areas, this fox occurs at high altitudes, where it seeks shelter among piles of boulders, or large rocks. The Tibetan fox has a long snout and powerful teeth, indicating that it feeds mainly on rodents. A dense coat and small ears helps provide protection from the cold. It is trapped for its pelt, which is used to make hats.

Dhole *(Cuon alpinus)*
Asia
Its remains suggest that groups existed in Europe. Today it ranges eastward from India as far as China

EURASIAN CANIDS
These include species such as the Arctic fox which have a distribution extending literally around the world, in northern latitudes. Highly opportunistic by nature, these canids are equipped to survive in harsh environments.

1 Corsac fox
2 Tibetan fox
3 Dhole
4 Bengal fox

and south to Java. Dholes live in packs of a dozen or more. Outside the breeding season, packs may form larger units of a hundred or more, described as "clans." This wild dog hunts large prey, including deer. It communicates by howling whistles.

Maned wolf *(Chrysocyon brachyurus)*
South America

This species is more closely related to foxes. The maned wolf stands 29 in (76 cm) high, which enables it to see for a long way in the grassland areas. Birds are a main part of its diet, with the wolf's speed and agility helping it to catch such quarry. Rodents and fruit are also eaten.

Culpeo *(Dusicyon culpaeus)*
South America

This fox occurs along South America, adjoining the western seaboard. It is the largest member of the genus. It will eat lambs, but feeds mainly on rodents and rabbits.

Crab-eating zorro *(Cerdocyon thous)*
South America

The Spanish word zorro is used for many foxes from this continent. The crab-eating zorro has a wide range, most common in Bolivia, Paraguay, Uruguay and Argentina. It eats land crabsand fruit

Azara's zorro *(Dusicyon gymnocercus)*
South America

This species occurs in a wide range of habitats. It has a solitary lifestyle, preying on small animals and birds. It displays great fear of people, often reacting by freezing, in the hope of escaping detection.

Gray zorro *(Dusicyon griseus)*
South America

This species is mainly gray, and is hunted for its fur. The gray zorro is small, weighing little more than 9 lb (4 kg). It ranges down to the tip of the continent.

Small-eared zorro *(Dusicyon microtis)*
South America

One of the most mysterious members of the genus, this small-eared zorro lives in ares of the Amazon Basin. It is around 14 in (35 cm) at the shoulder and weighs around 22 lb (10 kg). This zorro is said to be mainly nocturnal and omnivorous in its diet.

Hoary zorro *(Dusicyon vetulus)*
South America

The hoary zorro inhabits the southwestern region of Brazil, where it hunts in grassland and lightly wooded areas. It eats rodents as well as invertebrates. The young are born in underground dens, with females often taking over tunnels made by armadillos.

Sechuran zorro *(Dusicyon sechurae)*
South America

Occuring in southern Ecuador and the adjacent region of northern Peru, this fox is named after the Sechura Desert. It is the smallest of all the Dusicyon species. It scavenges along the shoreline, but has a varied diet, forced to survive on seed pods when other food is unavailable. It tends to be nocturnal.

Bush dog *(Speothos venaticus)*
Central and South America

Ranging from Panama to South America, the bush dog looks like an otter, with a short tail and underparts darker than the rest of its body. It is highly aquatic, and hunts rodents, such as the capybara.

Raccoon dog *(Nyctereutes procyonoides)*
Europe and Asia

This species inhabits eastern Asia, but was released in several parts of the former Soviet Union, hoping they could then be hunted for fur. It has since spread in Europe, extending eastward across Germany into France. The raccoon dog tends to be nocturnal, which, combined with the fact that it does not bark, helps to conceal its whereabouts.

WILD WOLF TO DOMESTIC DOG
Relationships today

It is not just coincidence that most people prefer to choose a puppy rather than an older dog when they are seeking a pet. Apart from looking cute, a puppy is likely to be more adaptable and so should settle more readily into a new home. Older dogs often prove to be shyer, and there may be problems associated with them which are not obvious at first, such as aggressive behavior.

It is not just coincidence that most people prefer to choose a puppy rather than an older dog when they are seeking a pet. Apart from looking cute, a puppy is likely to be more adaptable and so should settle more readily into a new home. Older dogs often prove to be shyer, and there may be problems associated with them which are not obvious at first, such as aggressive behavior.

It is also usually possible to introduce a puppy into a home where there is already an older dog, whereas a mature dog could be a liability in such surroundings. An established dog is likely to display far less resentment toward a puppy than to a dog which is more than a year old. Having a much younger companion can help give an older dog a new lease of life. It also means that, when the time comes to part with the elderly pet, the experience may not prove so traumatic for the household in general.

All these aspects of canine behavior can be related back to the social structure which exists in

ABOVE A young puppy will soon come to accept the family as its pack, and it is this ability to transfer their loyalty from other pack members to people which has led to dogs becoming such popular pets.

wolf packs in respect of the cubs. Cubs feature at the bottom of the regular hierarchical structure and are submissive in their behavior to other pack members. In turn, older wolves of both sexes treat cubs in a friendly manner.

Wolf cubs which have been reared in the company of humans lack the shyness and reserve that is associated with older individuals, in the same way that, in new surroundings, puppies are more friendly toward people than adult dogs are.

The level of aggression between the cubs in a pack does start to increase as they grow up,

Practical Pointer

When you are seeking to have a puppy as a pet, be sure to choose one that has been reared in domestic surroundings. It will be much more accustomed to human company, and to living in a home.

A young puppy will soon come to accept the family as its pack, and it is this ability to transfer their loyalty from other pack members to people which has led to dogs becoming such popular pets.

especially if food is in short supply, such as during the winter months. It is not necessarily matter of dominance. At this time, fighting can be linked very closely with feeding behavior. However, when aggressive encounters are geared to obtaining sufficient food from a kill, rather than to establishing a higher position in the social rank of the pack, they quickly pass.

In domestic surroundings, when conflicts do arise, they are usually associated with food, and the dogs should therefore be fed separately to eliminate the risk of any fighting.

ABOVE Wolf cubs show the same playful side to their natures as puppies, but they are much more wary than domesticated puppies of human contact.

Practical Pointer

Always try to find out as much as possible about the background of any adult dog that you are thinking of acquiring, particularly if it is a rescued animal. It could have been rejected by its previous owners because of some serious behavioral problems, or it could have become withdrawn as a result of being neglected.

Why are there domestic dogs?

The first wolves that were domesticated would have been even more unpredictable in terms of their temperament than today's hybrid dog. They would also have been much shyer. At first, there was almost certainly only a very loose association between them and the people who they lived alongside. Some orphan wolf cubs may have been reared and remained in the vicinity of a human settlement. They probably started to join in with hunting expeditions and so a routine was established, although it would not have been possible to train them in the same way as today's dogs.

These wolves would probably have bred and remained with the family group. Eventually they would have become tamer and more trainable. The

way in which they began to adapt their hunting skills, working alongside the tribes people to achieve kills, would have ensured they were valued, even by tribal elders.

The ability of the wolves to detect danger in the dark and alert the group to any threat would also have been a great asset. There could be attacks not only by neighboring tribes, but also by other dangerous animals.

Almost certainly, the domestication of the dog did not take place at a single locality, on any single occasion. This is partly a reflection of the wide range of the gray wolf through the northern hemisphere. Doubtless, a number of wolves were kept at different stages in history, and not all would have contributed to the evolution of the domestic dog.

BELOW This is an ancient Egyptian portrayal of the god Anubis, which has a dog-like appearance (second from left). Some experts suggest that this imagery was inspired by a jackal. Archeological evidence suggests that this domestication of the dog may have begun around what is now the Middle East. It was here that the origins of today's sighthounds, such as the grayhound, lie

Practical Pointer

You are unlikely to find much by way of remains of ancient dogs in museums, because early archeologists unfortunately ignored their bones, concentrating instead on human finds. A lot of potentially valuable information was probably lost from many sites as a consequence, before a more enlightened attitude prevailed.

Dogs for a purpose

There was a vital difference in those early stages, however, in that dogs were not kept primarily as companions. In fact, they were quite likely to be eaten if other food was in short supply. The use of the domestic dog as a source of food has continued throughout its subsequent domestication, notably in the East. The Chow Chow, for example, has been kept for this purpose in parts of China for centuries.

Dogs were also used to fulfill an enormous variety of other tasks, adapting to the changing needs of people. This has helped to ensure their continued popularity. As guns became more commonplace, in Europe for example, so a new type of dog evolved to assist in this activity. Instead of being a pack animal, like hounds, these retrievers were valued for working closely, and almost instinctively, with their owners in the field.

Dogs as companions

The keeping of dogs mainly as companions rather than for working purposes is a very recent phenomenon in their history that dates from the late 1800s. This developed partly as a result of the interest in the showing of dogs, pioneered by Charles Cruft, who founded the world-famous dog show that still bears his name. The interest proved infectious, to the extent that the American Kennel Club was set up in 1884 and, today, both the Westminster Show held in New York and Crufts still enjoy huge popularity.

This Roman statue shows the wolf suckling the orphans Romulus and Remus. Legend tells how the twins founded the city of Rome, paving the way for the Roman Empire. The wolf rescued the infants from the banks of the River Tiber, and her maternal instincts led her to carry them up to the Palatine Hill and shelter them in a cave until they were found by a shepherd.

ABOVE This Roman statue shows the wolf suckling the orphans Romulus and Remus. Legend tells how the twin founded the city Rome, paving the way for the Roman Empire. The wolf rescued the infants from the bank of the River Tiber, and her maternal instincts led her to carry them up to the Palatine Hill and shelter them in a cave untill they were found by a shepherd.

Practical Pointer

Paintings, carvings and other artifacts portraying early domestic dogs have helped to show where particular breeds originated. There are recognizable similarities between a number of today's hounds and their ancient Egyptian forebears.

The emergence of the domestic dog

The first clear evidence of a divergence in appearance of the domestic dog has been uncovered in the Beaverhead Mountain region of the United States, in the State of Idaho. By this time, there was a small beagle-like form and a distinctly larger, retriever-sized type of dog. Their remains date back approximately 9,000 years, indicating significant variations in the size of dogs from the same locality had begun about 3,000 years after the likely start of the domestication process.

The tendency toward smaller lapdogs took place at a relatively early stage in the dog's history. Unfortunately, it is very difficult to build up any real impression of a dog's appearance, in terms of key features such as color or hair length, just from Wits skeleton.

While a clear indication of its facial shape can be established from its muzzle, the appearance of its ears remains unknown, because the ear flaps themselves are comprised of cartilage rather than bone. This is why the discovery of the mummified remains of dogs of terrier size in Arizona was significant. These had long coats and were black and white in color, indicating that divergence from the coloration of the gray wolf had occurred by this stage.

Hounds

In Europe, evidence from Egypt reveals that the hound lineage was established early in history. Phoenician traders were probably responsible for carrying these hounds to other localities around the Mediterranean in their ships. This legacy is still apparent today, and a number of similar hounds, such as the pharaoh hound from the island of Malta, the Ibizan hound from Spain, and the Sicilian grayhound, originating on the island of Sicily, still survive.

These three breeds all have an unmistakably similar appearance, with broad, stiff, erect ears and a

Practical Pointer

The characters of dogs have evolved over thousands of years. If they were originally bred for outdoor work, not all will settle well in the home.

Certain sheepdogs can be included in this category.

BELOW The Ibizan hound has changed little over thousands of years. Egyptian artifacts show similar hunting dogs.

Practical Pointer

Do not be persuaded to buy a breed simply because it is fashionable. Ask yourself whether the dog would integrate well into your particular life style — otherwise you are likely to be storing up problems for the future.

short, smooth coat. In terms of their coloration, they are essentially red with white markings, which are typically confined to the vicinity of the chest. They are often considered to bear a striking resemblance to the ancient Egyptian god Anubis.

It is thought that they were first taken abroad from Egypt around 5,000 years ago and have since developed in isolation. They are athletic, agile hunters, and are able to hunt by both sight and sound, although evolution has led to other hound breeds developing other more specialized hunting skills. They have survived largely unchanged for so long because of this tendency to keep them in isolation. As a result there was little cross¬breeding, which would have altered their appearance and other characteristics.

Mastiffs

It can actually be harder to trace the ancestry of other ancient breeds, although the mastiff lineage is still quite clearly defined. Dogs similar in appearance to the Tibetan mastiff were brought westward at a relatively early period in history. In the early stages, these large, powerful dogs were aggressive by nature. They were used essentially for guarding purposes. In Europe, they were valued for their ability to protect livestock against attacks by rampaging packs of wolves, which were still numerous up until the 1800s, and beyond in some areas. Their aggressive traits were eventually turned into protective loyalties, however, and this characteristic is still markedly apparent in this breed today. They are friendly toward members of their own households, but generally prove to be aloof and very suspicious with strangers.

BASIC INSTINCTS

Wolf template

The variance in features such as coloration and size which existed in the different races of wolf through their range serves to explain the diversity which is apparent between different breeds of domestic dog. Selective breeding has reinforced characteristics of the dog's wild ancestor over the generations, creating breeds with specialist skills, such as scenthounds.

BELOW Tibetan mastiff — a strong, powerful breed.

Early Domestication
The dog through history

Sighthounds were already present in Britain by the time of the Roman invasion although how they reached there is a mystery. They too, could have been brought by Phoenicians. They were apparently similar to today's grayhounds and displayed the typical lemon and white associated with various breeds of hound today.

The Romans

The Romans highly valued a breed of dog called the vertragus, to the extent that a special official, known as the procurator cynegii, was appointed to obtain such hounds and arrange their shipment to Rome. They were similar in appearance to grayhounds and

Practical Pointer
A dog's pedigree will help you to trace its ancestry, and all pure-bred puppies should be sold with a pedigree. Keep this document in a safe place, especially if you intend to either show or breed from your dog in the future, as you may need to refer to it.

Practical Pointer

Cross-bred puppies result from the mating of two pure-bred individuals belonging to different breeds. Consequently, they may show features of both their parents. In contrast, mongrels are dogs bred from non-pedigree lineage.

BELOW Until comparatively recently, dogs were kept primarily for working purposes, helping to hunt as in this case, or used as guardians to watch over property.

able to outrun hares, which were apparently their usual quarry.

Another type of dog already established in Britain when the Romans arrived was the mastiff, believed to have been brought by the Celts. These dogs were large, courageous and fierce, and were often used to hunt wild boar, which were an exceedingly dangerous quarry. A number were sent to fight in Roman amphitheaters, where they could reputedly kill bulls with a single blow to the animal's neck.

With the spread of Roman civilization, there was also an increasing interest in small dogs, whose main role appears to have been as companions, although they could have been used to warn owners of the presence of intruders or visitors. These were equivalent in size to today's toy breeds, measuring just 9 in (23 cm) at the shoulder.

BELOW Dogs of mastiff stock were used in battle.

Domestication through history: purpose-bred hounds

The reliance on hounds to assist in the hunting of game led to increasingly strict laws being placed on the ownership of such dogs, to prevent all but the aristocracy possessing them.

Middle Ages

Ironically, the hunting of the gray wolf appears to have taken on a renewed urgency at this stage, with dogs being pitted against a wolf on a regular basis throughout the Middle Ages. The natural cunning and greater stamina of the wolf meant that it was often able to elude its domestic relative.

This period also saw the appearance of the largest breed that ever existed. This was the Irish hound, a possible ancestor of the Irish wolfhound, which measured over 48 in (1.2 m) at the shoulder. Contemporary reports describe these hounds as being a sandy shade. Hugely powerful, the Irish hound was kept both as a guardian and for hunting purposes. Its skull alone measured 17 in (43 cm) and,

Practical Pointer

Dogs will learn certain tricks, such as begging, almost instinctively, particularly if they are consistently rewarded. Poodles have a long history as circus dogs, being particularly playful by nature.

in terms of size, it undoubtedly would have rivaled the largest of the gray wolves.

Other dogs from this era which are now extinct include the fearsome Alaunt. These were used on the battlefield — Henry VIII of England (1509-1547) used 400 of them in his invasion of France — but, because of their ferocity, they did not survive once the invention of firearms rendered their original purpose obsolete.

One breed which has survived down the centuries is the mastiff, a breed which also saw service on the battlefield. It was a mastiff that guarded the wounded knight Sir Piers Leigh on the battlefield of Agincourt in 1415.

New types of dog began to evolve too, in response to the changes taking place in society in the Middle Ages. The forerunners of today's spaniel breeds began to emerge at this stage in history, being used for hunting birds.

Classification of dog breeds

The first attempt to classify dogs into distinct varieties was undertaken in the famous work De Canibus Britannicis, written by an English physician, Dr. John Caius in 1570. There were hunting dogs, such as grayhounds and the so-called "limor," which was probably a forerunner of the bloodhound, that tracked its quarry by scent. Also well established at this stage were terriers and harriers, which often assisted the hunt, while spaniels and setters were fairly recent introductions.

Interestingly, it is clear there was already a movement of developing breeds from one country

ABOVE This hunting scene clearly shows two types of hound. There are the fast, narrow-nosed sighthounds, reminiscent of a modern-day grayhound, and the broad-nosed forerunners of the scenthounds.

to another by the time that Caius's work appeared. He himself described one such black and white spaniel brought to Britain from France. Caius disliked the ladies' pets — equivalent to today's toy breeds — known then as "comforters". These small dogs were kept entirely as companions.

Some of the more interesting dogs of that period were to be found in Caius's so-called "degenerate" grouping. These apparently lacked any standardization in terms of their type, being kept instead for a variety of purposes. They included dogs which carried out tricks and danced as entertainers, and "turnspits" — small dogs trained to turn joints of meat as they roasted over open fires in the kitchens of large houses.

LEFT As hunting developed, so hounds were used to catch quarry in combination with falcons. The ladies were entertained by lapdogs, so-called because of their small size. These were essentially companion dogs, although they could also serve as guardians.

Practical Pointer

Today it is much easier than it was in Caius's day to prevent bitches becoming pregnant, thereby adding to the number of unwanted mongrels or cross-breds. Neutering provides the simplest solution in the long term.

Domestication through to modern times

From the late 1600s, a number of today's smaller breeds were popular at the royal courts of Europe.

King Charles Spaniel

King Charles II of England (1660-1685) actively encouraged the spaniel breed that was named after him, which actually originated in France. In those early days, these spaniels had relatively long faces, but by the 1920s, they had become much more compact.

An American spaniel enthusiast then put up substantial prize money for breeders who could produce spaniels that bore a closer resemblance to the original type. As a result, this effectively led to the emergence of two different forms of the King Charles spaniel. This recently recreated form, with a longer nose more akin to the original examples of the breed, is now described as the Cavalier King Charles spaniel, to distinguish it from its flatter-faced cousin.

Practical Pointer

Visiting dog shows can be a good way to meet breeders and also to learn what is involved in exhibiting. This is essentially a hobby — even a major win brings very little financial reward.

LEFT A King Charles spaniel — the appearance of this breed has been modified since it attracted the attention of King Charles II during the seventeenth century.

BELOW Selective breeding of hounds for their stamina took place well before the advent of dog shows. Foxhounds can be highly variable in terms of their markings.

Foxhounds

Other breeds were changing during the 1700s, most notably the foxhound, whose history was to provide a pointer to the subsequent development of other breeds. At first, these hounds were slow and often incapable of keeping up with the fox, let alone outpacing it. Interest grew in selective breeding to improve the stamina and pace of the foxhound.

The inspiration behind this project was Hugo Meynell, who resided at Quornden Hall, in Leicestershire, England. It ultimately led to the founding of the famous Quorn pack of foxhounds.

The first dog shows also revolved around this particular breed. Masters of Foxhounds frequently took their dogs to events in the summer months, outside the hunting season. Accurate pedigree records of foxhounds extend back further than those of any other breed.

Development of the modern dog scene

More general interest in dogs in the Victorian era resulted in the establishment, in 1873, of the Kennel Club, the oldest body of its type in the world, to oversee the development of pure-bred specimens. There was also a rapid expansion of the show scene, in which selective breeding and pedigree records were to play an increasingly significant part.

The origins of the modern dog scene began in the public houses of London, the proprietors of which encouraged dog shows as a means of providing entertainment for their customers. The first major event of this type pioneered separately was a show for terrier breeds. It was organized by a pioneering dog-food salesman named Charles Cruft and took place in 1886. He had been inspired by the Paris Exhibition, and enjoyed the support of wealthy members of the aristocracy who were keen dog-lovers.

ABOVE The modern dog show scene developed at the end of the nineteenth century. Show standards exist for recognized breeds, and judges assess the dogs in accord with these prescribed features.

By 1891, Cruft was sufficiently confident to launch an event for breeds from around the world. A great showman, he appreciated publicity and success. Queen Victoria, herself a great dog enthusiast, entered her Pomeranians at the event.

Cruft brought together the largest selection of breeds ever assembled, and the public responded enthusiastically. Not only did they come to see the breeds, but also to own them. Today's breeds have since attained a strong international following.

The development of the pet-food industry on a large scale after the Second World War has since helped to simplify the care of dogs, increasing their popularity as a result. So today more and more people enter their dogs in shows or take part in dog exhibitions.

Practical Pointer

Cruft's show is now organized by the Kennel Club and attracts visitors from around the world. Each day, the different groups are judged, leading up to the finale of the Best-in-Show award on the last day.

ANATOMY
Skeleton and skull Shapes

The pattern of the wolf's and dog's skeleton is very similar in terms of their components, but significant changes can be detected in the shape of the skull, while the length of some of the limb bones also differ markedly. This reflects the divergence in physical appearance of domestic dogs. Not surprisingly, those still resembling the gray wolf have a skeletal structure that most closely approximates to it.

Skull

The dog's skull can be classified into one of three basic groupings. Those breeds with relatively long nasal chambers, such as the grayhound, which hunt primarily by sight, have skulls similar to those of the gray wolf. These are described as being "dolichocephalic."

The skull structure is altered in the case of scenthounds, or breeds such as the pointer, which have broad noses to assist in the detection of a particular scent. These are the so-called "mesocephalic" breeds.

In the case of many fighting dogs, the length of the muzzle is greatly reduced, and the upper jaw is correspondingly shorter, with the skull itself becoming more curved in shape. The lower jaw is also shortened, but not as severely as that of the upper jaw, with the result that it displays a distinct curve. This shorter, squared jaw pattern helps the dog to maintain its grip, with more of the jaw being used for this purpose.

However, the reduction in the length of the jaws in these so-called "brachycephalic" breeds creates a potential problem, in that the teeth are likely to become overcrowded because they show no corresponding reduction in numbers. Furthermore, especially during hot weather, the severe reduction in the size of the nasal cavities leaves these breeds, as typified by the bulldog, at potentially greater risk of succumbing to the effects of heatstroke. You should try to avoid exercising any dog when the sun is very hot.

ABOVE Mutations have arisen affecting the appearance of the dog's facial shape, as well as its ears, compared with that of the gray wolf ancestor.

Practical Pointer
Dogs are more likely to make a mess when eating if they are forced to use their teeth to rip their food apart, so when feeding fresh or canned food, break it into reasonably small chunks

Dogs are unable to regulate their body temperature by sweating — sweat glands are restricted to the area between the toes, where they serve as scent markers. Instead, to dissipate heat, dogs rely on a combination of panting and the cooling effect of evaporation from their nasal cavities. The latter is essentially not possible in the brachycephalic breeds.

The pattern of dentition in wolves and domestic dogs, is surprisingly constant. They generally have 42 teeth, which, with the exception of the molars, are paired. The incisor teeth are curved, and help the dog to maintain its grip, while the pointed canines can be used to overpower prey. They are blunter than in some other carnivores, such as cats.

There is then a gap, called the diastema, leading back to the chewing teeth, which com¬prise the premolars and molars. The molars are unpaired, with two at each side of the upper jaw and three beneath, so that the last premolar above can work with the first molar in the lower jaws, to shear through meat.

Dogs use these teeth to chew, when they hold their head down to one side. They prefer to gulp their food, rather than chewing it into small pieces. This is a reflection of pack life, where eating in the shortest period of time can make the difference between survival and death.

Some breeds such as the Alaskan malamute retain a strong affinity with the wolf, in terms of their facial appearance and underlying skull structure. Other breeds from the far north like the Siberian husky share similar features.

In the case of other breeds, the skull shape may be broadened and slightly shortened, compared with that of the wolf. The enlargement of the nasal passages helps to improve the dog's scenting skills, and so it is most apparent in dogs such as the pointer.

Certain breeds show a more dramatic shortening of the skull, as exemplified by this bulldog. The nasal passages are greatly compressed, to the point that such breeds are susceptible to heatstroke, as dogs cool themselves by loss of moisture from the nasal cavities.

Vertebral column

One of the main reasons why dogs cannot climb effectively is because of the structure of their spinal column. It lacks the mobility of that of cats, and so restricts the dog's movements, although both wolves, and indeed dogs, can run at pace for relatively long distances if necessary. Yet, while the wolf may be seen as the general blueprint, there has been a trend toward specialization in the case of domestic dogs, which in a few instances has been potentially counterproductive.

The skull attaches to the vertebral column by means of the seven cervical vertebrae. These in turn are linked to the 13 thoracic vertebrae that form the upper part of the chest wall. The ribs extend from here down the sides of the body. The actual shape of the chest varies somewhat, according to the breed of dog. In those which are most active and have a high oxygen requirement, such as the borzoi, the chest is deep, to provide room for a large lung capacity and a suitably powerful heart to pump the blood around the body.

The breastbone, or sternum, is located at the front of the chest and extends along the lower side of the body, where it provides support to the rib cage. It is not a rigid structure, however, because otherwise the chest wall would lack the flexibility to move in and out as the dog breathed. Nor are all the ribs attached to the sternum. The last pairs, the so-called "floating ribs" are free of the sternum and are slightly shorter.

Behind the thoracic vertebrae, and running along the back above the abdomen, are the dorsal vertebrae, which may vary from six to eight in number. They are characterized by broad, raised vertical projections on their upper surfaces, known as the dorsal spines. These provide for the attachment of muscles, to assist the dog's movement. They also restrict the mobility of the spinal column, concentrating the dog's power into running or

Practical Pointer

When dealing with a dog which has suffered intervertebral disk problems, be sure to restrict its mobility. Otherwise the outlook for recovery will be bleak. Never encourage dachshunds (a breed predisposed to this condition) to jump, or to climb up flights of stairs.

LEFT Tail docking will alter the appearance of a dog permanently, with part of the tail being removed. This surgery is carried out soon after birth. The Pembrokeshire Welsh corgi puppy on the left has been docked, with its litter-mate retaining a full-length tail.

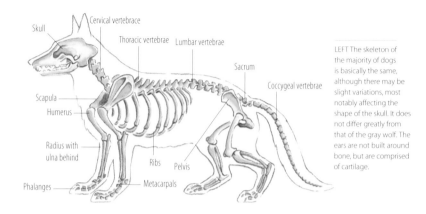

Skull
Cervical vertebrace
Thoracic vertebrae
Lumbar vertebrae
Sacrum
Coccygeal vertebrae
Scapula
Humerus
Radius with ulna behind
Ribs
Pelvis
Phalanges
Metacarpals

LEFT The skeleton of the majority of dogs is basically the same, although there may be slight variations, most notably affecting the shape of the skull. It does not differ greatly from that of the gray wolf. The ears are not built around bone, but are comprised of cartilage.

jumping. Further stability follows behind, where the sacral part of the vertebral column attaches to the hips, enabling the thrust from the powerful hind limbs to be maximized into movement.

Intervertebral disks

Sandwiched between the vertebrae themselves are intervertebral disks, which act rather like shock-absorbers. Degeneration of these disks at an early stage is especially common in dachshunds, which have relatively long backs. Should the disk rupture, it will impinge on the spinal cord, causing a variety of symptoms, which may include paralysis, depending on where the rupture occurs. The most likely sites are at the thoracolumbar junction Skull and in the cervical region.

Tail

It is at the rear end of the vertebral column that the greatest variation is to be seen, in the case of the bone structure of the tail. There may be between 14 and 23 coccygeal vertebrae, which narrow along their length to the tip of the tail. In the case of the

domestic dog, some breeds have a naturally short tail, which is described as a bobtail, but in other cases, the tail length is deliberately shortened by a process called docking. This entails cutting off a variable length of the tail when the dog is very young.

Proponents of docking argue that, in the case of working breeds, this saves the tail from being injured later in life. Those who are opposed to the concept highlight the fact that docking may be painful, even for a puppy, and that dogs use their tails as a means of communication.

ABOVE Sighthounds such as the greyhound have a particularly athletic build, as the sprinters rather than the distance runners of the dog world.

LEFT Stride length means that some dogs cover much more ground with a single bound than others, when running at speed. A deep chest provides good lung capacity.

Limbs

The wolf depends largely on its superior speed to overtake and kill its quarry. Injured wolves are unlikely to survive for long in the wild, particularly if they cannot keep up with the rest of the pack. They will then face a slow death from starvation. It is therefore not surprising that the domestic dog has inherited its ancestor's ability to run, and shows the same skeletal adaptions for this purpose.

Forelimbs

Dogs lack a functional collar bone because this would allow energy to be wasted by pulling the limbs laterally. Binding them tightly against the body increases the power of the propulsive thrust. The collar bone, or clavicle, is still present, however, but reduced to a thin wafer buried in the muscle mass in the shoulder region.

One of the features of the wolf, and of most other dogs, is that their legs are long in relation to their bodies. This allows them to cover more ground per stride. The flattened shoulder bone, or scapula, contributes to the length of the limb, and also the dog's stride, because it is bound tightly against the body.

The scapula attaches to the humerus beneath, while lower down the limb are the radius and ulna. Increases in the length of these bones can also be seen, while greater stability results from the tight binding together of radius and ulna. These form the wrist at their lower end, with the metacarpal bones (which are also found in our hands) actually forming part of the dog's limb, rather than its front paw, and increasing its length as a result.

The dog supports all of its weight on its digits and, as a result, runs in a digitigrade fashion. The pads on the underside of the digits are tough and horny, absorbing any roughness of the ground as the dog runs, although profuse bleeding is likely to follow if a pad is cut, typically on a piece of glass.

There are other bones present in the lower part of the limbs, and these are bound together with ligaments to prevent sideways movement. The

Practical Pointer

Cases of hip dysplasia often lead to osteoarthritis in later life. This may need treatment with painkillers, although today, in severe cases, it is possible to carry out hip replacement surgery successfully.

only exception to this pattern is found in the tree-climbing fox, in which rigid forelimbs make climbing impossible. Greater rotation of the bones means that they are capable of grasping and adjusting their position off the ground, so they are less likely to fall and injure themselves.

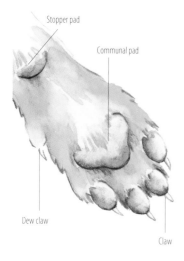

Stopper pad

Communal pad

Dew claw

Claw

Hindlimbs

In the case of the hindlimbs, the upper bone, known as the femur, fits into the hips, forming a ball-and-socket joint. In domestic dogs, typically those weighing over 24 lb (11 kg), there may be a developmental weakness which causes the socket to be too shallow. This results in the condition known as hip dysplasia.

The bottom of the femur, where it forms the knee joint, is more likely to be a point of weakness in smaller breeds. This particular joint is quite flexible, allowing the dog to jump effectively. If the kneecap slips, however, this creates the condition known as luxating patella.

The tibia and fibula in the hindlimb extend down to the ankle joint, with the structure of the lower part of the dog's hindlimb being not dissimilar from that of its forelimb. Stability is equally important here.

LEFT A dog's paw seen from beneath. The stopper pad gives support and prevents the dog from losing its grip on a slippery surface. The pads may appear tough, but are highly vascular and will bleed profusely if cut.

BELOW Some breeds, such as this basset hound, have short legs. This group of hounds arose in France and are used by huntsmen on foot. "Basset" is derived from "bas" meaning "low" and refers to the short legs.

Changes resulting from domestication

The incidence of skeletal problems is much higher in domestic dogs than in wolves. In the wild, natural selection pressures would ultimately prevent wolves that were suffering from congenital disorders, such as hip dysplasia, from making any significant input into the gene pool. A disability of this type would result in their acquiring lower social status, and so they would be unlikely to mate within the hierarchy of the pack. There are no such constraints with domestic dogs, and as breeding of closely related stock is not uncommon, in order to preserve and even improve on desirable features, there is a risk of emphasizing the effects of harmful genes — as can be seen in breeds such as the dachshund.

Leg length

One of the most significant changes in appearance within the domestic dog group, compared with wolves, is the emergence of dogs with dramatically shortened legs. These are frequently described as bassets, this name being derived from the French word bas, meaning "low." The size of the rest of the body in these dogs shows no alteration.

The various dachshunds are also short-legged, with long bodies, for functional purposes. This enables them to disappear underground without difficulty, where they were formerly used to pursue badgers, whereas this would be virtually impossible for a hunting dog with longer legs.

Claws and toes

There are also differences in claw structure between wolves and domestic dogs. As with the reduction in the length of the legs, what might well be harmful to the wild wolf has advantages for the owners of domestic dogs, and so such traits have been encouraged.

In all cases, however, the dog's claws are not retractable, being broad and generally blunt-ended. They serve to anchor the feet into the ground as the dog runs, helping to prevent it from sliding over. But although dogs have five toes, the innermost of these, equivalent to the human thumb, is held permanently off the ground. It can be used by the dog to hold down quarry if necessary, and is called the dew claw simply because it skims the grass, picking up the moisture of dew.

BELOW Shortening of the limbs as in the basset hound (above) has occurred without any corresponding reduction of the body. The length of their legs means that jumping is difficult, and should not be encouraged. This also applies in the case of the dachshund (below). Their vertebral column is quite weak, and they can be prone to intervertebral disk problems as a result.

Practical Pointer

Dew claws, when present, need to be trimmed back regularly. Since they are not worn down by contact with the ground, these claws have sharp points and continue growing, to the extent that they may even curl around and grow into the pad, which can be very painful for the dog.

An increase in the number of toes — known as polydactylism — is a notable feature of the Lundehund, or Norwegian puffin dog, which may have six toes on each foot, as well as extra dew claws. This assists these dogs as they climb around the sheer cliffs of their Norwegian homeland, hunting for nesting puffins.

Wild dogs lack dew claws on their hind legs, but these are a common feature in domestic breeds. The briard actually has double dew claws, which

ABOVE The lundehund or Norwegian puffin dog is unusual because it often has more toes than other breeds and extra dew claws, which help to give a better grip.

are considered to be characteristic of the breed. Because of this, they cannot be removed, but in other breeds, these claws are often excised early in life. Otherwise the dog may become caught up and tear the claw as a result.

Practical Pointer
Short-legged dogs are not adept swimmers, so keep them away from deep stretches of water, where they might encounter difficulties if they fell or jumped in.

COAT VARIATIONS
Development of colors and textures

All the colors seen in domestic dogs are present to a variable extent in the coats of wolves. Selective breeding of dogs has seen the emergence of breeds characterized by their so-called "self", or pure, colors. The range of colors available extends from white through shades of red to brown and black. So-called "blue" colors are the result of a combination of black and white hairs running through the coat.

Self coloring may be broken by small areas of white on the bodies of the darker-colored dogs, typically on the chest, or there may be more widely distributed white patches, a feature associated particularly with hounds. Wolves, too, can often be identified from a distance by their markings, but self coloration in wolves is very unusual. The Newfoundland white wolf (*Canis lupus beothucus*), which was white in color, as its name suggests (although in reality was a subspecies of the gray wolf), was the notable exception. It was finally hunted into extinction in 1911.

The natural coloration of the wolf is influenced to a large extent by the terrain in which it lives, and helps to provide camouflage. The tundra race of the gray wolf (*C. l. albus*), for example, has a much paler coat than the typical gray wolf (*C. l. lupus*), which used to range widely through the forests of Europe. There, dark coloring would help the wolves to blend in against the shadows of the trees. In desert areas, wolves with sandier-colored coats are likely to be encountered. Therefore, in spite of its name, the gray wolf occurs in a wide range of color variants.

In the case of the dog, as domestication has proceeded, so the coat in many cases has become longer. This would be a handicap to a wild wolf, as its fur would soon become matted and dirty. It is important to remember that long-haired breeds, such as the Afghan hound, need considerable grooming every day in order to maintain their immaculate appearance.

BELTON (English setter)

BLACK AND TAN (Hamiltonstövare)

BLUE (Basset bleu de Gascogne)

TRICOLOR (Beagle)

GRIZZLE (Old English sheepdog)

HARLEQUIN (Great Dane)

BRINDLE (Grayhound)

PARTI-COLOR (Swedish vallhund)

RED (Irish setter)

ROAN (Welsh corgi)

WHEATEN (Soft-coat wheaten terrier)

PIEBALD (Dalmatian)

ABOVE This is the lemon and white form of the beagle.

Other hounds, such as the beagle and foxhound, have short coats. This is partly because they regularly hunt in overgrown terrain where the long hair of the Afghan would be a distinct handicap. The coloration of these short-coated hounds of northern European origin is frequently tricolored — being black, white and tan — or sometimes lemon and white.

LEFT The coloration of many hounds is distinctive, being either tricolored as shown in the dog pictured, or bicolored. The markings are sufficiently distinctive to enable individuals within a pack to be identified without difficulty.

BASIC INSTINCTS

Wolf's thick coat

The coat also serves to protect the wolf from climatic extremes. The coat consists of two layers. There is the longer top coat, made up of coarse guard hairs, and a shorter, dense, insulating layer of hair beneath. The coat is of even length over the body, including the tail, with the weather-resistant guard hairs standing away from the body. The coloration of the gray wolf is variable, as shown above in these two individuals.

RIGHT This is the powderpuff form of the Chinese crested dog, one of a number of the so-called hairless breeds.

general, although obviously the care of such dogs is slightly different to that of other breeds.

In the first place, they are susceptible to the cold as a result of their lack of hair. The lack of hair can have a less obvious effect, however, particularly when the weather is hot. These hairless breeds are at risk of suffering from sunburn, because their skin is so exposed, especially in the case of those with pale bodies. Sunblocks will be needed and these dogs should be kept indoors as much as possible when the sun is at its hottest.

Practical Pointer
Hairless dogs that have pink skin are more vulnerable to sunburn than those with dark skin, because, in these pale areas, there is no protective melanin pigment present.

Unusual coats

There are some dogs which have a highly distinctive appearance, simply because they have virtually no coat.

"Hairless" dogs

A mutation has occurred giving rise to so-called "hairless" breeds, which do actually have some body hair, most noticeably on their heads. The origins of these breeds are something of a mystery, but they probably arose quite early during the domestication process.

The Chinese crested dog is the best-known example, but there are also Mexican and Peruvian hairless dogs. The skin coloration of hairless individuals still gives a clear indication of their coloration, with pink patches indicating what would otherwise be areas of white hair.

Litters typically consist of both hairless and normal-coated puppies, the latter being described as "powder-puffs". Hairless dogs are a good choice for owners who tend to be allergic to animal fur in

BELOW Hair is confined to the extremities of the body in the case of the hairless form of the Chinese crested dog. The pattern of pigmentation seen in the skin depends on the individual,

Wire-haired dogs

Another coat variant which has become established in the case of the domestic dog is the wire-haired form. This is associated with a variety of breeds, ranging from dachshunds and various terriers to larger dogs, such as the wire-haired pointed griffon. The coat of these dogs is coarse and wiry, as the name suggests, and provides them with good protection in undergrowth, being relatively impenetrable to thorns and other sharp projections.

The wire coat does not lie sleek against the skin, nor will it be molted as usual. This means that the dead hair here will have to be stripped out at least twice a year. Further trimming is often required prior to a show. While more frequent stripping of pet dogs of this type will be needed if the coat is basically clipped, rather than being dealt with by hand in the traditional but time-consuming manner.

Molting

Not all dogs actually molt their coats — poodles being a typical example. This may be helpful in terms of keeping the house clean, but instead the coat will need to be clipped about every six weeks or so. This may prove to be an extra expense, unless you feel confident enough to carry out this task for yourself.

Other breeds shed hair often throughout the year, although the peak molting times are in the spring, when the dense winter coat, most apparent in northern breeds, is lost, to be replaced by a lighter summer coat. Another period of molting then occurs in the autumn, as the winter coat starts to grow.

Practical Pointer

It is not just hairless breeds that may need protection against the elements. A number of thin-coated hounds, such as the whippet and Italian grayhound, should be fitted with a jacket to protect them from extreme weather. Dog jackets are sold on the basis of length, so measure your pet's back to obtain the correct size, or better still, take your dog along for a fitting!

BELOW Wire-haired variants have been developed in some breeds such as the dachshunds. This change in coat texture gives better protection in undergrowth.

EVOLUTION
Breeds and selective breeding

Changes in the appearance of domestic dogs have occurred because of various mutations which, in the first instance, affected coat length, face shape, and similar features. Geneticists believe that just 20, or even fewer, such primary changes could account for the wide diversity apparent in the various breeds of dog which now exist.

Selective breeding has also subsequently played a part. It is likely that there have been as many as 5,000 generations of domestic dog since the domestication process began, enabling desirable features to be developed and emphasized. Dogs started to evolve distinctive types long before the onset of dog shows, but these events have proved to be the major factor responsible for the standardization and division of dogs into today's breeds.

Defining a breed

What defines a breed is now laid down in the breed standard. This specifies the ideal "type", or appearance, of that particular breed, to the extent that, in the show ring, dogs are not judged against each other, but with respect to the standard. The dog which is considered to be closest to the ideal will win the class. Not all breeds are recognized for show purposes, however, usually because they are either very scarce in a particular country or are a new breed that has yet to achieve standardization in appearance. Also, the number of new breeds being created today is relatively small. One of the most recent is the kyi leo, which, in spite of its name, is of North American origin, having been developed in California. It was evolved from crossings of Maltese and lhasa apso stock as a companion breed suited to an apartment life style.

Today, throughout the world, there are between 350 and 400 different types of domestic dog. However, as some are added to this list, so equally, others are becoming extinct, like the Tahltan bear dog, bred by the Tahltan indian tribe of North America.

LEFT One of the forms of the Belgian shepherd dog, known as the Tervuren, named after the region of Belgium where it was developed.

ABOVE Variations in coat length have been emphasized in the domestic dog, as shown by the smooth collie (left) and the long-haired collie (right), but they are also apparent in gray wolf populations.

Practical Pointer

Try not to be too influenced by the latest trends when selecting a breed. It can be harder to obtain good-quality stock of a fashionable breed, simply because unscrupulous breeders may be tempted to produce as many puppies as possible to meet the increased demand, without worrying about the dogs' welfare.

Popularity of breeds

It is something of a mystery as to why some breeds manage to attain a strong international following, whereas others remain highly localized. The shepherd dogs of Europe are an example. All are believed to share a common ancestry, but while the German shepherd dog (formerly known as the Alsatian) is one of the best known of all breeds, the Belgian shepherd dog group is far less common. Meanwhile the Dutch shepherd dog is virtually unknown outside its homeland.

Fashion does undeniably, and possibly increasingly, play a part in the relative popularity of the different breeds. The "Lassie" character, for example, generated a huge following for the rough collie breed, while more recently the film "101 Dalmatians" has led to considerable interest in this breed.

PROTECTING RARE BREEDS

There is a growing awareness on the part of dog-lovers today to conserve the rarer breeds. One of the great success stories in recent years has involved a Chinese breed called the Shar Pei. The plight of this ancient breed was brought to the attention of American breeders by the writings of Matgo Law, in the dog press. Stock was taken to the United States in the late 1970s and reached the United Kingdom in 1981. Since then, the breed has become well established outside its southern Chinese homeland, and its future is now secure.

Possible weaknesses

Domestic dogs show far more diversity in both appearance and size compared with cats. This is in part a reflection of the fact that the gray wolf naturally shows a much greater variation in size through its range, and this trait is apparent in domestic dogs today, with such divergence being encouraged by selective breeding.

In the case of the poodle, for example, the standard variety was scaled down, resulting first in the miniature poodle and subsequently the toy poodle. Loss of soundness does appear to be a problem, however, once the dog's size falls dramatically. Many small breeds are at risk from luxating patellas (kneecap) in the hindlimbs (see page 37).

Selective breeding has, of course, meant that a number of today's breeds would have difficulty in reverting to a free-living existence.

Interestingly, the domestic dogs that most closely resemble the gray wolf are those which are still kept essentially for working purposes in northern areas, such as the Siberian husky. Sled dogs have another feature in common with their gray wolf ancestor — they are kept in groups and so their behavioral patterns have not altered dramatically. In many ways, they live much as the early wolf-dogs would have done. Even their coloration in many cases clearly resembles that of the wolf.

Nevertheless, members of this group can suffer from various genetic and congenital disorders. Siberian huskies, for example, are known to suffer from Von Willebrand's disease, which is a disorder affecting the blood-clotting system, so that blood loss following injury, or even as the result of a season in a bitch, can be both unduly severe and prolonged.

Practical Pointer

You can tell the likely adult size of a mongrel puppy by looking at its feet. Large paws at this stage indicate that the puppy will grow up into a relatively large dog.

BELOW The Siberian husky retains a similarity to the gray wolf, partly because it has not been subjected to the same selective pressures as breeds from elsewhere in the world.

BELOW Scaling down in size has led to breed weaknesses becoming more apparent in breeds like the miniature poodle. Generally however, small dogs have a longer life expectancy than their larger relatives.

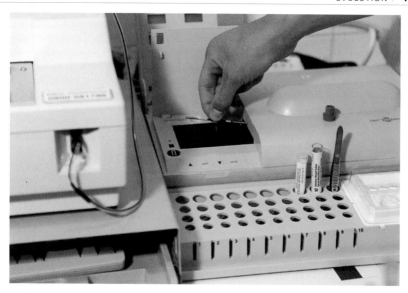

ABOVE There are now various ways of screening dogs for potential breed weaknesses, depending on the likely type of problem concerned. Skeletal weaknesses may be highlighted by X-ray examinations, whereas metabolic problems can be checked by laboratory tests of different types.

A large number of these type of problems have been recorded, with at least one disorder of this type, and frequently more, being associated with the majority of breeds. Thankfully, the incidence is generally low, but the effects can be serious in some cases. While breeders may be aware of the vulnerability of their particular breed to specific complaints, it may prove a difficult task to trace the incidence of the affected genes within a bloodline. By the time a puppy is born with a hereditary defect, it could well be that the genes responsible have been widely distributed, making. other cases more likely to arise in future generations.

Screening programs involving breeding stock are, being set up wherever possible to lessen the likelihood of these genes being passed on from one generation to the next. Already the results

with hip dysplasia and progressive retinal atrophy, a disorder affecting the cells of the retina at the back of the eyes, have led to a noticeable decline in these widespread conditions.

While it is often said that mongrels are healthier than pure-bred dogs, this is not necessarily true. Any canid — wild or domestic — is likely to be equally vulnerable to the major infective illnesses, such as distemper, if not protected by vaccination. The incidence of inherited afflictions is, however, far lower in the case of mongrels.

Practical Pointer

If you are seeking a relatively quiet breed, the basenji would be a good choice. It is sometimes called the barkless dog, although, in reality, it is not silent but sometimes utters strange yodeling and chortling calls.

HYBRIDS
From folk tales to science

Few animals are capable of inspiring so much terror in people as the gray wolf. Fear of wolves has been etched into human consciousness over the course of generations and reinforced by childhood stories, such as "Little Red Riding Hood". But now, at last, with the wolf largely eliminated from much of its former range, there are signs that this situation is changing, especially in North America.

The truth is that attacks by wolves on people have always been decidedly uncommon, even when the numbers of wolves were far higher than today. Partly struck by guilt over the way that wolves were trapped and killed, often needlessly, people have begun to reappraise their relationship with the wolf.

Wolves have already been reintroduced into areas where they were previously eliminated, and "wolf-watching" has become a popular pastime, especially in parts of North America. Unfortunately, however, this newfound affinity with the wolf has also had less desirable consequences.

Hybrids

The genetic links between gray wolves and domestic dogs remain today, to the extent that they can breed together successfully and produce hybrid offspring. This has already occurred in some parts of the wolves' former range in Europe, where just a handful of them still survive. They have mated with domestic dogs, usually strays out scavenging on garbage dumps and similar sites, to which the wolves are also attracted by the prospect of food.

ABOVE It is the unpredictability of gray wolves which can make them dangerous, and particularly if they are cornered, then they are likely to attack. Wild wolves infected by rabies are especially dangerous.

Some breeders have sought to produce deliberate hybrids by pairing captive wolves with established breeds, typically those of northern stock, such as the Alaskan malamute, which resemble the wolf most closely in appearance, but have far more stable temperaments. Such wolf-dog crosses have become quite popular in the United States, especially over the past decade, to the extent that an estimated 500,000 or more are now being kept there.

Practical Pointer
Do not be tempted to consider a wolf-dog hybrid puppy, no matter how cute it may appear. Such hybrids will be a dangerous liability and you could well find yourself in court if your wolf-dog injures or even kills someone.

However, whereas the wolf itself has a natural caution with regard to people, these hybrids tend to lack such reserve and may readily attack as a consequence, particularly once they are mature. Even greater problems with aggression in such hybrids is likely if domestic dogs bred primarily for guarding purposes, such as rottweilers, are used. Many American states have banned wolf-dog hybrids, which have already been responsible for the deaths of a number of people.

Hybrids may result from the matings of domestic dogs with other species of the genus Canis, which are their closest relations, but, as a rule, these are uncommon. They take place in areas where there are a large number of stray dogs. Cross-breeding with foxes, however, does not appear to be a viable option because they are not so closely related.

ABOVE This gray wolf is four months old, and looks similar to a puppy. Dogs are easy to train but wolves remain intractable even if attempts are made to train them from an early age. They are more nervous especially if kept on their own rather than with other wolves.

BASIC INSTINCTS

COYDOGS

Male coyotes do mate quite readily with domestic dogs, however, producing what are often described as "coydog" offspring. In many cases, these hybrids actually appear to be more tractable than those bred from wolves, although they may be unpredictable in terms of temperament and can still be aggressive. Some coydogs do respond to training though, and often have a friendly side to their natures, particularly toward those who they know well. It may seem strange, therefore, that gray wolves and coyotes do not themselves hybridize where they occur together in the wild. There appears to be a strong antipathy between them, certainly on the part of the wolves, which will often kill their smaller relatives. Nevertheless, successful hybridization between these two species has been carried out on at least one occasion, in zoo surroundings.

Saarloos's program

Wolf-dogs are not a new phenomenon, and the legacy of such hybridization can be seen in Europe today. During the 1930s, a Dutchman named Leendert Saarloos, working together with a local zoo, began a special breeding program that was to entail the cross-breeding of gray wolves and domestic dogs.

Saarloos believed that the domestic dog had become weakened by selective breeding over the course of many generations, and that this had

led to problems such as hip dysplasia. His aim was to eliminate these faults and introduce vigor into the domestic dog by hybridizing it back to its original ancestor.

He chose the German shepherd dog for this purpose, but his theory received a serious setback in its early stages when the original wolf he selected for the program died of a viral infection, that it had possibly contracted from its canine companion. Later he encountered behavioral problems in the wolf-dog puppies that resulted from the second pairing. They were less responsive to training than domestic dogs and were also shyer by nature. They also proved keen to roam and displayed a strong pack instinct.

Practical Pointer

Hip dysplasia is one of a number of inherited problems for which breeding stock is now commonly screened. The larger breeds, such as the German shepherd dog and labrador retriever, are especially vulnerable — only buy from reputable breeders whose stock has been screened. Otherwise, before long, your young dog is likely to be displaying signs of hindlimb weakness, depending on the degree to which the hip joints are affected.

BELOW This is a Saarlooswolfhond — a breed that was created by the reintroduction of wolf genes to a domestic dog lineage during the 1930s.

LEFT The German shepherd dog was the other contributor to the development of this breed. Saarloos believed its vigor was declining and sought to remedy the situation by hybridization.

Saarloos continued with his breeding program, concentrating on reducing the lupine (wolf) influence over successive generations by pairing the offspring repeatedly back to German shepherd dogs. The intention was that wolves would play no further part in the breeding strategy after the first pairing.

The undesirable traits which Saarloos originally observed had largely disappeared by the time of his death in 1969. Other enthusiasts subsequently took up the challenge of his work. Six years later the breed was finally accepted for registration purposes by the Dutch Kennel Club. It was given the name of its creator and so became known as the Saarlooswolfhond. Saarloos's own belief, which originally led to the development of the breed, remains unproven.

Today, these dogs can be seen at major European dog shows, but they are not common. They are carefully protected by their supporters from any possible threat of exploitation as a result of their ancestry, and are far removed from today's wolf-dog hybrids in terms of their temperament. Nevertheless, they do still retain a slightly withdrawn side to their natures, especially toward strangers, and are often most settled when kept in pairs rather than as single companions, reflecting the influence of the wolf's recent genetic input into their development.

Practical Pointer

Always be sure to establish a clear impression of a breed's likely temperament and needs before making any decisions. Dogs do differ significantly in such respects, with sled dogs, such as Siberian huskies, being strong and athletic, and requiring plenty of exercise.

DOMESTICATION
Where breeds originated

The origins of today's dog breeds owe much to the former distribution of the gray wolf. The majority are from the northern hemisphere. Relatively few have come from Africa, where the gray wolf never ranged. The notable exception is the basenji, a hunting dog from Central Africa, which is probably descended from the early Egyptian hounds. More recently, in the late 1800s, the Rhodesian ridgeback was bred in the south of the continent by Boer settlers. The distinctive raised ridge of hair running down its back is a feature inherited from the extinct Hottentot dog.

LEFT The lean, fit appearance of the azawakh means that its ribs show — like the grayhound, this North African breed carries no body fat. It has good lung capacity.

Other probable descendants of the Egyptian hounds are the azawakh, a very fast, long-legged breed, kept by the Tuareg tribespeople in the southern Saharan region to hunt gazelle, and the sloughi, also from the northern part of Africa and now becoming better known in other parts of the world as well.

South America

A similar situation exists in South America, which is the other area that is uninhabited by wolves. There are the ancient Peruvian hairless dogs, which may be related to the Mexican hairless breed occurring further north. Recognized breeds from further south, such as the Fila Brasileiro and Dogo Argentino, are of much more recent origin, with an ancestry relating to breeds brought there from other parts of the world.

North America

Companion breeds are virtually unknown from North America, where it was essential that dogs were able to work alongside people, hauling sleds or tracking game in what was, and still can be, a particularly harsh environment, where only the fittest survive.

The power of these dogs, working in teams of six, is quite phenomenal. Alaskan malamutes regularly pull sleds weighing over 700 lb (355 kg) for distances of over 50 miles (80 km) a day.

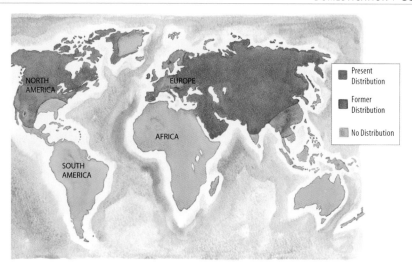

Practical Pointer

Breeds which originated in other parts of the world are generally no more difficult to manage than those that evolved in the region where you live, but you may have to provide them with extra protection in the winter if the weather is cold.

Eurasia

It was in Europe and Asia, where life was more settled, that the toy breeds were developed. These breeds were strictly protected in many cases, with ownership being confined to the nobility. At the Imperial Palace in Beijing, the Pekingese was guarded to the extent that anyone who was caught trying to smuggle one of these dogs out of China faced certain death. It was only after British forces stormed the palace that this breed was seen in the West for the first time.

Few dogs can ever have led such a pampered existence as the Pekingese. They were sometimes called "sleeve dogs", as they were small enough to be carried in the flowing sleeves of courtiers. Their puppies were even wet-nursed on occasions.

ABOVE This map shows both the former and current ranges of the gray wolf, revealing how its distribution has been curtailed in recent times, particularly in Europe. The distribution of the wolf helps in turn to explain the pattern of evolution of the domestic dog

BELOW The Dogo Argentino — a South American breed developed from imported European stock in the 1920s. Relatively few breeds of dogs have originated on this continent.

Today's Pekingese have more compact faces and longer coats than their Chinese ancestors.

Practical Pointer

New breeds are usually obtained by breeders in the first instance, because of the need to import at least several dogs so that unrelated bloodlines can be established. Subsequently, surplus stock may be sold as pets, but new arrivals are usually costly to purchase, because of their relative rarity compared with established breeds.

The lineage of the domestic dog is thought to stem from several distinct lineages of wolf, which occurred through North America, Europe, the Middle East and Asia.

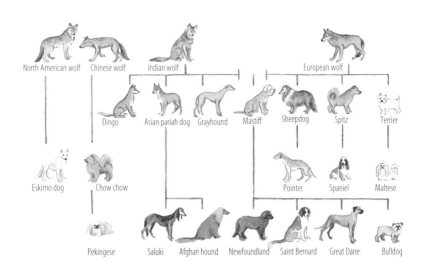

North American wolf | Chinese wolf | Indian wolf | European wolf

Dingo | Asian pariah dog | Grayhound | Mastiff | Sheepdog | Spitz | Terrier

Eskimo dog | Chow chow | Pointer | Spaniel | Maltese

Pekingese | Saluki | Afghan hound | Newfoundland | Saint Bernard | Great Dane | Bulldog

BASIC INSTINCTS

Sled team

Dogs served as a vital means of keeping communities in touch, never more so than in the case of Nome, in Alaska, when it faced a diptheria outbreak in the early 1900s. With no other means of reaching this outpost, it took the bravery of a sled team to get through under the most appalling conditions.

BREED GROUPINGS
How are breeds defined?

The classification of breeds for show purposes differs somewhat from one country to another. Under Kennel Club rules for example, there are five basic divisions, comprising gundog, hound, terrier, toy, and utility groupings. The situation in North America is somewhat different, with non-sporting and sporting sections, and no separate utility or gundog categories.

BELOW The Chihuahua is accepted as the smallest breed in the world, and is kept as a companion. It is classed as a toy breed. This is the long-haired variant.

ABOVE LEFT The Irish wolfhound (not shown to scale) is the largest breed of dog in the world. With its hunting ancestry, its breed is classified as a hound.

There are also considerable differences in the recognition of breeds, and, in some cases, even in the breed standards themselves. The greatest number of breeds is recognized by the European body called the Féderation Cynologique Internationale (FCI), which has also sought to divide breeds more on the basis of their functions. In most cases, the dogs in each category have features in common — in terms of both their appearance and temperament.

The hound group

The hound group traces its ancestry back to the earliest days of the domestication of the dog, in the vicinity of the Middle East. While the older breeds tend to hunt by a combination of sight and sound, just like wolves, there is also evidence of increased specialization within the group. The sighthounds, as epitomized by the Afghan hound and the greyhound, are highly athletic, with a long, loping stride. A so-called "roach back" is typically seen in this type of hound, which slopes noticeably from the shoulders down to the hips.

Since their sense of smell is of relatively little

Practical Pointer

Lurchers are not a standard breed of hound, but the result of cross-breeding between grayhounds and collies, frequently for poaching purposes. This is why many Lurchers are traditionally dark-coated, to conceal their presence at night.

significance, the nasal chamber of these sight-hounds is narrow, giving their head a rather pear-shaped appearance. Although built for speed, these hounds also have stamina and are sure-footed, being able to turn at speed to prevent their quarry from eluding them.

Sighthounds are independent rather than pack dogs. As pets they are active and lively companions. Early training can be difficult because they are prone to follow their instincts, and run off readily. Ex-racing grayhounds are often offered as pets once their career on the track is over. They will prove to be gentle dogs, and are very trustworthy with children.

It is good idea to muzzle such hounds when taking them for a walk, however, particularly where they might encounter other smaller dogs, which they may instinctively regard as potential quarry. Grayhounds tend to be sprinters and, after brief burst of running, will they be content to return home. This makes them a good choice if you do not have a lot of time each day to walk a dog.

Scenthounds are built for stamina rather than speed. Their noses are broad, to maximize their abilities to follow a trail. Often working in packs, such dogs are friendly and boisterous, as well as gluttonous, and are often very ready to steal food.

ABOVE Classification of dogs only began with the development of the show scene toward the end of the nineteenth century. There were various types of bulldog in existence at that stage.

RIGHT Today's bulldog is rather different in appearance, with a larger head and shorter legs than its ancestors.

Terriers and toys

Both these groups are comprised of small breeds, but they can show a remarkable difference in temperament. Terriers tend to be tough, wiry, tenacious characters whereas many toy breeds are much more docile and compliant, having been bred essentially as companions. While the vast majority of terrier breeds originated in Britain, the origins of toys are much more diverse.

Terriers

In many cases, terriers were originally bred as hunt companions. They were required to drive foxes and other creatures out of their burrows, so that the hounds could then pursue their quarry. Faced with a determined and cornered fox within the confines of a burrow meant that such dogs needed to have a bold and brave nature. It is no coincidence that many terriers have wiry coats, because originally they spent much of their time outdoors.

BELOW Rats were a health hazard and hunting them was a vital activity that terriers could be relied upon to undertake with enthusiasm. Even pet terriers will still instinctively catch and kill these rodents today.

Another feature of terriers is their ability to kill rodents, to the extent that, in the nineteenth century, rat-killing contests used to be held in London public houses. A leading ratter of the period, named Billy, managed to kill a hundred rats in just six minutes and thirteen seconds. With increasing urbanization at this stage in history, terriers became much in demand as a means of curbing the growing rodent populations.

The bravery of terriers was also used in a far more negative way, in the form of dogfighting contests. Staffordshire and English bull terriers were kept for

ABOVE Other dogs such as the Staffordshire bull terrier were pitched against each other in vicious dog fights that often resulted in death for one or both dogs.

this purpose after bull-baiting itself was banned. Even today, these particular terriers will not agree well with others of their kind, and can be a liability in areas where there are many other dogs.

More recently, the notorious pit bull terriers, which have been responsible for many vicious attacks on people, have shown the undesirably aggressive side of these dogs. Restrictions on their ownership have been introduced in a number of countries, although the situation has been made difficult because these terriers are not a recognized breed. Rather, they are cross-breds, being a combination of a bull terrier and often a rottweiler, or similarly dominant breed.

ABOVE The Pomeranian is the smallest member of the Spitz group of dogs, complete with a fox-like face.

Toys

Members of the toy group include the tiny Chihuahua, named after the Mexican province of this name where the breed is believed to have originated. Its origins are now obscured, but it occurs in both a long- and short-coated form. A distinct anatomical peculiarity that is associated with the Chihuahua is its open molera. The roof of the skull is not fully formed, to the extent that an opening can be cautiously discerned under the skin. In behavioral terms, this breed is also unusual in that it will shiver when nervous or excited and not just when it is cold.

A number of scaled-down versions of larger breeds are also to be found in the toy category. This includes the very popular Pomeranian, which is one of the smallest members of the spitz group, whose members bear the closest similarity to the gray wolf.

The Pomeranian itself stands around 11 in (28 cm) high, only slightly smaller than the shamanu, or Japanese wolf (*Canis lupus hodophilax*), which was hunted to extinction around 1905. It measured 14 in (39 cm) tall, and was mainly a pale shade of gray.

Many of the Oriental breeds which still survive today are in fact in the toy category, although there

is no evidence to suggest that they are descended from the shamanu wolf. It is only quite recently, however, that such breeds have become well known in the West. Both the Tibetan terrier (which, in spite of its name, is not a terrier) and the Lhasa apso, also from Tibet, were first seen in the West in the 1930s. The pugs, Pekingese and shih tzu are also of Oriental origin.

Toy breeds usually have appealing personalities and develop into loyal companions. They often prove to be alert and courageous guardians as well. In spite of the problems of soundness, these small dogs generally have a longer life expectancy than their larger relatives.

BELOW Many of today's toy breeds originally evolved in the East, such as the Lhasa apso.

Herding dogs

The use of dogs to protect livestock against predators is an ancient tradition that extends back to the early days of farming. Herding dogs can be divided into two categories. The larger breeds, such as the Bergamasco from Italy, or the Tibetan mastiff itself, are primarily flock guardians. These often worked in the company of smaller dogs that were actually responsible for controlling the animals.

The true herding breeds were evolved mainly to work with sheep and goats. Across Europe, a number of such breeds evolved in isolation and, in some cases, are quite dissimilar in appearance. One feature that they do tend to have in common, however, is the water-resistant nature of their coats, as they would be outside working in all weathers.

Old English sheepdog

The Old English sheepdog is one of the best-known members of this group internationally, with a long, shaggy coat that needs daily grooming to prevent it from becoming matted.

Welsh corgis

Some herding dogs have been evolved to work with cattle rather than sheep, and perhaps surprisingly, these are often smaller in size. The Welsh corgi is a typical example, measuring just 12 in (30 cm) in height. There are two different types — the Cardigan, which has a long tail resembling that of a fox, and the Pembroke, also named after a county in Wales.

They are both old breeds, dating back centuries, and bear a strong resemblance to the Swedish vallhund, although the relationship between these breeds is unclear. Their small size is advantageous, because it means they can move easily among the cattle, encouraging them to move forward by nipping at their heels, with relatively little risk of being kicked, which could obviously have fatal consequences.

Corgis once played an important part in driving herds of cattle to market, but unfortunately their tendency to nip is still apparent in the breed today, and they may respond almost instinctively in this way on occasions. Firm training from an early age

LEFT In common with other sheepdogs, the Bergamasco is a lively and intelligent breed that will not thrive if kept confined in urban surroundings. Behavioral problems will inevitably develop under these circumstances.

BELOW Dogs have been used for herding and guarding stock for centuries, and working sheepdogs in particular are a common sight in many countries.

will deter this type of behavior, but even so there are probably other breeds better suited to a home with children.

Australian herding dogs

Herding dogs with excellent stamina and adaptable natures were required to work in Australia and one of the best-known breeds evolved for this purpose is the Australian cattle dog. It is slightly larger than the corgi, measuring up to 20 in (51 cm) high at the shoulders. A wide selection of breeds is thought to have contributed to its ancestry, including possibly the dingo, as well as the Dalmatian, which is why Australian cattle dog puppies are white at birth.

While the dingo helped to contribute the required stamina, its semblance to a wolf-dog hybrid means these dogs are not responsive to training. The Dalmatian, bred to trot beside the carriages of the rich in Britain and elsewhere, has a more malleable nature, as well as the ability to cover large expanses of ground at a fair pace.

Another Australian herding breed with an interesting ancestry is the kelpie. These sheepdogs are descended from a pair of collies, sent out from England in 1870, that produced puppies on their arrival. In due course, one of these then mated with a local dog, which was called kelpie.

Various colors, ranging from shades of red to brown, are seen in the case of the Australian kelpie. Black dogs in this instance are called barbs, although they are in fact the same breed. Like all good sheepdogs, they have the ability to control the sheep not so much by running around after them as by using their eyes and fixing them with their gaze.

One member of this group becoming increasingly popular on the international show scene at present, is the Australian shepherd. Confusingly, however, this breed has actually been developed mainly in the United States, with its origins lying in France and Spain.

BASIC INSTINCTS

Adapted to heat

The fennec fox is a type of wild dog that is found in hot, arid climates. There is no cover for hunting purposes, so it relies on its large ears to locate rodents and other creatures that it can catch. The fox has to hunt after dark when the temperature is much cooler. During the heat of the day, it often hides away in burrows or rocky outcrops.

ABOVE The Australian cattle dog is a tough, hardy herding breed, with excellent stamina.

ABOVE The Swedish elkhound is very similar in appearance and coloration to a gray wolf. It is the largest of the elkhound breeds that are native to Scandinavia.

ABOVE The Karelian bear dog is a hunting companion, bred in Finland. In contrast, the doberman (BELOW) is a breed developed primarily as a guardian, and still retains a rather dominant nature. Both may be considered to be working breeds.

Working dogs

This is one of the most diverse categories, corresponding roughly to the utility breeds featured in the Kennel Club classification. As a result, the members of this group have a range of backgrounds and have been used for a variety of purposes. It is therefore particularly important to look into the breed history very carefully, in order to gain a reliable indication of the dog's likely temperament. A number of these breeds are now no longer kept for their original purpose and are at risk of dying out, unless they attract the attention of dog-lovers.

Spitz breeds

Already the Tahltan bear dog has disappeared from North America, while in Europe, a similar breed, the karelian bear dog, underwent a decline in numbers in the 1960s. It is named after the province of Finland where it evolved. Today, this striking black and white breed has undergone a revival in numbers and its future is much more secure.

Similar spitz-type breeds from Scandinavia, characterized by their pricked ears, resembling those of wolves, and a well-furred tail that will curl to one side of the body when the dog is standing. They have been kept in this part of the world for centuries, as multi-purpose dogs used to herd stock as well as hunt. Some, such as the Swedish elkhound, which stands up to 25 in (64 cm) tall and is the largest member of the group, have a coloration similar to that of the gray wolf.

An alert disposition combined with a friendly nature is a feature of these dogs, which means that, in more recent times, they have appealed to those seeking a companion breed. They are not always as well disposed toward others of their own kind.

Rottweiler

A number of the working dogs are large and powerful in build, as typified by the Rottweiler. This breed is very popular in many countries, especially the United States, having originated in the German town of Rottweil during the last century. Standing up to 27 in (69 cm) at the shoulder and weighing 110 lb (50 kg), it is a formidable guardian when aroused, and firm training is essential from puppyhood to keep its aggressive tendencies under control.

Doberman

The Doberman, another German breed, is often similarly colored to the rottweiler, with black and tan markings, and a sleek, short coat. It has a narrower muzzle, however, and a lighter build. Bred originally to protect a tax collector called Louis Doberman, this breed is potentially aggressive toward those whom it regards as strangers, although great efforts have been made by breeders to remove this particular trait from its character.

Dobermans which show any indication of this behavior in the show ring will never be among the

ABOVE The St. Bernard first attracted attention because of its mountain rescue skills, and it is now a popular pet worldwide, in spite of its tendency to dribble.

winners. But it is vital that this type of dog is kept under control at all times, and never left alone in the company of children.

St. Bernard

Other working breeds are recognized for their friendly dispositions, in spite of their large size. Among them is the St. Bernard, which can weigh as much as 200 lb (91 kg). Its origins can be traced back over 1,000 years, to the Hospice of St. Bernard de Menthon, in the Swiss Alps. The nearby treacherous mountain pass claimed the lives of many travelers and these large dogs were used to rescue those in difficulties. Over the centuries, they are reputed to have saved more than 2,500 lives.

Gundogs (sporting dogs)

A range of today's most popular breeds of dog are to be found in this grouping. This is not entirely surprising, because they were evolved to work at close quarters with people, and so are very responsive to training, as well as being friendly by nature. Although shooting with guns did not become widespread until the 1800s, the ancestry of a number of these breeds goes back much farther. Prior to this, dogs such as spaniels were used to locate and then retrieve birds, such as waterfowl for example, that had been shot with bows.

Water dogs

One of the characteristics of many members of the gundog grouping is their readiness to enter water. While wolves themselves are able to swim, they tend not to do so unless for a particular reason. It may seem hard to believe, based on its appearance, but the poodle was originally bred as a retriever. The manicured and distinctive coat associated with the breed stems from this era.

The limbs, especially the area around the joints, were shaved of fur to assist the swimming abilities of these dogs, but much of the hair on the body was left, to give better insulation against the cold water.

Leaving the hair long on the tip of the tail meant that it was easier to watch the poodle's progress.

Wildfowling abilities are apparent in a number of these sporting breeds, including the curly-coated retriever. Like the poodle, it also has a dense and tightly curled coat. The curls are most apparent on the body, with the legs again being used to assist the dog to swim well. The tapering tail acts rather like a rudder.

The third representative of this group with a curled coat is the Irish water spaniel. The advantage of this type of coat structure is that it is relatively water-resistant. As a consequence, the dog can shake much of the water out of its coat when emerging onto land and thus can continue working without risk of being chilled.

Pointers

The keen scenting abilities of the pointer have been valued for centuries. Its role is at the start of the search for game. Part of its amazing scenting skill is thought to have come from crossings involving bloodhounds.

Apart from the pointer itself, there are a number of similar breeds that originate from various European countries, such as the large French

ABOVE An Irish water spaniel — it has a dense water-repellent coat, not unlike that of the poodle which may be descended from this ancient breed.

ABOVE A curly-coated retriever. Its dense coat again helps to trap air close to the body, so the dog does not become rapidly chilled in cold water.

LEFT The pointer has a broad nose which means that it has an acute sense of smell and, once it has located potential quarry for the hunter, it will then pause and adopt its characteristic position, effectively pointing out the direction of the creature.

pointer, the German wire-haired pointer, and the old Danish pointer. Many of these still remain localized in distribution, even within their country of origin. This applies particularly in France, where a number of different Pointer breeds are to be found.

Setters

Another group that has evolved because of its ability to locate and indicate the presence of game is the setter, many of which, particularly the Irish setter (often incorrectly called the red setter), are now popular as household pets. The name "setter" is derived from an old English word "set", which means "sit" and describes the way that these dogs respond having scented game. Setters have broad heads and relatively long coats, with longer hair, known as "feathering", present on the back of the front legs and along the underside of the tail.

Spaniels

Smaller in stature are the spaniels, which, today, are often kept purely as pets, although they are equally at home as working gundogs. There has been a divergence in type, with show dogs having more profuse coats than their working counterparts. They are used to flush game and also to retrieve.

Golden and labrador retrievers

The most adaptable gundogs are the golden and labrador retrievers, which are now among the

PURPOSE-BUILT SWIMMERS

In the case of some gundogs, the feet have become modified to assist their swimming abilities. The Chesapeake Bay retriever, named after the area of the United States where it was developed in the 1800s, has webbed toes for this purpose, combined with very powerful hindquarters. Its coat is relatively smooth but oily, which again protects against waterlogging and chilling.

most popular breeds in the world. Their scenting skills and intelligence are applied in many different situations, both in the home and elsewhere. They may work as guide dogs or hearing dogs and are equally suited for working in airports seeking out drugs or explosives. In the field, they are still used as retrievers, while their responsive, lively personalities also make them popular as family pets.

Feral dogs

Around the world, there are a number of feral dogs. These are domestic dogs which have reverted back to an independent, free-living life style, as distinct from strays seen on city streets.

Dingoes

The dingo is the best-known example of a feral dog, and is believed to have been taken to Australia by the early Aboriginal settlers. It is now clear, however, that the links between dingoes and the Aborigines are not as strong as previously thought. These dogs are generally tolerated rather than encouraged by the Aboriginal people, and do not play a significant role in their culture. This may be because dingoes have proved almost impossible to train.

Their ancestry remains a mystery, but there are a number of similar dogs to be found further north in Asia. As might be expected, dingoes show considerable variation in size, as they are not a standardized breed and they have now diverged from their ancestral roots.

One of the features of the dingo which is distinctive is its coloration — this is a reddish-brown shade, often with white markings on the underparts. Subtle changes are occurring, however, because of hybridization between dingoes and other dogs in parts of their range.

There are several significant anatomical differences which set dingoes apart from domestic dogs. The most obvious is probably the fact that their canine and carnassial teeth are larger, while in temperament dingoes are relatively quiet, notably when hunting. This may be because, in many areas, they do not associate together like wolves. Instead, they rely on an element of surprise to achieve a kill, rather than on the collective abilities of a pack.

However, where there are packs, the structure is similar to that normally associated with wolves. There is a matriarchal hierarchy, to the extent that only the dominant female will breed. If another female in the pack becomes pregnant, the matriarch will kill her rival's pups. Unlike most domestic breeds, dingoes

BELOW The New Guinea singing dog is kept in a state of semi-liberty around settlements on that island. Some of these dogs are now being kept and bred in the U.S.

BELOW The dingo has been hunted heavily in Australia because it is blamed for attacking sheep. These feral dogs are thought to have been resident in Australia for more than 8, 000 years

come into season only once a year rather than twice. Mating usually occurs in March or April, with as many as ten young being born nine weeks later. It will be around six months before they are fully independent.

Dingoes have been heavily hunted because of the damage they might inflict on Australia's sheep industry, especially at lambing time, but, in reality, they prey readily on the country's native animals, such as wallabies.

New Guinea singing dog

On islands to the north of Australia, similar feral dog populations are found, and these are attracting interest from dog-fanciers. Currently, the best known of these is the New Guinea singing dog, although others can be found on New Ireland and elsewhere. It, too, has a reddish coat, often broken with white markings, and an unusual, almost melodic call.

Canaan dog

Feral dogs are sometimes also known as pariahs. In the Middle East, successful repeated domestication has occurred, resulting in the emergence of the Canaan dog. The breeding program began in 1935 in Israel, and Canaan dogs are now kept in many countries. Their appearance has become standardized, but they retain the features of a typical pariah dog.

Their ancestors were probably first kept around 4,000 years ago, to guard herds of goats from predators, such as jackals. As a result, they are quite amenable to training and this has helped to ensure their popularity.

ABOVE The Canaan dog is a breed which, having lived in a feral state, has now been domesticated again.

BASIC INSTINCTS

A tough life

Many dogs live in a state of semi-liberty in places such as Africa. They often have to forage for much of their own food, but benefit from being in contact with people as well, since they receive shelter and some care. This particular dog, drinking at an African water hole is in poor condition. Many such dogs are heavily infected by internal and external parasites, and they are vulnerable to illnesses which they may acquire from their wild relatives. Not surprisingly, their life expectancy tends to be lower than that of truly domestic dogs.

EARLY LIFE

The social coherence and pack structure of the gray wolf is one reason why the domestication of these wild canids proved to be successful. The domestic dog has effectively transferred its allegiance from the pack to people, although there is a key socialization period early in a puppy's life that is vital to its future development. If deprived of contact with people at this crucial stage, it will prove difficult to win the dog's confidence as it grows older. The hierarchy that exists within a pack means that a young puppy will normally adapt well to domestic surroundings, and will be eager to win approval from its owner and other members of the family.

BREEDING
"Heat" in seasons

Domestic dogs in general tend to reproduce more prolifically than the gray wolf. Bitches usually have two periods of reproductive activity, known as "heats", each year, whereas female wolves only come into season once. However, there are breed differences, with the Basenji, for example, generally having only one heat annually. This often occurs in the fall, rather than in spring or summer as in most breeds.

There are differences between individuals, and also a variance due to latitude. The basenji, unlike most breeds, originates from equatorial areas, where there are no significant seasonal distinctions. In contrast, breeds from the far north, and wolves living in this area, benefit from coming into heat in late winter. The pups are then born in late spring or early summer, when the climate is likely to be favorable for their survival and prey easier to acquire.

The importance of factors such as climate is now far less important to domestic dogs, simply because, in most cases, they are no longer dependent on obtaining their own food, nor on the temperature.

Bitches will come into heat throughout their lives, beginning at around six months. Smaller breeds mature more rapidly than larger ones, probably because they attain adult size at an earlier stage. Large dogs may not have their first period of heat until they are over a year old.

It is not recommended to allow a bitch to mate until her second heat at the earliest, which means, in the case of a larger breed, she could be approaching two years old before she has her first litter of puppies. Although she will have two periods of heat each year, the bitch should not be allowed to

ABOVE The basenji displays the typical reproductive pattern of the gray wolf, with bitches coming into season just once a year, rather than twice like most domestic dogs

Practical Pointer
Check that male dogs, especially toy breeds, have two testicles in their scrotum. It can happen that one is retained within the body, giving rise to the condition known as cryptorchidism. This requires surgical correction, since the retained testicle can give rise to a Sertoli cell tumor.

have more than one litter in a year, because of the demands of raising the puppies.

Male dogs mature at a similar age to females, although there are significant breed differences — with male beagles, for example, usually attaining maturity at a much earlier stage than females. Even so, it is inadvisable to use them for breeding purposes until they are at least a year old.

Domestic dogs are usually more promiscuous than wolves. If unsupervised, they will mate at the earliest opportunity, which is why a bitch on heat must be closely chaperoned to prevent her from becoming pregnant. Only in a very few breeds, notably those developed largely in isolation, such as the saluki from North Africa, is the bitch likely to reject the advances of dogs other than her own breed.

BASIC INSTINCTS

Mating wolves

In the case of wolves, it is likely to be only the dominant pair which actually mate. Young animals which have just attained puberty, and therefore are at a relatively low level in the social hierarchy of the pack, are unlikely to be reproductively active.

By concentrating all the pack's resources on one litter of cubs, there is an increased likelihood that a significant number of them will survive to maturity. If there were many cubs, the pack would be likely to face difficulties in finding sufficient food and chaperoning a group of cubs of different ages.

Male and female cycles

Although male dogs can mate at any time of the year, they will only attempt to do so when the female is on heat. Chemical messengers, known as pheromones, are produced by the bitch at this time and serve to attract males. These molecules are wafted in the breeze and can carry a considerable distance, which is why male dogs may be drawn from afar when there is a bitch on heat in the neighborhood.

Onset of heat

The earliest visual indication of heat is swelling of the vulva, and a blood-stained discharge which originates from the uterus. In contrast to menstruation, this bleeding precedes ovulation. The blood loss is variable, but can usually be detected on the bitch's bedding. She will also spend longer than normal licking her hind-quarters at this stage.

Her behavior also alters, and she becomes more playful, encouraging the male's interest. However, male dogs which do approach at this stage will not be permitted to mate while the bitch is still in pro-estrus. This typically lasts about nine days and, subsequently, the bitch then enters the estrus phase, during which copulation is likely to occur.

Estrus and ovulation

As estrus proceeds, so the vaginal discharge changes from being bloody to becoming clearer. Instead of bounding away when approached by a male, the bitch will stand with her tail to one side of her body, indicating a readiness to mate. She will not necessarily

Practical Pointer
Be particularly careful with a bitch in season, because her desire to mate may be so strong that she will slip out of the garden in search of a mate. Do not allow her out unsupervised.

BELOW Although a number of male dogs may be drawn to a bitch in heat, it will be the dominant individual, not necessarily the biggest dog, who will mate with her.

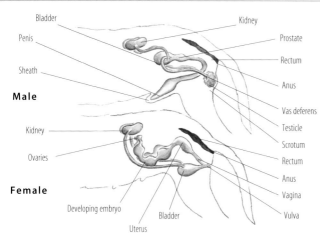

Bladder
Kidney
Penis
Prostate
Rectum
Sheath
Anus
Male
Vas deferens
Kidney
Testicle
Scrotum
Ovaries
Rectum
Anus
Female
Vagina
Vulva
Developing embryo
Bladder
Uterus

LEFT The anatomy of the reproductive systems of the male dog (top) and the bitch (bottom). The female in this case is already pregnant, with signs of the developing fetuses already evident as swellings in her uterus. Whereas the bitch's genital opening is at the rear of her body, it is located underneath the body in front of the hindlimbs in the case of the male.

accept all dogs which approach her. She has to perceive the male as being more dominant than herself, as occurs in the case of wolves.

Ovulation itself usually takes place within a few days of the beginning of estrus, but because there is no accompanying increase in temperature, as there is in humans, it cannot be detected easily. As a result, breeders tend to mate bitches twice between the tenth and fourteenth day from the start of the breeding cycle, in order to increase the likelihood of a successful mating.

Mating

The male clasps the female tightly during mating. In most cases, a so-called "tie" is formed, in which the swollen tip of the male's penis is anchored into place by the muscles of the bitch's vagina. The bone in the dog's penis helps to provide rigidity during the mating process.

The spermatozoa are ejaculated at an early stage, after which the male, still inside his partner, switches position. He drops down off her back and swings round so that, ultimately, their hindquarters

are together while their heads are pointing in opposite directions.

As with the wolf, this serves to provide more safety at what is a vulnerable time for both dogs. During this period, which can occasionally last for over an hour, secretions from the prostate gland are released into the female's reproductive tract, which enhance the prospect of fertilization. Finally the dogs separate and clean themselves.

It is not strictly essential for a tie to take place in order for fertilization to occur, and in certain breeds, notably the chow chow, a tie is unlikely to be formed. In any event, avoid separating the dogs during mating, because this could cause injury. Once they are tied, it is too late to prevent any transfer of sperm and you will need to arrange for the bitch to have a special injection if you wish to prevent her conceiving puppies.

Practical Pointer

Bitches may mate repeatedly during estrus, so do not allow your bitch to wander, even after mating, because she may well seek another mate.

The puppies in a litter may be the offspring of more than one father.

Pregnancy

Assuming that mating is successful, pregnancy is likely to last approximately nine weeks. In other cases, the signs of estrus will subside, usually after a period of roughly two weeks, so that the period of heat extends for just over three weeks on average. There will then follow a lengthy anestrus phase, lasting perhaps five months or more, until the next period of heat.

Signs of pregnancy

It is difficult to tell for the first month whether or not mating has been successful. During this stage, the fertilized eggs move down the oviducts to the uterus, which has a short body and long horns. This is because there are normally a relatively large number of puppies and the horns actually provide a

Practical Pointer

It is quite normal for milk to appear at the nipples prior to the puppies being born. Equally, pregnancy may vary in length, extending for up to seventy days without necessitating any cause for concern, although a veterinary check-up under these circumstances is recommended.

means of accommodating them all successfully.

The fertilized eggs implant into the wall of the uterus, where they develop a placental connection. The placenta serves to nourish the puppies as they grow. In the early stages, do not be tempted to prod the bitch's abdomen to see if you can feel the pups because this could cause a fatal injury. Obvious signs, such as abdominal distention and swelling of the mammary glands, become apparent about five weeks into the pregnancy. This parallels the situation in the wolf, where the physical growth in size of the cubs occurs in the final stages, so as to minimize the encumbrance to the female, who still needs to keep up with the pack and hunt.

Care of the bitch

During most of the pregnancy, the bitch will not require any special treatment. She can be allowed to exercise normally, which will help to maintain her muscle tone, but toward the end of the gestation period, she should be discouraged from jumping. Only in the latter stages, when the puppies are growing in size, is she likely to require additional food.

It is better to offer her extra food in the form of additional meals, rather than simply increasing the amount of food given in her regular feeding schedule, because her abdomen will already be distended by the presence of the puppies. You should seek advice from your veterinarian about the amount of food she will require. It is also important to deworm the bitch to lower the risk to the puppies of early infection.

It is important to choose a quiet area in the home where the dog can give birth and the puppies can be reared through to independence. The kitchen can be too busy and may be positively dangerous,

LEFT This sheepdog is near the end of her pregnancy, with her nipples being more prominent than usual. She gave birth to 12 puppies. Wolves may have up to 11 offspring although 6 is probably an average litter.

especially when cooking is taking place, unless the puppies are duly constrained. The bathroom may be an alternative, but here again, there will inevitably be disturbances at certain times of the day. A spare bedroom is the ideal situation, if available, although you must be prepared to cover the floor with a sheet of linoleum or similar material that can be easily cleaned.

ABOVE Wolves are very vulnerable as cubs, and the mother may need to move her offspring from potential danger, carrying them individually in her mouth.

WHELPING BOX

A whelping box is recommended for when the bitch is ready to give birth and this should be made available to her during the last ten days of pregnancy. The box should be large enough to allow her to lie out comfortably. It should have a barrier extending about 3 in (7.5 cm) around the sides so that there will be no risk of the bitch crushing her puppies soon after birth. This can be a particular problem with some of the larger breeds. Easy access to the box is important, so the sides should be correspondingly low, while ensuring that the puppies will be securely contained. Line the box with a thick layer of newspaper, and before the puppies are due, put in an old blanket, or similar bedding, to encourage the bitch to sleep there.

Birth

Female wolves and domestic dogs both seek a quiet haven when the birth is imminent. Wolves may use a cave or a similar den, while a dog, if she dislikes the position of the whelping box, will seek another locality. There is little point in trying to dissuade her under these circumstances, although you may be able to compromise by moving the whelping box to the part of the home which your bitch prefers.

Restlessness is one of the most likely signs that birth is really imminent, and a bitch also sometimes loses her appetite and vomits at this stage. Other indicators include swelling of the vulva, which also becomes a darker shade of pink. Immediately prior to the birth, you may also notice that the pelvic ligaments slacken, so that the upper points of the hips appear more pronounced.

Birth process

In the vast majority of cases, birth proceeds without problems, although the bitch may appear to be rather distressed, particularly if she has not given birth before, frequently panting or even shivering. When the puppies are soon to be born, abdominal contractions become quite apparent. The puppies themselves are produced head first, often with the allantoic sacs surrounding them still intact.

The bitch instinctively breaks this sac with her teeth and then licks the puppy to start it breathing. Should the puppy still be attached to its placenta, via the umbilical cord, she will also bite through and sever this connection. Once the birth process begins, the puppies are born in quite rapid succession, typically at about thirty-minute intervals.

Placentas

It is important to count the placentas, which will be expelled after each puppy. These are usually eaten by the bitch — such behavior is quite normal and not indicative of impending cannibalism. Female wolves behave in the same way because, by disposing of the afterbirth, there is less to attract predators to the den. Should the placentas be retained in the body, this can give rise to a serious infection.

Litter size

Where there is a difference, however, is in the numbers of offspring produced. Larger dogs, with bigger reproductive tracts, have larger litters than smaller breeds, but all puppies are of a similar size at birth. The upper limit for a litter for smaller breeds of dog is six pups, while up to fourteen puppies may be born to large bitches.

LEFT It is vital that puppies start suckling without delay after being born, because the first milk or colostrum contains protective antibodies. These border collie puppies are just a day old.

ABOVE In the case of the gray wolf the average size of a litter comprises six cubs although there may be some variation. The gestation period for both wolves and dogs is similar, usually lasting 63 days.

Problems

Should you suspect any problems during the birth process, contact your veterinarian for advice. One of the most common is a breech birth, when the puppy is born tail first rather than head first. It can become stuck in this position, with fatal consequences unless it is freed without delay. Some breeds, notably those with large heads, such as the bulldog, are more prone to difficulties in giving birth than others.

In the case of the gray wolf the average size of a litter comprises six cubs although there may be some variation. The gestation period for both wolves and dogs is similar, usually lasting 63 days.

BASIC INSTINCTS

Security
Both wolves and domestic dogs seek out a quiet spot where they can give birth. Caves or underground retreats are favored by all wild dogs for this purpose. Here the offspring can remain in relative safety while their mother seeks food, or water, which is vital in order to maintain a sufficient flow of milk. The young will remain in close proximity to each other at first, to conserve their body heat.

GROWING UP
Young puppies

Healthy puppies grow surprisingly fast. Their eyes will begin to open when they are about a fortnight old and their hearing will be effective in a further week. Their mother will watch over them closely at first, attending to all their needs while they are helpless. By licking them, she regulates their body functions until they are about three weeks old and starting to move around on their own.

This is also the stage at which the puppies are likely to start eating on their own, although it will still be several weeks before they are independent. At this stage, in common with her wild relatives, the bitch is likely to respond by vomiting food for them. This is quite normal behavior, and not a cause for concern. Vomiting food may also be easier for the puppies to digest, as it will have been exposed to digestive juices in the bitch's stomach (although the majority of enzymatic action occurs lower down the digestive tract, in the small intestine).

Weaning

The attitude of the bitch to her puppies will change from this stage onward. She will spend less time with them and will discourage them from suckling, so they will be more inclined to switch to solid food. Her milk output also declines as the puppies suckle less, but it will not be until they are about six weeks old that their first teeth start to emerge.

Puppies are all weaned at a similar age, in spite of the difference in the size of the various breeds. The main divergence in growth rate actually takes place in the post-weaning period. The diet for puppies from this stage onward is therefore important; they will need on average about twice the amount of food compared with an adult dog of the equivalent weight.

Choosing a puppy

When it comes to choosing a puppy, it is quite usual for the litter to be viewed before they are independent. Purchasing direct from the breeder provides much greater insight into the background of a puppy. One which has been reared in domestic surroundings is likely to be instinctively more friendly than a young dog that has lived in kennels throughout its early life. There is actually a crucial period, often described as the socialization phase,

RIGHT Puppies will be keen to explore, and this is the stage during which they are most likely to encounter problems. It is possible that this young dog could end up with a flower pot stuck on its head for example.

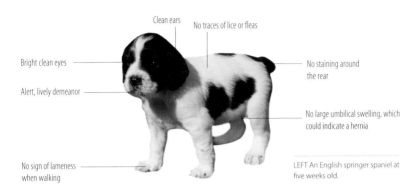

Clean ears

No traces of lice or fleas

Bright clean eyes

Alert, lively demeanor

No staining around the rear

No large umbilical swelling, which could indicate a hernia

No sign of lameness when walking

LEFT An English springer spaniel at five weeks old.

lasting from the first three to fourteen days of the puppy's life. If the young dog does not have any close contact with people at this stage, it is likely to remain shy throughout its life.

When choosing a puppy, there are several aspects to consider, such as whether or not you want to exhibit your pet in the future. A puppy from show stock is likely to be correspondingly more expensive than one bought from an ordinary pure-bred dog, which may be slightly mismarked for example, which would make it unsuitable for the show ring.

If you are concerned about breeding from your puppy in the future, then obtain a bitch. You can arrange for her to be mated with a suitable stud dog in due course. Bitches may prove more affectionate than dogs and are also less likely to stray, but you will have the problem of their periods of heat to cope with, unless they are neutered.

A healthy puppy

Healthy puppies tend to be very lively when they are awake, but they will also sleep for long periods. This is quite normal. Their skin is loose and pliable, and they should feel plump. Their eyes should be clear, with no sign of any discharge onto the surrounding

ABOVE When picking up a puppy, the most important thing is to restrain the hindquarters properly, to prevent the young dog from struggling. Puppies should be lifted up regularly from an early age, so they become used to the experience and then will not resent it in later life.

fur at the time of weaning, and their ears should be clean.

Check the coat for any signs of parasites (see page 159) and also check under the tail — any staining here is indicative of diarrhea. This need not necessarily be a cause for concern as it can be linked with a deworming treatment. The puppy should move about freely and also needs to be alert.

CHOOSING YOUR PUPPY

It is important to think very carefully before deciding to acquire a puppy. They are demanding animals and have to be trained to integrate fully into family life.

The responsibilities of obtaining a puppy

Owning a dog can be a great source of pleasure as millions of people worldwide will testify, but not everyone is able to devote the time and care necessary to ensure a dog's well-being.

Keeping any pet places certain obvious restraints on the person involved in its care, and dogs rank among the most demanding of companion animals. A dog will need to be fed, exercised and groomed on a regular basis, and this is likely to take up at least an hour every day throughout the year. The cost of keeping a dog can prove a significant burden on finances too. There will be expenditure on food, equipment and routine veterinary care, and certain breeds may require professional grooming. Other incidental costs are boarding kennels and licensing.

Introducing a dog of any type into the home will inevitably cause some disturbance to the domestic routine, and it is certain to result in extra work. For example, all dogs shed dead hairs and these rapidly accumulate unless they are cleaned up daily. Some damage to the home or furnishings may also result from ownership of a dog, especially a puppy. This is more likely to happen if the animal is bored. As much time and attention must be given to a dog, as to an individual member of a family.

Mongrel or a Pedigreed dog?

A mongrel is a dog which belongs to no specific breed, whereas a pedigreed animal, as its name suggests, has been carefully bred over generations to conform as closely as possible to the prescribed

ABOVE These Norfolk Terrier puppies will probably all grow up to be gentle and even-tempered dogs but it is wise not to select the most dominant nor the most submissive one of the litter. Ideally, your puppy should fall between these two extremes in temperament and be alert, curious and playful.

standards for that particular breed as laid down by the appropriate authority in the country concerned. The likely adult size and shape of a young pedigreed dog can, therefore, be assessed with much greater accuracy than can that of a mongrel puppy. The feet can prove a useful indicator of the potential size of a young mongrel, however; relatively large feet compared with body size suggest that the puppy will develop into a big dog. By the age of four months, any dog, including a mongrel, should be about two-thirds of its final adult size.

Mongrels can often be obtained at little or no cost, but the purchase of a pedigreed dog is likely to prove an expensive undertaking, reflecting the time and care that has been expended on developing the bloodline. For those wishing to show their dog later in life, however, a pedigreed animal is clearly essential. It is often said that mongrels are less prone to illness than their pedigreed counterparts. While this is untrue in the case of infectious diseases, it is certainly correct that mongrels are less at risk from the inherited and congenital disorders that can afflict most pedigreed breeds.

Making the choice of getting an adult dog or puppy

A young puppy is likely to prove more adaptable than an adult dog and is certainly preferable for a home with children. Older dogs can prove nervous, especially if they have had several homes previously, and they may not be used to children. They will take longer to settle into the domestic environment and are likely to be relatively unresponsive to training. Difficulties that can arise are, for example, the inability of the dog to respond to a new name and its initial reluctance to remain with its new owner when let off the leash. Given time and patience, however, such problems can be overcome to a great extent, but the settling-in period for an adult dog can be a difficult time, especially for the novice owner and particularly if the dog's origins are unknown.

If you intend to exhibit your dog later, you may want an older individual whose show potential can be assessed more easily than a puppy's. But a dog that has lived most of its life in a kennel will also have difficulty adapting to a domestic environment. Studies have shown that there is a so-called socialization period in the life of young dogs between the ages of about six and thirteen weeks during which time they need to be exposed to human company. The more attention they receive during this time the better they will settle in the home. A particular difficulty associated with dogs kept under kennel conditions during the early formative months of their life is that they have never been housetrained, and this can prove difficult to teach at a later stage.

Male and females dogs

As a general rule, male dogs are more prone than females to escape and wander off, particularly in an area where there are a number of dogs and perhaps a bitch in heat nearby. They can also prove less responsive to training. For these reasons, bitches are preferred as guide dogs for the blind. The major drawback in owning a bitch, however, stems from the two periods of reproductive activity each year and the risk of an accidental mating during these "heats" leading to unwanted puppies. Another troublesome side effect can be the occurrence of phantom pregnancies.

LEFT Selecting a puppy from a private home means that You can meet the mother, note how the puppies behave among their littermates, and pick one out at your leisure. Puppies from a private home are usually well balanced, due to the benefits of good personal care and early contact with people.

The differing temperaments of dog breeds

The various pedigreed breeds have been developed for specific purposes and thus do exhibit some variation in temperament. Nevertheless, there is obviously pressure for all breeds to be sociable in human company! The difference in temperament is perhaps not marked in the training sphere. Gundogs such as the Retriever are relatively responsive to training compared with others such as the so-called sight hounds like the Afghan Hound, which have been developed for chasing game over considerable distance. Guard dogs such as the Rottweiler are often highly suspicious of strangers but generally tolerant of those they know well. Perhaps the least satisfactory group of dogs in terms of temperament for use as family pets are those bred specifically for fighting, such as the Staffordshire Bull Terrier. They can be easily provoked to bite by children as well as by other dogs; of course, some individuals are more tolerant than others, and firm training can help to overcome such tendencies. Breeders have also mad strenuous efforts to purge aggressive traits from contemporary bloodlines.

Nevertheless, temperamental disorders do occur and often receive widespread publicity, particularly in popular breeds such as the German Shepherd (formerly known as the Alsatian). Certain bloodlines exhibit neuroses more often than others, and it is a good idea to look into this by talking to breeders before obtaining a dog. Not only the large breeds can be affected; indeed, some smaller dogs may well exhibit such behavior. In Britain, temperament problems may be encountered quite often in Cocker Spaniels, Dobermanns and certain other breeds. Always consult a local veterinarian for advice as soon as possible if a dog starts showing aggressive traits.

BELOW LEFT The Komondor has an unusual coat (above) that consists of cords which must be separated if the coat becomes wet, to prevent matting. This breed also needs firm control and training.

BELOW The varying size of dogs is irrelevant to their compatibility — a Great Dane can be seen in harmonious company with a Yorkshire Terrier (left). The various breeds have been evolved for different purposes, and their temperaments may vary somewhat as a result.

The bond between a child and a dog can become very strong, but in the first instance, the child must be taught not to tease or hurt the dog in any way. Mutual trust is important

Different breeds, different challenges

A large dog will need more space than a smaller one, and the bigger breeds, in their exuberance, may inflict accidental damage on the home by knocking a cherished ornament off a low table with a sweep of the tail, for example. Some breeds such as the St. Bernard have a tendency to drool saliva from their mouths, and this can be deposited on furniture or carpeting. The majority of dogs moult, and some hair, even with fastidious daily grooming, will be deposited around the home. There are certain breeds, however, including the Bedlington and Kerry Blue Terriers and poodles, which do not lose their hair in the conventional sense. They will need regular clipping and stripping to keep their coats trim and free of dead hair respectively. The flattened faces associated with the achondroplastic breeds such as the Bulldog, Pug and Pekingese may lead to snuffling because of their compressed and shortened noses. This habit tends to worsen as the dog gets older and can become a source of irritation to some owners.

Buying a dog if you have a child who suffers from asthma

It would be sensible to seek medical advice first since allergies to dog hair and dust are certainly not unknown and may complicate an existing medical problem. Consider one of the breeds which do not shed in the conventional way or opt for one of the so-called "hairless" dogs such as the Chinese Crested. Unfortunately, this, like its Mexican counterpart, is a relatively scarce breed, and it also needs special protection during cold weather.

Buying a dog if you have young children

The choice of a dog for a home where there are young children necessitates particular care. A dog of a fairly tolerant breed such as a Whippet or a Labrador Retriever is to be recommended. Small dogs are not always to be encouraged because they themselves may be injured if handled roughly and are more liable to bite as a result. In any event, always supervise contact between the children and the dog, particularly in the early stages when they are unfamiliar with each other. Children must be taught not to hurt the dog by playing roughly with it, and they should always be encouraged to participate in its care, even if only to offer the dog its food bowl. It is of course vital to follow a strict deworming schedule, as advised by your veterinarian, because of the slight risk of the transmission of parasitic worm eggs from dog to child. This is more likely to occur outdoors, and dog excrement should be removed from the environment on a daily basis.

ABOVE As companions for elderly people, dogs are ideal. But, the choice of dog needs to be considered carefully — obviously, a large, boisterous puppy would be unsuitable in many cases.

Which dog breed to buy if you are away from the home most of the day

Use the money you would have spent on a dog either to install a burglar alarm or to increase your insurance coverage. Dogs are social creatures by nature and should never be shut up all day without attention on a regular basis. Puppies in particular will prove highly destructive under such conditions and may well attract complaints from neighbors as they are likely to howl for attention. It will be virtually impossible to train a young dog kept in this way, and the inevitable soiling of carpets will be a source of constant frustration to you. Older dogs may be left occasionally for short periods, but be sure to encourage them to use the garden beforehand and always leave a fresh supply of drinking water available when you are away.

BELOW Puppies are inquisitive, and will naturally be interested in other pets, such as cats and so scenes such as this Norfolk terrier playing with a tabby kitten are not unusual. Indeed, a strong bond can develop between a puppy and kitten as they grow up together.

Buying a dog for an elderly relative who lives alone

Studies being undertaken into the relationship between pets and their owners are confirming the importance of pet ownership, particularly for people living alone. As to whether an elderly person would be better suited to another type of pet such as a budgerigar, the decision depends to a great extent on the physical health of the person, and on the amount of assistance the family can offer in caring for a dog. The type of dog should be considered very carefully. A puppy may prove too difficult, as would a large dog. Ideally, this is a situation where an older small dog, known to be of reliable temperament, would be ideal, but unfortunately a dog of this type is often difficult to find. Try to help with exercising, particularly during the winter months when pavements can be slippery. A dog could cause an elderly person to fall and hurt themself.

ABOVE An older dog may well appreciate the company of a young individual (right), although care must be taken during the early stages to ensure that the established dog does not feel challenged by the newcomer. There are various ways of minimizing the risk of such conflict.

Buying a puppy if you already own a cat and dog

Cats tend to ignore a new canine resident in the home, but this does not mean that the cat accepts the newcomer at once! The animals will need time to come to terms with each other. This stage must not be forced, but conflict must be avoided in the interim. The same applies when a new dog is introduced alongside an established dog. Feed them separately so there is no risk of fighting over food, and reassure all concerned. Remember that the newcomer is invading the territory of the resident dog, particular reassurance needs to be given to the older dog so that it does not feel that its position as the dominant individual is being usurped by the newcomer. Hierarchy is important to dogs and invokes strong instinctive feelings that are derived from their ancestors — packs of wolves.

There is less likelihood of conflict when a puppy is introduced; an older dog may challenge the hierarchy. The rigid social structure existing within a pack of wild dogs serves to prevent serious conflict, and this arrangement still exists in their domestic counterparts. Keep favouring the established dog so there is less likelihood of a challenge from the new arrival, but remember that the temperaments of the individuals concerned will vary. It may be a good idea to introduce them first on neutral territory outside the confines of the home — in a nearby park, for example. Bitches as a rule tend to be less aggressive than male dogs, and they are more likely to live alongside each other in harmony than are two male dogs. The introduction of a younger companion to an older dog can encourage a more lively disposition in the existing pet once both are accustomed to playing with each other.

The best time of year to obtain a puppy

In an ideal world, the best time is probably spring so that when inoculations are completed, the young dog can be trained out of doors at a time when the weather and day length are most favourable. Do not obtain a puppy in the summer if you are just going off on vacation, as this will disrupt the training routine. And most reputable kennels will be reluctant to take a young dog before it is fully protected by inoculations. It would also be extremely disturbing for a dog to be transferred to a new home and then moved again to a kennel within the space of a few weeks. Also, never buy a puppy at Christmas when the home is likely to be in disarray and full of visitors, as there will be little time to take care of the needs of the newcomer. It is no coincidence that most dogs are abandoned or discarded by their owners at these times of year.

Caring for "high maintenance" dog breeds

Certainly the long-haired breeds, such as the Afghan hound, will need more attention by virtue of their coat type. This applies not only to grooming, but also to drying the coat after the dog has been out in the rain. And the long hair around the feet will attract mud. Certain light-colored dogs may require regular washing around the eyes where the tear fluid stains the coat. Apart from considerations of coat care, some smaller dogs can also prove fussy and faddish eaters, and this may necessitate additional care and be a source of worry to owners.

BELOW The Afghan Hound (left) is one of the most fashionable breeds to acquire but people do tend to overlook the fact that it is also one of the breeds that demands most attention. The Afghans' long, soft coat needs plenty of grooming, training them may be difficult and they need considerable exercise.

LEFT Animal welfare organizations (right) provide many delightful pets — both mongrel and pedigreed. Litters of puppies are frequently given to these organizations and if new homes are not found for them, the puppies may have to be destroyed.

Finding a puppy of a particular breed

There are various ways to find a specific breed of puppy. Attending shows can be particularly valuable if you are seeking a dog for exhibition purposes at a later date. You can see which bloodlines are winning regularly and also the type of dog preferred by the judges. Details of shows can be found in the various national dog periodicals. These may also carry advertisements from breeders offering surplus stock for sale. A puppy of a popular breed will not be too difficult to obtain, but one from a scarcer breed may involve a wait. In some countries, directories, produced and revised annually, give details on breeders and the breeds they have available. The national Kennel Club will also be able to give you details. There are no recommended prices; generally, rare breeds and puppies from acclaimed bloodlines are relatively expensive. Occasionally, a breeder may have a poorly colored or marked puppy available at a substantially reduced price. Beware of any that have physical defects, since these may prove more expensive in the long term as veterinary fees mount up. Actually, a veterinarian may be able to suggest a reliable breeder in the neighborhood, provided the breed is not too rare.

Finding a mongrel puppy

You could look at local advertisements in newspapers; they often offer both pedigreed and mongrel puppies. Alternatively, some pet shops do have puppies for sale, but check such dogs closely. Staff may not be as knowledgeable as a breeder, and the mixing of young dogs from various premises can present disease problems less likely to arise in a dog purchased directly from the breeder. This also applies to animal sanctuaries, which have a constant input of dogs. Some are unlikely to have been inoculated and could be incubating diseases such as distemper. Such organizations usually have a surplus of older dogs rather than puppies, but litters are brought in from time to time. Do not be surprised or offended if you are asked questions and visited at home before being given a dog from an animal welfare organization. It is simply doing it's best to ensure that the dog does not have to suffer the trauma of moving to another home for a short time and then being discarded again.

When a pedigreed dog is homed by such organizations, its pedigree documents are not usually handed over, to discourage breeding from the dog. Indeed, some organizations may even insist on a neutering agreement. The problem of unwanted dogs is now so great that many breed associations have established their own rescue groups for specific breeds, unlike the more traditional organizations which care for all unwanted dogs. Indeed pedigreed dogs are just as likely to end up homeless as mongrels. Those who try to home such dogs are invariably self-financed. Do not forget to give a donation to help their work continue. Hopefully, the public can be educated eventually to adopt a more responsible attitude.

Guidance from breeders

The vast majority of breeders are genuine, trustworthy people who are concerned that their dogs have a good home, and they will go to great lengths to advise a potential purchaser. Nevertheless, do not rely entirely on what you are told; look at the puppy and its surroundings. When making a preliminary telephone call to arrange a time to visit, it is possible to get an initial impression. Explain what you want and ask questions such as the price of the puppies for sale and whether breeding stock has been checked for inherited defects such as hip dysplasia and progressive retinal atrophy. A conscientious breeder will acknowledge your interest in the breed and arrange a convenient time for a visit. Always try to visit the premises, even if it means traveling a fair distance, because traveling is preferable in the long term to receiving a puppy of the wrong type or one that is sick.

Breeders operating on a small scale frequently have litters of puppies living in the house. This ensures that the young dogs are used to the domestic environment from birth — unlike those that have been reared in kennels. Individual puppies will vary in temperament; there is a distinct social order established almost from birth, and some are more dominant than others. These are usually first to the food, pushing their contemporaries out of the way. Young puppies will sleep for quite long periods, and such behavior is not necessarily associated with illness. Watch them for a short time before focusing on a particular individual.

Points to check

Are their surroundings clean? Any excrement evident on the floor should be relatively firm, unless they have been dewormed shortly beforehand. Healthy puppies are relatively fat, and when handled (with their owner's permission) they will have loose, pliable skin. Starting at the head, look at the eyes. These should be clear and free from any discharge which could stain the fur, particularly at the sides of the eyes nearest the nose. The nose should be moist in appearance, and the ears should appear clean. Moving down the body, look at the fur closely for any signs of fleas or lice. The ribs can be felt but should not be evident when the puppy is held.

Underneath, check that there is no swelling in the midline which might indicate an umbilical

HIP DYSPLASIA

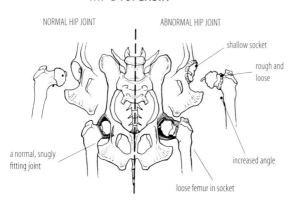

NORMAL HIP JOINT

ABNORMAL HIP JOINT

shallow socket

rough and loose

a normal, snugly fitting joint

increased angle

loose femur in socket

LEFT The hip joint is of the ball and socket type, with the head of the femur fitting into the socket of the pelvis. Hip dysplasia occurs when the development of the joint is faulty, or the socket is abnormally shallow. Radiography is used to screen breeding stock for this inherited problem, and also for diagnostic purposes.

hernia. This, although not serious, might need to be corrected at a later date by surgery. The belly should not appear pot-shaped as this can indicate a heavy parasitic worm burden and shows a lack of care on the part of the breeder. The anal area should appear clean. Any swelling around the groin could be a sign of an inguinal hernia, which in this locality is more serious than in the umbilical position. Once back on the ground, the puppy should move nimbly, with no signs of lameness. It will also respond readily to noise, provided it is not deaf; this can be a particular weakness in dogs which have pure white coats, irrespective of breed.

If you are not happy with the puppies for any reason, do not purchase one. Remember, the puppy will become an integral part of your life for at least a decade; it is better to wait than to rush into an acquisition you will soon regret. A more thorough medical examination can be undertaken by your veterinarian when the puppy is taken for its inoculations. No reputable breeders are likely to want to sell a dog that is unsound, since this would be embarrassing and potentially damaging to their reputations and could also render them liable to legal action.

Questions to ask the breeder

Prospective customers often view a litter of puppies before they are weaned. This enables the new owner to make preparations before taking the puppy home. Many breeders will provide you with a diet sheet giving details of the food that the puppy has been eating. Always keep to this regimen for the first few days after picking up your puppy to minimize the risk of digestive upsets, and, for the same reason, carry out any changes to the diet gradually rather than suddenly. Check to see what inoculations the puppy has received, and if possible, get a certificate showing the date and type of inoculation that was administered. This can be of value to your veterinarian at a later date, particularly as there are now so many types of vaccine available. It is also important to know how many times the puppy has been dewormed and the date of the last deworming.

In the case of pedigreed dogs, you should receive the appropriate documentation: the pedigree, setting out the ancestry of the puppy over the preceding generations, and either details of registration or a transfer card which must be returned to the appropriate authorities to notify them of a change of ownership. This is particularly important for dogs which may later be shown. The national kennel club is the final authority on what constitutes a breed, and if the dog is not registered as pure bred, it is called a mixed breed.

1

2

3

There are various points that should be checked before deciding upon a particular individual. The head should be examined for any evidence of lice (1). The eyes should appear clear of any discharge, with no tear staining visible and the ears should be free from any unpleasant odor (2). Finally, with a puppy in particular, check that there is no trace of an umbilical hernia (3). In addition to these physical indicators, the puppy should be active and alert.

SETTLING IN AT HOME
Puppy principles

Having arranged to collect your puppy, ensure that all the preparations are made at home in advance. Obtain a diet sheet from the breeder, setting out the feeding regimen to which the puppy has been accustomed, and obtain similar food for it, at least at first. This will greatly lessen the likelihood of any serious digestive upset. You can then introduce changes gradually as your puppy settles into its new home with you.

Transporting your puppy

Rather than allowing a young puppy to sit on your lap on the way home, a special traveling crate is recommended. This will also be useful when taking your new pet to the veterinarian, for example, and, in the case of a small breed, it should suffice throughout its life. Larger breeds should be housed behind a dog-guard in the back of a station wagon. It is never a good idea to allow a dog freedom in a car, because of the risk of it distracting the driver and causing an accident. Also, a young dog left on its own in a car might be destructive and could rip up the upholstery.

At home

When you first arrive home with your new puppy, be prepared to allow it to sleep, as it will probably be tired. You can then start to accustom it to its new life

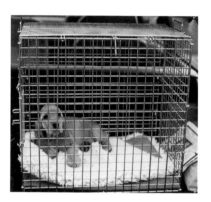

ABOVE Being able to travel with your pet safely and securely restrained in the car is vital. This type of carrying cage can double for transport purposes, simply needing to be lined with old newspaper and a blanket on top.

Practical Pointer

It can help to have your dog microchipped as a second means of identification. The microchip unit, about the size of a small grain of rice, can be inserted under the dog's skin by your veterinarian. It contains a unique code, which can be recognized by a special reader passed over this area of the body. This helps should its medallion be lost.

with you. Puppies are naturally more adaptable than older dogs. In the wild, young wolves will themselves split off from the family group and wander on their own for a time before joining with another pack.

If you already have an older dog, then introducing it to a new puppy needs to be carried out carefully, to avoid conflict. Your established pet is otherwise likely to view the newcomer as an interloper, and may attack it. Therefore, introduce them on neutral ground, in a park for example, and then walk them home together. It is not advisable to place both dogs together in the back of a car unless

they are well acquainted. Otherwise they may start to fight, with potentially serious consequences.

ABOVE Puppies often play boisterously, but if you also have an older dog, supervise them carefully, to prevent a game from escalating into a fight.

Equipping your puppy

A new pet is most likely to stray when out for a walk, for example, and will be less inclined to return to you. This is why, at first, it is not a good idea to allow the dog to roam off its leash.

A puppy should also be fitted with a collar and you can begin training at an early stage, even before the age of three months, when the initial vaccinations will be completed. When purchasing a collar for your puppy, bear in mind that its neck will expand and buy one which allows for its growth. Check the collar regularly as well, to ensure that it is not becoming too tight.

It is also useful to buy a leash to match the collar at the same time. You may prefer a colorful nylon leash, although more traditional leather collars and leashes are equally durable. For leash-training, and for exercising an adult dog that cannot be allowed to run free, an extensible leash is a good idea. It can be played out, giving the dog freedom to roam without the risk of it disappearing too far.

ABOVE In the case of an older dog that is used to going out for walks, it is vital to fit a collar with a medallion or capsule giving your address or telephone number.

THE ELDERLY

DOG

As time passes, so the dog will begin to show signs of aging. In most cases, however, dogs remain reasonably active up until the end. Modern medicines have done much to relieve many of the common troublesome symptoms of old age, although clearly it is not possible to cure certain ailments such as a deterioration in kidney function, diabetes and other metabolic disorders. Regular veterinary check-ups are therefore likely to be increasingly necessary at this stage in the dog's life, to ensure that all possible care can be given and medication adjusted according to need. However, an elderly dog will still provide you with years of pleasure.

THE SENIOR CITIZEN

The problems of age in dogs, as in humans, are usually insidious in onset. A range of diseases — cardiac, renal and tumorous — become an increasing danger.

Life expectancy of a dog

As a general rule, the bigger breeds tend to have a shorter lifespan than their smaller cousins. Giant breeds such as the Irish Wolfhound are unlikely to live more than 10 years, but some small terriers and toy dogs may live until well into their teens. There are of course exceptions to every rule, and dogs have lived into their thirties. While it is sometimes said that every year of our lives is equivalent to seven years in the life of a dog, this is essentially untrue. It arose from the idea that humans lived for the biblical "three score years and ten", or 70 years, and that dogs had an average lifespan of 10 years.

ABOVE Dental problems such as this build-up of tartar which has led to gum disease tend to afflict dogs in the older age bracket. These teeth will have to be cleaned by a veterinarian, with the dog under anaesthetic

The visible signs of aging

Aging is a slow process, even in the dog, and changes tend to be gradual. They are not necessarily evident at a casual glance. The coat color is likely to become paler over successive shedding; the Golden Labrador, for example, becomes whitish rather than golden, while its black counterpart becomes paler around the muzzle with silvery white hairs evident. You are likely to notice a decrease in activity in your dog; it will not want to walk long distances and will be content to potter along slowly rather than racing along like a young puppy. Its teeth, after a lifetime of service, may be showing signs of wear, and the

It is important for the owner to be aware of the pack order between two dogs in the same family. Trouble is likely to arise if the owner gives more attention to and favours the new dog as the natural order is upset (1).

The dominant member of the pair — the older, established individual of the household — will naturally defend his position by attacking the newcomer (2).

To counteract this natural behavior, the owner should show attention to the dominant, older dog so that the position of both dogs will be defined and the hierarchy accepted (3).

1

2

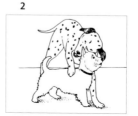

3

dog may appear reluctant to chew as it used to do when younger.

Obesity is a common adjunct to aging, because the dog's level of activity declines, but it often receives the same quantity of food it ate as a young adult dog. Obesity can create and worsen other problems of aging, such as osteoarthrosis (a loss of the cartilage lining certain joints). Failing senses may also be apparent, with a decline in eyesight being perhaps most noticeable. Deafness is also common but may not be detected by owners because they just assume their dog is becoming more stubborn and disobedient in old age. But dogs are adaptable by nature, and an individual that is perhaps almost totally blind can live quite well without injuring itself in familiar surroundings.

Constipation may also afflict the older dog as the gut tone declines. This can be overcome by the administration of mineral oil. In certain instances, as the uptake mechanisms in the gut begin to fail, the faeces become more liquid, and diarrhoea results. Urinary incontinence, often associated with kidney failure, can also accompany the aging process, and treatment can prove difficult. This kind of problem affects the owner as much as the dog.

Dental care for dogs

Certain breeds are more prone to dental decay than others. Yorkshire Terriers, for example, often lose most of their teeth when they are in middle-age. Dental decay may be linked to diet; soft diets based on home-prepared foods or on cans of dog food, tend to encourage the build-up of tartar on the teeth. Tartar contains bacteria which cause both tooth decay and gum disease. It is a good idea to provide hard items, such as dog biscuits, on a regular basis to reduce the tartar accumulation. The teeth can also be cleaned with a special canine toothpaste. An older dog that has lost the majority of its teeth will still be able to eat adequately if offered soft foods. In any event, dogs do not use their teeth for chewing purposes but for catching prey and tearing strips of flesh that can be swallowed whole. Neither of these functions are of significance for the pet dog.

LEFT In old age as synthesis of melanin is reduced the coat and nose color became paler and as in this Beagle, white hairs begin to show, particularly around the muzzle.

The skeletal problems your dog may encounter in old age

These are likely to be degenerative conditions such as osteoarthrosis, a loss of the cartilage lining certain joints, especially those of the hip and stifle. This affects bigger dogs in particular, and causes lameness, which is most marked after a period of rest. The condition usually improves following movement, but some medication to relieve the pain in bad cases may be indicated. If the dog is overweight, the problem is worse because the joints have to carry a greater burden than normal.

Slipped discs are more likely to occur in a slightly younger group of dogs, but the weakness remains throughout an affected individual's life. The discs themselves occupy the intervertebral spaces between the vertebrae and prevent friction — they act as shock-absorbers. If there is a weakness in their outer layer, however, the inner core of the

ABOVE Dogs with short legs and a long body such as Dachshunds, Beagles and Basset Hounds are prone to suffering from occasional back pain and sometimes even a slipped disc. This is due to the vertebral canal enclosing the spinal cord being made up of a number of vertebrae, each joined to the next by a flexible pad — the so-called intervertebral disc, consisting of outer fibrous layers and an inner gelatinous area. If the spine is flexed too vigorously, especially in an older, long-backed dog, a prolapsed or 'slipped' disc may occur, as the soft center of the intervertebral disc bursts up into the spinal canal, causing serious injury.

disc expands and presses against the spinal cord. This in turn causes considerable pain, and results in paralysis of either the front or hind legs depending on whether the disc concerned is in the neck or toward the tail. It is a very common complaint in dachshunds and may be related to their long bodies. Dachshunds should be discouraged from jumping on chairs or climbing stairs as these activities can predispose them to slipped discs.

Treatment tends to be supportive. The dog is kept as quiet as possible and confined to a small area so that it cannot injure itself further. Medical treatment decreases the inflammation and eases the pain. Given the sensitivity of the neck region of the dachshund, especially in the older dog, it makes sense to use a harness rather than a collar to remove stress from a sensitive part of the dog's anatomy.

Dogs and cancer

The incidence of tumors in dogs averages about four in a thousand and about one-third of these are likely to prove malignant (cancerous). Older dogs are most likely to develop both benign and malignant tumors. The benign tumor relatively slow-growing and does not spread and invade other tissues. As a result, it can be removed fairly easily (depending on its location in the body). New tumors will not develop from it in other parts of the body, a process associated with malignant tumors and known as metastasis.

The skin is the most common site for tumors in the dog, and this facilitates early detection. Other likely sites include the mammary glands of bitches. In this instance, studies have revealed that bitches spayed before their first heat are 200 times less likely to develop such tumors than bitches neutered later in life. To offset this of course, possibly one in ten young bitches may develop urinary incontinence later in life because of spaying. Older dogs are increasingly susceptible to tumors in these two locations, but most of these tumors are

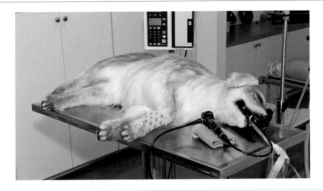

ABOVE Modern breakthroughs and innovations in veterinary medicine have resulted in a much improved survival rate for dogs suffering from a variety of conditions.

not malignant. The incidence of major malignant tumors in dogs appear to peak between seven and ten years of age. These afflict the skeleton and the lymphatic system. Large breeds are most likely to have bone cancer.

Treating cancer

The treatment depends largely on the type, size and locality of the tumor. It may be possible to operate and excise the tumor, but there is always a risk of recurrence, particularly with a malignancy. It may recur at the same site or elsewhere in the body. A refinement of the surgical approach is cryosurgery, in which a liquid gas such as nitrogen at a very low temperature is applied to the affected tissue. The intense cold kills the cells and thus obviates the need for any incision. The area round the tumor is masked off to protect it while the probe is being used.

Cryosurgery has a number of advantages over traditional surgery, particularly in the case of skin tumors. The patient does not have to be fully anaesthetized in some instances, and this can be a distinct advantage with an old dog in declining health. Since there is no bleeding, there is less likelihood in the case of a malignant tumor that cells will spread around the body to set up secondary tumors elsewhere. Using cryosurgery it is also possible to treat areas of the body, around the anus for example, that would bleed quite profusely if attempts were made to cut away the tumor. There is also less risk of an infection following surgery.

The major drawback to cryosurgery is that the tissue that has been frozen does not drop off at once, and waiting for this to occur may be unpleasant. It may be necessary to repeat the treatment if some of the diseased tissue remains unaffected. This applies also in skin conditions such as warts where there is little fluid present. The ice-crystals formed will disrupt the cellular structure of living tissue after freezing. It is now accepted practice to inject warts with water to achieve the best effect.

Cryosurgery does not provide a means of treating every tumor, especially those within the body. Here radiation therapy can lead to a remission, often in conjunction with chemotherapy which entails the use of drugs. The side-effects of these drugs are not usually as unpleasant in dogs as in humans. If radiation therapy is not available in your area, you may have to travel several times to a veterinary school doing research into radiation therapy to obtain this kind of treatment.

Incontinence in an elderly dog

If your elderly housetrained dog is starting to urinate indoors, it may be a problem linked to the kidneys. If the dog is drinking more, more urine will be produced, and the bladder will need to be emptied more frequently. For this reason, it is not unusual for older dogs to soil their quarters overnight while remaining clean for the rest of the day when someone is on hand to let them out to urinate more frequently. Keep a close check on the amount of fluid that your dog is consuming and inform your veterinarian. Note whether urine trickles out of the vulva in the case of a bitch, especially without its knowledge. This will stain the coat below the vulva. Be more responsive to your dog's requests to go out. Try to leave it alone in the home for only short periods, and let it out beforehand to empty its bladder.

Heart failure in elderly dogs

Dogs rarely succumb to coronary thrombosis (a condition in which blood clots occlude the pulmonary arteries nourishing the heart). Similarly, fatty deposits within the circulatory system are also uncommon. But the incidence of heart disease in elderly dogs is quite high and relates to the valvular structure of this vital organ. The four chambers of the heart are separated by valves, and left-sided failure is most common. The mitral valve becomes thickened so that blood does not leave the heart as usual. The actual symptoms of valvular disease vary. When the mitral valve is affected, the dog is likely to cough frequently and to tire easily when out for a walk. Coughing is most apparent either after exercise or at night and may be coupled with difficulty in breathing.

In the case of right-sided failure, the tricuspid valve is affected. Fluid builds up in the tissues because of increased pressure in the circulatory system from blood unable to enter the heart at the usual rate. Organs such as the spleen and liver also become engorged with blood and swell in size. These changes can be detected when your veterinarian examines the dog. If both valves are failing, a combination of symptoms will be seen.

Once the condition has been diagnosed, it can be stabilized with drugs, and you should see an improvement in your dog's condition. The cardiac glycosides, of which digitalis is best known, control the heart rate. By slowing its pace and improving its

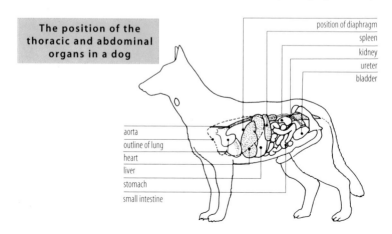

The position of the thoracic and abdominal organs in a dog

position of diaphragm
spleen
kidney
ureter
bladder

aorta
outline of lung
heart
liver
stomach
small intestine

contractibility, they increase cardiac output. Diuretic drugs remove excessive fluid and sodium salt from the blood via the kidneys and thus decrease the pressure on the heart itself. The initial dose of drugs will be higher than the maintenance dose, which will then be administered throughout the dog's life, especially if the dog is seriously ill. This may result in symptoms of toxicity such as vomiting. If you are concerned, contact your veterinarian.

Amputation for a dog with bone cancer

A veterinarian may recommend amputation for a dog with bone cancer, but the choice ultimately has to be yours in this kind of situation, but you can rely on the sympathetic and understanding support of your veterinarian. Surprising as it may seem, dogs do adapt quite well to life on three legs and can live a relatively normal existence without appearing distressed. The idea may be abhorrent to you, however, and if so, you should opt to have your dog put to sleep before the malignancy spreads further within the body. Before deciding, ask your veterinarian if you can see a former patient that has undergone such surgery. This will give you a better idea of what to expect, and you can talk to the owner who, like you, would have been equally concerned at the outset. The surgery itself is unlikely to result in complications, but when you take your dog out for walks afterward, be prepared for strange looks or comments from other people.

Dogs with chronic kidney failure

All dogs are afflicted to a greater or lesser extent by kidney failure in old age. This is a progressive condition, and one of the first signs of it is the dog's foul-smelling breath (often linked with bad teeth). The body has a high reserve of functioning kidney tissue, but once the level falls to only 30 percent of the total available, kidney or renal failure follows and the waste products of body metabolism that are normally filtered out of the body by this route remain in the blood. Various infectious causes of chronic renal failure exist including both infectious canine hepatitis and leptospirosis. Damage from these diseases at an early age will become more noticeable later in life.

Your dog will drink more fluid and urinate more often. In order to diagnose the condition and assess its severity, the veterinarian may want to have a urine sample for testing. This can be collected in a broad plastic saucer such as those used for potted plants in the home. These are easier and more practical to use than a bottle. The large surface area means that at least some of the urine will be collected. And, in any case, a large volume of urine is not necessary. Once you have the sample, transfer it to a clean, dry, screw-top container. Never use jars that have previously held jam because any remaining deposits of sugar are likely to interfere with the results

In cases of chronic renal failure, there is no effective curative treatment. But you can modify the diet in order to improve your dog's state of health. Special canned foods are available from your veterinarian for this purpose. The protein level of the diet needs to be reduced overall, while the protein itself must be of higher biological value in terms of its amino acid content. Eggs, example, are a useful source of such protein. Vitamin B supplementation may also be required since these water-soluble compounds will be lost in increasing quantities via the kidneys. A deficiency of nicotinic acid will cause the tongue to turn blackish in color, and this is a typical symptom of long-standing renal degeneration. Other changes, especially in the skeletal system, may occur in cases of chronic renal failure because a form of Vitamin D known as 1,25 DHCC is synthesized in the kidneys and it acts on the intestines to regulate calcium absorption there. It also exerts an influence on calcium stores within the body itself. A similar compound which stimulates the bone marrow also originates in the kidneys, and thus anaemia and resulting complications can also arise from kidney failure.

THE BIG SLEEP

If your dog is suffering and there is not hope of recovery, it is kinder for you to end your pet's misery and have him or her put to sleep. This is invariably a traumatic decision.

Putting your dog to sleep

The usual method involves the administration of a barbiturate by injection into a vein. It is quick and effective and mimics the procedure used when an intravenous barbiturate is given for anaesthetic purposes but a stronger drug is used. Within seconds, the dog will be unconscious, and its heart stops almost immediately. With a dog that is known to be aggressive, a strong sedative in pill form may be given in meat beforehand. The process can be carried out efficiently after this medication has taken effect.

After you reach the decision, arrange a time with your veterinarian to leave your dog at his surgery and say farewell. While you can stay to the end, it is usually preferable from everyone's viewpoint, including the dog's, if this unpleasant task is carried out with minimum fuss. Dogs are very sensitive to the mood of those around them and will detect the emotion on this occasion. This could cause them to be more difficult. For this reason, it is better to have the task carried out at the veterinarian's surgery than at home.

ABOVE The decision to have a dog put to sleep can be difficult and the advice of your veterinarian may be helpful at this time. The actual process is painless—an intravenous injection of barbiturate being administered by the veterinarian—and the dog loses consciousness in seconds.

What will happen to the body of your dog afterward?

This will depend on your instructions. Many owners request that the veterinarian arrange the disposal of the body. Alternatively, it may be possible to arrange a private cremation. In some areas, you can purchase a plot at a pet cemetery, and the organization concerned may arrange burial and a headstone if required. It is not always possible to bury your dog in your garden because of local laws. If you do opt for this method, make sure that the grave is at least three feet (one metre) in depth to deter scavengers such as foxes that might otherwise be attracted to the carcass.

Dealing with depression after your dog has died

The loss of a dog can be a devastating emotional blow, especially for people living alone with no other form of companionship. Indeed, it can be like losing a close relative. But the grieving process when a relative dies is recognized by society while the death of a dog passes largely unnoticed, except by the person directly affected. Grief in this instance is not usually expressed and builds up because the person is unable to unburden his or her sense of loss. Talking about the loss can be therapeutic.

It may be that another dog would help, but many people reject this by saying that another dog could never replace the recently departed pet. This is a perfectly natural reaction, but a new dog would not substitute directly for the deceased pet but be an individual in its own right. Given time, most people accept a new dog with enthusiasm. If you feel that you cannot cope with another dog, you could get another pet that is not such high maintenance, such as a budgerigar. The positive benefits of owning a pet are becoming increasingly appreciated, and in some countries such as France, dog ownership is a right for all citizens, embodied in the constitution.

Explaining to children that your dog is to be put to sleep

How you go about this depends to some extent on the age of your children; it may be easiest to explain it by saying that the family dog went to sleep and will not wake up again. Children are often very upset by the death of a pet. Lacking the acquired reserve of most adults, they express their deep grief openly by crying and gradually come to terms with their sense of loss. Acquiring another dog may be helpful in overcoming this feeling.

Deciding on the right time to put your dog to sleep

After a lifetime's companionship, it will be a difficult decision. Although your veterinarian can guide you, the ultimate responsibility is yours. Clearly, you do not want your dog to suffer unnecessarily when there is no hope of recovery. The decision may also be influenced by your personal circumstances. In the case of a paraplegic dog unable to stand on its own, you may be able to obtain one of the special dog carts available to assist paralysed dogs. The hindquarters are fitted to the cart and the forelegs, functioning as usual, pull them along. Not all dogs are happy with these attachments. And you may not be in a position to provide the extra attention that a dog of this type needs. Under these circumstances, consider euthanasia.

General guidelines must revolve around the normal daily habits of your dog. Can it walk? Is it able to eat and drink properly? Is it continent? Does it still appear to enjoy life? These are the type of questions that you must honestly ask yourself before arriving at your decision.

If you do opt for euthanasia, it should be carried out by a veterinarian. You may be asked to sign a consent form. This transfers the legal right of deciding your animal's future to your veterinarian.

LEFT There are plots that can be acquired as a final resting place for your faithful dog (right). Alternatively, your veterinarian will be able to arrange for a cremation or, you may wish to bury your pet in your garden, in which case a deep grave of at least one metre (three feet) will be necessary.

TRAINING
&
EXERCISE

Within a wolf pack, the young cubs learn the vital skills necessary for survival, even in inhospitable terrain, by following the example of the older members of the pack. As domestication has proceeded, so this characteristic has been emphasized by selective breeding, with puppies learning readily from their trainers. The training process itself actually serves to strengthen the bond between dog and owner much as it helps to maintain the social fabric within the wolf pack . The training responses of certain groups of domestic dog have become more highly developed than others. This is apparent especially in gundogs that are used to working on a one-to-one basis with people, compared with pack hounds that are more independent by nature.

TRAINING
First steps

Training may sometimes be regarded as a rather one-sided activity, with the owner imposing their will on their dog, but in fact, the reason that dogs can be trained so successfully stems largely from the social structure present in the wolf pack. Domestication has simply served to refine the submissive behavior of the dog within a different hierarchy.

Sound training is actually of benefit to dogs themselves. A well-trained dog will not simply run away into the distance when first let off the leash. It will stay when told, which means that its owner can ensure as far as possible that potentially dangerous situations, such as a road with fast-moving traffic, are avoided. In the home itself, a dog which is house-broken and responds readily will also be a much more amenable companion.

ABOVE Young puppies like this English springer spaniel will be keen to learn, but bear in mind that they have a relatively short attention span. Short sessions are therefore recommended.

House-training

Dogs of all ages respond best to a routine, such as the wolf establishes in the wild, seeking food and resting during certain parts of the day. Start by feeding the puppy regularly at approximately the same times every day. Then start toilet-training by placing the puppy in the required spot in the garden. It helps if this is a tiled area that can be cleaned and disinfected quite easily. Eating stimulates movement in the puppy's digestive tract, so after a meal is the time that it is most likely to want to relieve itself.

Dogs are naturally clean animals and the puppy will soon learn what is expected of it, and before

ABOVE It is important to keep a watch on your puppy to prevent it from getting into trouble. Try not to leave it unsupervised, particularly out-of-doors, as it may soon become bored on its own.

Practical Pointer
Check-chains are a popular training aid to stop dogs pulling on the leash, but they must be used correctly or they can cause injury. Remove your dog's usual collar and then fit the check-chain in such a way that it slackens when pressure is relaxed. The dog should respond to the tightening of the chain by not pulling ahead or walking more slowly.

long, it will return to use this spot regularly, just like wild dogs. The Southeast

Asian dhole, which lives in packs like the gray wolf, even has specific, so-called "dunging sites", used by all members of the pack and located some distance from their burrows, which are never soiled.

Care outdoors

At first, always stay with your puppy in the garden, to ensure that it comes to no harm. It could encounter problems, for example if it fell into a fish pond with steep sides, although dogs can swim quite efficiently. In any event, you should check the perimeter of the garden very carefully for any gaps or weakness in the fences. It only needs a relatively small gap for a puppy to escape, basically one that is equivalent to the height of its body. Puppies can crouch down on all fours in order to slip under a fence or gate. All such potential exits need to be securely blocked off in advance because, once a puppy does discover a route out of the garden, it will often continue to slip out at this point, possibly with fatal consequences.

It is equally important, as a precautionary measure, to insure your puppy or dog from the outset, not only to guard against unexpected health costs, but also for public liability cover, in case your pet runs off and causes an accident.

Importance of regular training

Start carrying out regular training exercises by encouraging your puppy to walk properly on its leash. In the first instance, this can be accomplished by effectively sandwiching the dog between your left side and a wall or fence, thus encouraging your pet to walk in a straight line. Almost inevitably it will start to pull ahead, at which point you should give a quick pull on the leash and the command "heel", but pause to ensure that the puppy adopts the correct position before continuing the session.

Puppies are naturally enthusiastic, so try and use this energy in a positive way by making training an extension of play and keeping the sessions relatively short. A maximum of perhaps ten minutes tuition time will be adequate, and several lessons given through the day are usually better than one marathon course.

ABOVE Puppies will learn the command to sit quite readily, since they will naturally adopt this posture. You can teach it either in conjunction with leash training or prior to a meal. If the puppy does not respond as required, then apply gentle pressure to the hindquarters as shown in the top photograph. The puppy should then stay in this position for a period of time. Always make training a positive process, and never forget to praise the puppy when it responds as required.

Practical Pointer

Puppies can usually start to attend training classes once they are about six months old. Details of local courses can be found through your veterinarian, or possibly at your neighborhood library. Having mastered the basics, there are also advanced classes which you can participate in with your dog.

ABOVE Puppies are a similar size at birth, with larger breeds such as this great dane then growing more rapidly than smaller breeds. Don't over-exercise the bigger breeds especially, as this can cause permanent harm.

Discipline

Training needs to be a positive experience for your dog in order to encourage it to respond in the desired way. However, there will be times when you are unhappy with its behavior, and have to resort to scolding it. In fact, the voice is one of the most potent tools in the trainer's repertoire, rather like the growling threat of the dominant wolf. The puppy will accept the scolding and register your displeasure by dropping its ears and adopting a hangdog look.

Coping with soiling

Nevertheless, there may be occasions when a scolding is likely to have very little effect, no matter how annoyed you may be. This applies particularly when the puppy has soiled in the home — rubbing its nose in the soiled carpet will actually serve no useful purpose, any more than shouting at your pet. It will simply not understand the cause of your anger unless you actually catch it in the act.

This is one situation which can be dealt with far more effectively by prevention. Try to anticipate

when your puppy is likely to want to relieve itself and place it outside at these times. It is likely to take at least six months before the young dog will ask to go out of its own accord.

There may be a particular difficulty when the puppy does soil in the home because, as with wild dogs, it will be attracted back to the same spot by the scent. Apart from obviously cleaning up thoroughly and disinfecting the whole area, it is therefore advisable to use a descenting preparation too.

If you are going out and suspect that you may be delayed, and that your puppy may need to relieve itself, confine the young dog to part of the house, such as the bathroom, where it will be possible to clean up easily. As well as leaving its bed and a water bowl, cover the floor area for some distance around them with layers of old newspaper. With luck, if your puppy cannot wait until your return, it will use these sheets, which will absorb its urine.

Practical Pointer

Always praise your dog when it responds as required, but do not give it an item of food on every occasion, otherwise this is likely to become a habit. When you do give a reward, a small piece of fresh carrot will be a healthy treat.

BELOW Once a dog will sit readily, it can be persuaded to offer its paw in this way without great difficulty. Training can be viewed as a progression through different steps.

ABOVE Within the framework of a game, one individual is likely to be dominant to the other, as can be seen with these Dobermans. The dominant individual is climbing up on the back of the other.

Discouraging bad habits

The excitement of a puppy greeting your return is likely to result in it jumping up at you. This may not be a particular problem at this stage, although its claws could scratch you, but a large adult dog behaving in this way could easily knock over a child. It is therefore vital to establish acceptable patterns of behavior from the outset — bad habits, once acquired, will be much harder to eliminate later in life. This also calls for consistency in your approach. It is not fair to encourage your puppy onto furniture alongside you, or to let it sleep on your bed, if you then want it to desist from behaving in this way in the future.

In terms of preventing your dog from jumping up, which is a natural display of exuberance seen in wolves and other wild dogs, you must therefore encourage it to sit. This command is one of the most important and yet easily taught because dogs

BASIC INSTINCTS

Pack commands

Dogs can be trained due to their wolf ancestors who had to learn and follow strict rules within the wolf pack. It is the trainer who assumes the dominant role, with the dog learning to fit within the hierarchy and respond as required. It is more effective to shake a puppy on the ground gently by the loose skin at the back of its neck, rather than any other form of punishment if it is caught misbehaving.

ABOVE Training should first be carried out in a yard or a quiet locality where there are no obvious distractions nearby. This will ensure that you can hold your dog's attention. Only once the basic lessons have been mastered should your pet be exercised off the leash.

Territories and vaccinations

Since dogs, unlike wolves, tend to live singly rather than in packs, they do not establish such strong territories. Territories not only provide security in the sense of ensuring access to prey, but they can also serve as a barrier to disease. There is no such security available to domestic dogs, especially those living at relatively high densities in urban areas. Diseases can be spread rapidly in parks and similar localities where dogs are exercised and strays may be present.

Danger of disease

Before allowing your puppy out onto the street therefore, it is vital that it is fully protected against the killer diseases which may affect dogs. Puppies frequently receive their first vaccinations at about eight weeks old, although this will not actually guarantee them complete protection. Therefore a second course is usually given when the puppies

are twelve weeks old. Then annual boosters will be necessary throughout the dog's life. It is very important to maintain the protection through into old age, because the dog's ability to fight infections may decline in later life.

Your veterinarian will provide you with a vaccination certificate, which should be kept in a safe place along with other household papers. You are likely to need it if you book your dog into boarding kennels, and if you register for dog training classes. Apart from offering the opportunity to ensure that your dog is well trained, these classes will also give your pet an opportunity to socialize with other dogs. This can be important, especially for a puppy which is living on its own. It means that it is less likely to react adversely when, for example, encountering another dog while out for a walk.

Practical Pointer

If your dog starts to disappear into the distance when you first let it off the leash, stand your ground rather than chasing after it. Otherwise the dog will assume that it is a game and will continue running rather than returning to you.

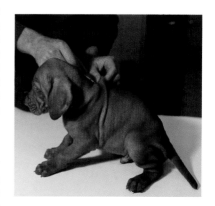

ABOVE The loose fold of skin also allows vaccinations to be given without upsetting the puppy in many cases. Protection against the killer diseases such as distemper must be maintained, even if they appear to be less common than in the past.

Training out of the home

Having mastered the basics of training within the confines of the home and garden, you will reach the point when it will be necessary to repeat these lessons with your puppy in a strange environment. Try and choose a quiet spot for this purpose, away from any roads, other dogs, and any farm animals. Do not be surprised if, at first, your dog does not respond as you had hoped in these strange surroundings. There will inevitably be a lot of exciting distractions for the dog in the environment, such as interesting scents and unfamiliar noises.

It can be of help to have a friend or family member with you at this stage, particularly when you call your dog to you. At first though, keep the dog on an extendible leash — otherwise its curiosity will almost inevitably mean that it will run off rather than to you.

Ask the other person to hold the leash, having extended it to its maximum distance, and ensure that your dog sits with him or her. Then walk away and call the dog to you. It should then run to you, although its attention may be diverted elsewhere at first.

If you continue to use the same location for training purposes, you will ultimately be able to let your dog off the leash there, repeating the exercises which you have previously taught it. Sound pleased and enthusiastic, and always encourage your pet with plenty of praise when it responds as required.

Practical Pointer

Try to keep to a routine when walking your dog. It will soon recognize the time at which it is taken out for a walk and will become restless if you ignore it. Two walks each day — morning and evening — are to be recommended.

BELOW An extendible leash is a very useful training device, until you are sure that your dog will behave properly, and not seek to run off. It provides plenty of training opportunities. You can play out the leash for example, and then ask your dog to sit and stay, walking toward it rewinding the leash at this stage.

EXERCISE
Dangers of taking your dog out

Once your dog is well trained, you can allow it much greater freedom when out walking, although try to avoid letting it stray out of sight. Otherwise it could encounter difficulties without you being aware of the situation.

The lost dog

If your dog does disappear, with no indication of where it could have gone, and fails to respond to your calls, stay in the general vicinity of where you last saw it, for perhaps ten minutes or so, before retracing your steps. If you have driven to the area, you may actually find that your pet is back at the car waiting for you.

If this turns out not to be the case, report your loss to the police and to any local animal welfare organizations without delay. You can also advertise in shop windows and in local newspapers, while some radio stations also run slots for lost and found pets. You should also return with friends to search the area where your pet disappeared.

It can help to have a mobile telephone with you when walking your dog, especially if you intend to venture off a main track along woodland paths. Should an accident befall you or your pet, you can then obtain assistance without delay.

Poisonous snakes

In many areas, although not particularly common, there are poisonous snakes, which can represent a hazard to dogs, especially puppies. Puppies lack the caution of older dogs, and can end up receiving a

ABOVE Two hounds from Africa — a basenji (left) and an azawakh (right) — meet for the first time. In most cases, such encounters pass off without problems, but on occasions, displays of aggression do occur, and you should be alert to this possibility.

fatal bite as a consequence. If you suspect your pet has been bitten by a snake, try to prevent the poison becoming widely circulated into the dog's body by applying a tourniquet to the limb, above the bite, making sure that it is not too tight. The feet or the legs are the most likely areas of the body to be bitten — the situation will be much more severe if the face is attacked.

The fur around the bite is likely to appear slightly moist, while the puncture holes made by the snake's fangs will be apparent on closer inspection. If you hear the puppy yelp, and are close enough to see the snake, try to identify it, or at least write down a description, so that your veterinarian will be able to treat the poison appropriately. This is especially

---

Practical Pointer

Buy a safe toy for your dog to retrieve when you are out walking, such as a flying disk, rather than simply throwing a stick for it. Otherwise this could cause injury if it hits your pet in the face.

Practical Pointer

Avoid areas where there could be hidden dangers lurking, such as sinkholes or disused mineshafts, when exercising your dog. It is also a good idea to keep your dog on its leash when taking a clifftop route.

important in areas where there may be more than one species of venomous snake.

Ice and water

At certain times of the year, some routes may become more hazardous for dog-walking than others, particularly those close to water. In fact, with a young dog, it is a good idea to avoid these if possible, in case it falls in. Ice on the surface during the winter can be equally hazardous, although the weight of a dog, with its four legs, will be more evenly distributed than in our case.

Never be tempted to follow your dog across ice, because it could easily give way, plunging both you and your pet into the chilly water beneath. Ironically, your dog is more likely than you to survive this experience, because its thick coat will help to insulate it from the cold, and it may also find it easier to clamber out onto the bank again.

Coast and clifftop

On the coast, try to avoid allowing your dog to wander along a pier head, or groyne, when it is off the leash, because it could lose its footing, especially if the surface is slippery, and it might end up being swept out to sea by the current. If you do take your dog on the beach, be sure that it does not upset fellow beach-users, and take a bottle and bowl so that it can drink fresh water if it becomes thirsty.

ABOVE Scent marking with urine is very common in dogs, especially males. They will regularly lift one of their hind legs as shown here to leave their scent in prominent localities, such as lampposts. It is also possible for urine-borne diseases to be acquired from such activities, and by sniffing, so this should be discouraged as far as possible.

LEFT Some dogs are naturally better swimmers than others, but always be careful, especially if your dog goes into the sea, as currents can be dangerous.

COMMUNICATION
&
BEHAVIOR

Dogs communicate in similar ways to wolves, although they rely more strongly on vocalizations, whereas wolves are shyer and more reluctant to reveal their position by this means. Scent marking is very important for both wolves and dogs. Urine serves as an indicator of the dog's social ranking, and is an individual marker that males deposit as an indicator of their presence, on lampposts, trees or similarly prominent sites where other canids are likely to be passing. When dogs or wolves meet, their body language will provide subtle clues to whether the encounter will prove friendly or is likely to lead to aggression. Dogs use a clearly defined series of gestures of increasing intensity that are normally employed as a deterrent before violence results. This serves to defuse conflicts without the risk of physical injury.

COMMUNICATION
Barking

Members of the wolf pack keep in touch with each other by howling. Their baying call echoes across the landscape, but the risk is that the wolves may reveal their positions not only to fellow pack members, but also to members of neighboring packs, which may be seeking to invade their territory. As a result, wolves will not always acknowledge the calls of their neighbors.

In the case of dogs, their ability to sense danger and to indicate the threat by barking was clearly of great value right from the outset of the domestication process. Just the barking of a dog could be sufficient to deter a potential aggressor. Barking, as distinct from howling, became a positive trait which was actively encouraged by those owning dogs.

Different-sounding barks

Today, the sound of a dog's bark differs, according to the breed. Howling remains a feature typically associated with those breeds from northern latitudes, which remain most closely allied to wolves in terms of their appearance. This so-called "sled-dog" group, as exemplified by the Siberian husky, will engage in communal howling, just like wolves. They only call in this way when standing still.

Many hounds have a baying call, which is used to keep in contact with other members of the pack, when they are in undergrowth for example, and also when they are following a scent. The sound of the bark is not necessarily a reflection of the size of the dog concerned, however, as some small breeds, such as the Cavalier King Charles spaniel, have a relatively deep bark suggestive of a much larger dog. In fact, some of the smaller dogs often rank among the most noisy.

ABOVE At close quarters, a dog will rely on its sight to locate its owner. Domestic dogs tend to be noisier than wolves, barking intently if they detect strangers or any possible danger. More casual barking may relate to a cat in the vicinity.

RIGHT The sound of wolves howling at night can be very eerie, with their calls being audible over long distances.

Control of barking

It is possible to teach dogs not to bark, or even to operate on them for this purpose, as happened in northern Europe during the First World War. At this time, many dogs were used as messengers in the trenches, and barking for any reason could have had very serious consequences for all concerned.

In those situations where barking may be desirable, alerting you to someone at the door perhaps, it is equally important to encourage your dog to stop once you are aware of the situation. Puppies should be trained to be quiet at this point, rather than being allowed to continue barking.

This behavior is often caused by excitement, so it is important to keep the young dog calm, rather than allowing it to become overexcited, at the prospect of a visitor for example. Barking begins early in puppyhood, starting when dogs are as young as three weeks old.

Barking difficulties

Today, barking can create problems under certain circumstances. Dogs may become conditioned to bark, as the result of their owner going out for example, and this can be very disturbing, particularly for close neighbors, and often leads to complaints and ill-feeling. Described as "separation anxiety", this problem is most likely to arise in the case of dogs that have spent part of their lives in kennels.

ABOVE When you need to leave your dog on its own, be sure to exercise it first, allowing it a good run off the leash. This may encourage it to sleep rather than pine in your absence. Leaving the radio on may also be helpful.

Separation anxiety

This can usually be overcome with patience, provided that the owner is aware of this situation. Always remember that the dog is behaving in this way because it is very distressed and agitated. Dogs do still retain the pack instinct of the wolf, although this trait may be more apparent in some breeds.

The dog relates to its owner as a pack member and so it barks when it is left in apparent isolation, uncertain as to when its owner will return. At the sound of its owner's footsteps or voice, such behavior is likely to cease.

Actual treatment of separation anxiety depends on you going out of your home for variable periods of time, typically between five minutes and half an hour, although you will need to stay within earshot. If your dog barks, and possibly scratches at the door as well, ignore it when you go back into the home.

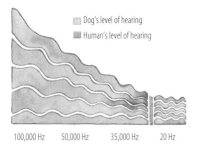

Dog's level of hearing
Human's level of hearing

100,000 Hz   50,000 Hz   35,000 Hz   20 Hz

LEFT Dogs have a much better sense of hearing than ourselves, being able to detect sounds at higher frequency, and so they can pick up sounds which are quite inaudible to our ears.

LEFT Domestic dogs seek to establish and mark territories just like wolves, although their instincts in this respect are generally not as strong. This may be related in part to the fact that many dogs live alone, rather than in packs.

Scent

Dogs rely heavily on scent-marking as a means of indicating their presence in an area, much as a pack of wolves will signal the borders of their territory. This will be particularly noticeable if you take your dog on the same route each time that you go out for a walk. It will pause to sniff at the same sites, such as tree stumps and posts for example, with male dogs in particular often urinating on the site afterward.

Male dogs are far more likely to scent-mark in this way, cocking one of their hind legs for this purpose. Interestingly, puppies of both sexes will keep their feet on the ground when urinating, rather like a bitch, until sexual maturity is attained and this distinction becomes evident. Raising its leg allows the male dog to direct its urine more accurately — some dogs will urinate with either leg raised off the ground, whereas others show a distinct preference for one particular leg.

Practical Pointer

Dogs have no difficulty in locating food concealed out of sight, for example in a bag left on the kitchen floor. You may then come home to find the bag ripped apart, and the food consumed. Therefore avoid leaving food within easy reach, even if it is hidden.

The volume of urine that is passed at each of these localities is often quite small, with males typically urinating about three times more frequently than bitches when out on a walk. Areas that are commonly passed by dogs, such as lampposts, are most likely to be sprayed in this fashion, because the scent of other dogs will encourage your dog to leave its mark as well.

In contrast to more solitary members of the dog family, the domestic dog produces a urine which has far less of an odor than that of foxes, for example, but it still contains pheromones — chemical messengers which can be spread on the air currents, with the scent being picked up by other dogs.

Dogs rely on a special adaption of their nasal pathway to help detect this scent. Located in the roof of their mouth, they have a so-called "vomeronasal organ", also known as Jacobsen's organ. Air containing scent molecules can be detected by this organ, which is connected by a neural pathway to the medial parts of the hypothalamus and preoptic area of the brain. This part of the brain is more concerned with sexual activity than feeding behavior.

After urinating as a means of scent-marking, a male dog may also scratch the ground, if it is earth or

ABOVE Some dogs have a much more acute sense of smell than others, with the bloodhound being one of the most effective trackers in the world. They can follow scents which were made days earlier.

something similar. This provides further evidence of its territorial claim by giving a visual indication as well. Glands between the toes may also leave a further deposit of scent.

It is not uncommon, if you decide to take on another dog, for your established pet to display a breakdown in its toilet-training. This is actually a means of trying to assert its continued dominance in the home. This phase will generally pass once the dogs become better acquainted.

The ability of the dog to detect scents is not a constant feature, but it is influenced by various factors. A hungry dog is likely to be able to track far more effectively than one which has just been fed. Although it is often said that a dry nose is a sign of illness, this is not necessarily the case, but a dry nose will depress its scenting skills. The moisture inhaled along with the molecules of scent aids the dog's scent detection.

The surface of the leathery tip of a dog's nose, is kept moist by means of the nasal lachrymal duct, which acts as a conduit, enabling tear fluid to drain down the nose. The flexible nature of the nostrils also means that they can be flared, which may help them to capture more scent molecules as the dog sniffs.

BASIC INSTINCTS

Scent marking

Male wolves behave in a similar way to dogs, scent-marking trees, for example, within their territorial boundaries. They constantly use the same localities, so the wolf or dog is able to reinforce its presence in the area. The ability to cock the leg is important, because otherwise, male dogs would have great difficulty in directing their urine. Bitches, like puppies of both sexes, will squat when urinating. Their urine tends to be more acidic, and it can lead to dead patches of grass developing on a lawn over a period of time.

Practical Pointer

Apart from pheromones, a number of potentially serious diseases can be spread via dog's urine, which is why it is so important to keep vaccinations up to date.

BEHAVIOR

Contact with other dogs

Two dogs meeting when out for a walk are likely to be slightly wary of each other. They will probably circle around, sniffing cautiously at each other's hindquarters. Size is not necessarily a reliable indication of which dog may prove to be the dominant individual, as a small dog will not necessarily be intimidated by a larger rival.

You may actually miss the key moment which will probably determine the order of dominance, because it is not obvious. When the dogs sniff noses, they also stare at each other — the one which looks away first will be the submissive individual.

Age also plays a part in seniority, just as it does in wolf packs. Recently weaned puppies will inevitably have a lower social ranking than an older dog, which is why it is usually easier to introduce a puppy rather than a middle-aged dog alongside an established individual.

The subordinate dog will react by cowering if threatened, while the dominant individual may place its paw on the other dog's back, depending on their relative sizes, and keep its tail erect. The encounter is likely to end with the weaker dog retreating back to its owner. There is rarely any conflict under these circumstances if the owners are in the vicinity.

However, a dangerous situation may arise in the case of ex-racing greyhounds. Once their track careers are over, these athletic hounds can make excellent pets as they have extremely gentle natures. Nevertheless, greyhounds have been trained to pursue a toy hare, and when out walking, they are liable to react to small dogs, such as Yorkshire terriers, in a similar way, except that the smaller dog may be seized and killed. For this reason, always ensure that a greyhound is muzzled when off the leash. Its sheer pace means that, if it spots a small dog in the distance, you will have no hope of catching it in time to prevent an attack.

Contact with cats

Although dogs are often ready to chase any cats which cross their path, it is usual for a cat living in a home with a dog to be the dominant individual.

LEFT Two wolves fighting. Here the contest is virtually over, with the weaker individual on its back. It will get back on its feet and run off, probably being pursued for a short distance by its opponent.

ABOVE Unusual friendships can form between dogs and cats. This bonding is most likely when the animals have grown up together and the dog's social instincts have been directed toward its companion.

LEFT When one dog encounters another, it may respond by raising its hackles — the fur at the back of the neck, as in the top photograph. This does not mean fighting is inevitable.

This is often a lesson which puppies need to learn. If cornered, the cat is likely to stand its ground and hiss loudly. If this is not a sufficient deterrent, the cat will be prepared to use its claws in order to stop the puppy's advances.

In such cases, the puppy is unlikely to display the behavior typical of a subordinate, but will simply withdraw. The one situation where your dog may respond aggressively, however, is if the cat tries to steal its food. As a precaution, be sure to exclude the cat when feeding your dog.

Contact with other pets

It is not a good idea to allow your dog any opportunity of coming in contact with small pets. Terriers, for example, will instinctively kill rats, while hounds will often pursue rabbits. Even a tame dog may instinctively respond in this way, particularly when the other animal moves, hopping off in the case of a rabbit. These creatures have no way of defending themselves if cornered.

Practical Pointer

If your dog is scratched or even bitten by a cat, be sure to wash the wound without delay, using an antiseptic solution. Otherwise, particularly following a bite, an infection may develop at the site because of the unpleasant bacteria in the cat's mouth.

Signs of aggression

Over the centuries following the start of the domestication process, the dog has spent so much time with humans that it regards people with whom it has regular contact in the same way as pack members. The dog has developed body language to communicate with humans and has lost some of its ability to establish bonds with its own kind. This is a reflection of the fact that, in many cases, dogs are tending to live more solitary lives, isolated from their own kind for much of the day, apart from when they are out walking.

Practical Pointer

Disputes between dogs may arise not just over food. Playthings can also provide a source of conflict. Offering a choice should help to prevent any serious aggression arising, although dogs that know each other well may play with a toy together.

BELOW Serious combat between two wolves. Contests are most likely to be bloody when the leader of the pack is challenged by a subordinate. The opponents are likely to be well-matched, with neither backing down readily.

Fighting instincts

Selective breeding has also played a part, and in some cases, the dog's natural territorial and aggressive tendencies toward its fellows have been deliberately reinforced. This was undertaken to create breeds, such as the Staffordshire bull terrier, for use in dogfighting. In spite of the fact that breeders have worked hard to eliminate aggressive traits from this and other similar breeds today, such dogs can still, on occasions, be very unpredictable in the company of others.

The actual appearance of breeds that are bred for dogfighting is similar, for practical reasons. They all have a relatively short, square, powerful muzzle, which enables them to exert a strong bite and take a firm grip on their opponent. Their eyes are relatively small and deeply set to protect against injury, while the skin on their necks is quite loose, so that a bite here is more likely to result in a superficial rather than a deep injury.

ABOVE Although they are not generally aggressive, ex-racing greyhounds in particular should be muzzled when walking in parks and other places where they could encounter small dogs. The greyhound may otherwise chase and catch its smaller relative.

ABOVE Pack rivalry within a group of hounds. Fighting is much more common among male rather than female dogs.

Pack behavior

In contrast, the situation with pack dogs is markedly different. This is not to say that they always agree, particularly in the case of sled dogs, which retain the closest resemblance to wolves. Arguments over dominance are not uncommon among this group — each team has its canine leader, and especially with new dogs, it will take time for the social order to become established.

But they will then bond and work as a team, which serves to reinforce the pack instinct between them, preventing disputes at this stage in the same way that wolves will not fight when hunting together. It is highly unlikely that wolves would have become such successful predators if their ability to cooperate had not evolved. A single wolf, on its own, is virtually unable to tackle large and dangerous prey, such as moose. The availability of prey is one of the main influences on pack size.

Practical Pointer

Adult dogs are often far more tolerant of the attentions of puppies than of another adult dog, because they are perceived in a different way — not as rivals, but rather as natural subordinates. Maintain this situation by not favoring the puppy in the presence of the older dog.

Cooperative hunting is a feature of many hound breeds, such as beagles and bassets. The social nature of dogs is one of the reasons why they have proved to be such popular companions, as they see the family as a pack, and adopt a subordinate role in the group. Pack hounds, in spite of the fact that they were originally developed for hunting prey, are actually very friendly, genial dogs by nature. If you are seeking two dogs which will live in relative harmony with each other, choosing from this group of breeds is recommended.

The fear factor

When purchasing a puppy it is virtually impossible to tell whether or not an individual will prove aggressive later in life, especially since this will depend in part on how the dog is reared. Much will also depend on its environment and particularly its training, although, especially in the case of bigger dogs, males are likely to be more dominant than females.

Levels of aggression

The overall level of aggression in a wolf pack, even among cubs, starts to rise during the winter period. Male cubs will often begin to build up a dominance over their female siblings, based in part on their larger size. Soon they will start interacting increasingly with the pack members of lower rank, and gradually start to establish a place for themselves in the hierarchy. This change in behavior becomes apparent once the young wolves are two years old, by which time they are also becoming increasingly aggressive.

With naturally assertive breeds of domestic dog, such as the rottweiler or the Doberman, problems are therefore most likely to develop not in puppyhood, but from two years of age onward. This is why firm training from an early age is so important, so that dogs do not start to challenge their owners, or other members of the family, at this critical later stage in their lives.

Fear of dogs

Some people are fearful of dogs, and this is something which a dog will be able to detect and interpret as a sign of submission. The temperament of domestic dogs is, however, far more stable than that of wolves. Certain breeds, notably those of the toy group, have in fact been specifically bred as companions. Not surprisingly therefore, these are the most suitable breeds as family pets.

Some breeds have acquired a reputation for aggression, which may be heightened by their appearance. Ear cropping is outlawed in many countries, but it serves to give breeds, such as this Doberman, a fiercer appearance with its ears raised.

A child brought up with dogs is unlikely to be afraid of them in later life. Young children see their dogs as both friends and protectors. However, always supervise contact between them — dogs are not toys!

It tends to be breeds that most closely resemble the wolf in terms of their appearance, such as the German shepherd dog, which inspire the greatest fear. Human antipathy toward the wolf is very deep-seated, and probably dates back to the time when people were switching from a nomadic, hunting life style to a pastoral existence.

Flock guardians

Wolf packs would have represented a serious threat to herds of sheep and goats in particular, at a time long before the development of firearms. Up until this stage, apart from the alertness of those watching over the animals, the main defense was by means of the wolf's domestic relative, in the form of flock guardians such as the Maremma sheepdog in Italy, or the komondor in Hungary.

Other, similar types of dog were developed throughout Europe. They tended to be whitish in color, as this helped them to blend in among the flocks that they were protecting. It also served to distinguish them readily at a distance from the dark-colored wolf.

Additional protection for these large dogs was provided by large, spiked collars, which guarded the vulnerable area of their throat. However, since the demise of the wolf during the late nineteenth and twentieth centuries in this part of the world, these flock guardians have become much scarcer, although some are now being seen in the show ring with increasing frequency.

Practical Pointer
Delve into the history of any breed which appeals to you before making a final decision about which to choose. This will give you a clear insight into a dog's likely temperament. Dogs evolved for guarding purposes are most likely to display aggression toward their owners and other people.

SIGNS OF DANGER

Menacing growl The first stage of threat behavior.

Bared teeth The second stage is a display of the dog's main weapons against a "trespasser"

Full threat A ferocious bark is the final warning. A dog will enact this three-stage ritual as a warning to avoid a fight, but will attack if the threat is not heeded.

The body language of dogs is very important, particularly because a dog will usually make a series of gestures before, for example, attempting to bite. If these are not detected by a young child, the outcome could be serious, with the child possibly being badly injured as a result. Never leave a child alone with a dog. It is not just coincidence that children are more likely to be bitten than adults. They may also play more roughly with the dog, pulling its tail for example, and be less aware of the warning signs.

Aggression toward people

Dogs rarely bite without some provocation, although some breeds are potentially more aggressive than others, because they will not accept a subservient role, and so are more likely to challenge younger family members in particular. Dominant breeds of this type include the rottweiler and other large dogs that are used as guardians.

A dog will often display its aggression by raising its hackles — the area of fur at the base of the neck — and drawing back its lips to reveal its canine teeth. This is often accompanied by growling, while at the same time, the dog will keep its tail raised. If these signs are ignored, then the teeth will be fully exposed before the dog launches into an attack.

ABOVE Avoid taking on an adult dog if you have a young family, unless you know the dog's history in detail. It may have been rehomed because of its aggressive tendencies, although the animal shelter may not have been told this by the previous owner. Regaining the confidence of a mistreated dog can also be difficult.

Displays of territorial aggression are similar, although the dog may not bite as readily as when it is in pain. Barking is also more common in such cases, providing a means of deterring the intruder without having to resort to physical violence.

Effect of past experience

Past experiences may also exert an effect on the dog's reactions. If it has been repeatedly teased for example, then, as a result, it may be more likely to bite with less warning. One of the potential difficulties with rescued dogs is that you cannot be sure of their previous experiences, with the result that something from their

ABOVE Lips drawn back with the canines exposed is a clear warning sign that this dog will attack if challenged any further. It will also be giving a menacing growl. Dogs rarely launch into a sudden attack, but display a series of signs of increasing aggression.

ABOVE There are times when aggression in a dog is required by its handler, as here in the case of a police dog that is being trained to apprehend a fleeing criminal. The dog is taught to seize the lower part of the arm, and not to inflict any serious injury.

BELOW A snarling gray wolf curls its lips to show its displeasure. This is an early sign of aggression, prior to direct physical contact. Wild dogs, and domestic dogs to a lesser extent, may be afflicted by the deadly rabies virus and infected animals can be unpredictably aggressive and violent.

past, even as simple as a particular color or style of coat, may cause them to display signs of aggression and start to growl.

Try to isolate the cause under these circumstances, and never force the dog to confront the situation directly, because this is highly likely to result in its becoming more and more distressed and aggressive. In this case, you should seek the advice of a behavioral consultant to address the problem and, in due course, perhaps overcome your dog's fear.

Practical Pointer

It is not just in the home that dogs can display territorial instincts. They may behave in a similar way if they are left in a car. This behavior is especially likely to arise if passers-by have teased your dog in the past by banging on a window. In any event, avoid leaving a dog in a car when the weather is very warm, because of the risk of heatstroke.

ABOVE This greyhound is making a "play bow" indicating that it wants to play.

Playtime

Dogs are naturally playful from puppyhood onward, although, with advancing age, they often become less inclined to use toys. Play has important social implications for dogs, helping to establish their social ranking at a relatively early age, as happens with wolf cubs. It can help to avoid the need for fighting, by testing their strength without overt signs of conflict. Dogs will very rarely injure each other during the course of a game.

One of the most distinctive indicators of a dog's desire to play is the so-called "play bow." The dog crouches down on its front legs and, if ignored at this stage, may bark excitedly to attract attention. It then bounces up and may run off for a short distance before repeating this performance should there be no obvious reaction from the other dog or its owner.

Practical Pointer
With all toys, it is sensible to train your dog to relinquish the item on command. Otherwise you could find that the dog becomes possessive to the point where it snaps if you try to take its toy away.

When playing together, dogs will often tend to jump and bounce, rather than walking normally. They may chase after each other and rear up on their hind legs, pawing at each other with their front legs. Small dogs tend to be more playful by nature than their larger relatives, with poodles, for example, often being great clowns. They often circle tightly and ultimately one may roll over on its back. This is a gesture of submission, also seen as a sign of surrender in a fight, but in this case, the body language is decidedly different. Instead of avoiding eye contact, as in the case of a fight, the dog on the ground will continue staring at its companion and will not fold back its ears as a gesture of appeasement.

Toys

Play between an owner and a dog is equally important as a means of reinforcing the bonding process. An ever-increasing range of toys for this purpose can be found in pet stores. They can be broadly divided into three categories. The first includes toys such as balls, which the dog can chase and retrieve. Many dogs appreciate toys of this type, although they perhaps have the strongest appeal for spaniels and retrievers, which will instinctively seek out and return with such items.

LEFT Agility events such as this one at Crufts are open to dogs of all types and sizes, with the dog being judged on the time it takes to get round the course rather than on its appearance. Agility courses harness and test the natural abilities of dogs. Their trainers play a vital role in encouraging the dog.

Practical Pointer

Only use toys which are safe for your dog to play with. It is not unknown for dogs to choke on unsuitable items used as playthings, which end up being swallowed and causing an obstruction in the throat.

OPPOSITE AND BELOW Flying disks are very popular with dogs, with the unpredictability of their flight adding to the excitement of the game. Choose special disks intended for dogs because they are generally made of softer material than those sold as toys. Dogs also enjoy tug toys, but it is important to ensure that your dog is trained to drop the item on command.

Throwing a ball for your dog to bring back to you means that your pet will get far more exercise on even a short walk than would be the case if it trotted alongside you. Special flying disks have also become popular toys for dogs — these are made with soft material which should not damage your pet's teeth, unlike those sold as children's toys or for beach use.

Second, there are chew toys, which help to keep your dog's teeth in good condition. They have largely replaced the typical marrow bones, which used to be sold for this purpose, proving to be more hygienic and less messy around the home. Domestic dogs have relatively little opportunity to exercise their teeth on bones in the same way as wolves, and so such toys can be valuable, especially for puppies during their teething phase, when they are about five months old.

Finally, pull toys are also popular with dogs, but need to be used more cautiously, especially with an older dog, whose teeth may not be in the best condition. Toys of this type may be either solid or comprised of fibers, which often tend to become rather congealed with the dog's saliva.

ABOVE It starts as a desire to come in. The dog tries to push open the door but if the door is closed it may decide to scratch, and this immediately attracts your attention. A pattern of behavior may then form which can soon develop into a serious problem.

Dog damage

Some degree of damage around the home is inevitable, particularly if you start out with a puppy. Carpets and doors are likely to bear the brunt of the puppy's attentions. By trying to anticipate its needs, however, you will be able to minimize the likelihood of any serious damage. Placing the puppy outdoors after meals, and both first thing in the morning and again at night should help to prevent soiling in the home. By dealing with antisocial behavior on the part of your puppy, you should prevent this from becoming habitual.

Conditioning can be significant in this respect. Your puppy may be in the garden and scratching at the door to be let in. If you immediately respond, you are likely to set off a cycle in which your dog scratches repeatedly at the door on every occasion when it is ready to come indoors, with its claws soon damaging the wood. Prevention in this case will depend on you anticipating how long your dog should be left outside and then calling it back inside before it becomes bored.

Practical Pointer
Bored dogs are more apt to become destructive. To prevent this try and provide plenty of toys and exercise for your pet.

Damage in the home

Try to avoid shutting your puppy in a room, certainly on a regular basis, because here again, it will start scratching, potentially damaging both the door and carpeting. It is much better to have a special pen in which your puppy can be safely confined when it is not possible to allow it a free run around the home.

The teething phase can result in quite severe damage to furniture should your puppy seek to relieve the irritation of its developing teeth by gnawing, for example, on a table leg. You will need to keep a close watch on your puppy at this stage and provide a good selection of chew toys to minimize damage around the home.

BELOW He may look cute but this lurcher puppy is likely to cause some damage around the home. Note the torn cloth on which he is lying — providing dogs with their own bed will help to safeguard furniture.

If you have any particularly valuable items, perhaps within your puppy's reach, it is always a good idea to move them to another part of the house, especially since most household insurance policies will not cover you for damage of this type.

Damage in the garden

Dogs can also cause problems in the garden, often digging in flower beds and lawns. Any fertilizers applied need to be selected carefully — a dog may delight in rolling in manure, or even want to eat it. Dogs will also dig to bury food items, such as bones. This behavior mimics the way in which wolves seek to hide surplus food in the hope of returning to it and eating it at a later stage. Burying food means that it will be more likely to escape the attention of scavengers.

There is little to be gained by interfering once the hole is dug, although you may want to remove the item before it is retrieved again. Dogs will eat rotting food, and while this may not upset the digestive system of wolves, it is certainly much more likely to disturb that of their domestic relatives.

Although dogs usually prefer to dig in flower beds, where the soil is softer, and can be excavated more readily, they will equally seek to dig in a lawn if there is no other option available. Their relatively short, blunt claws are ideal for ripping through the turf and either foot may be used for digging.

Neither is it uncommon for them to forage for food in the garden. While fallen apples being used for play, and gnawed, will cause little worry, a dog which chooses to help itself to a row of carrots is unlikely to enjoy a favorable reception from the gardener in the family. Unfortunately, this type of behavior can also soon become habitual — for example, after obtaining several carrots, the dog will return in search of more. The only solution is to fence off this part of the garden to exclude the dog.

BASIC INSTINCTS

Digging

Dogs will readily dig in the garden, particularly if you have buried any edible items in a compost heap or trench for example. This can have longer term and serious consequences, should it cause the dog to fall in. This behavior originates from that of wild dogs, which use their powers of scent to locate edible items such as roots when other food may be harder to obtain, or retrieve food which they have themselves buried previously. Most wild dogs are essentially scavengers. Their adaptability and resourcefulness in obtaining food is responsible for the wide natural distribution of the family today.

Practical Pointer

If you have a male dog which suddenly digs a hole under a fence and heads out of the garden, there is probably a bitch on heat in the neighborhood.

BODY LANGUAGE

Dogs use a combination of body postures facial expression, vocalizations and scent markings to communicate their feelings to their owners and other doges.

How dogs communicate with each other and their owners

The ears have a very important role in communication and are not just for detecting sounds. The posture of the tail is significant, and the fur along the back may also be used to signal the dog's mood. When a dog greets its owner, for example, it usually wags its tail while its ears remain-in their normal position. In a wary encounter with another dog, the tail is carried low and the ears are also lowered. One dog circles the other to pick up their respective scents. Direct eye contact is usually avoided because this is a gesture typically associated with a challenge and aggression. Dogs rarely bite without first signalling their intention to do so, usually by snarling and baring their teeth. A dominant individual in any

encounter will stand with tail and ears erect and often raise the hackles along the back to emphasize an aggressive posture. Faced with this challenge, a subordinate dog will normally turn away and retreat, sometimes being pursued for a short distance by the other. By following a clearly delineated series of gestures, dogs negotiate a potentially harmful encounter without an actual fight occuring.

Stylized behavior is also seen in other contexts such as in inviting another dog to play. The instigator drops down on to its forelegs in the so-called "play bow," with its hind legs standing. The dog may then leap up and bound about, wag its tail and in some cases bark to give further encouragement. A similar invitation is extended to an owner when a dog is in a playful mood.

ABOVE The "play-bow" when a dog bends forward on its front feet and then bounds off for a short distance before returning, is indicative of wanting to play.

ABOVE The tail is a significant indicator of a dog's mood, recognized by both owner and other dogs — the familiar wagging being a typically friendly gesture.

Sense of smell

In addition to body language of this type, smell also provides a potent means of communication, both directly and indirectly. Dogs have a much keener sense of smell than humans, and it is for this reason that dogs always sniff each other when meeting. They start at the head and then switch to the inguinal region between the hind legs. The significance of scent markers, known as pheromones, has been increasingly appreciated during recent years. These chemicals are present in the urine, and male dogs especially urinate very frequently when out for a walk to leave traces of their scent for other dogs passing on the same route. Male dogs urinate by lifting one of their hind legs; this enables them to direct urine to a particular spot such as a lamp post to which other dogs will also be attracted. This behavior is not seen in young male puppies however, which squat like bitches when urinating. There may be a hormonal cause for this behavior since dogs only start to urinate by this means after puberty. The actual administration of the male hormone testosterone, however, does not appear to have a direct influence other than increasing the actual frequency of urination once the puppies are independent of their mothers.

ABOVE LEFT Aggressive encounters between dogs are rare, since the subordinate individual usually backs down, although both will make threatening gestures, including snarling, up to this point. A distinct hierarchy is apparent in these Eskimo dogs, reminiscent of the pack behavior of their wolf ancestors.

ABOVE Sense of smell is vital to dogs and they recognize each other on the basis of scent, either directly, or from scent markers, notably urine. A male dog is not suffering from incontinence if he attempts to urinate at each lamp post while out for a walk — this simply serves as a territorial marker.

Faeces also may convey a characteristic scent to a dog, and wild dogs certainly use their excrement as territorial markers. The anal sacs or glands produce a secretion which under normal circumstances is transferred to the faeces. A dog rubbing its rear end along the ground is more likely to be suffering from impacted anal glands than leaving a scent trail. The scratching on the ground sometimes seen after urination or defecation, usually on grass or a similar surface rather than concrete, may however be a deliberate means of leaving an auxiliary scent. Between the toes of its feet, the dog possesses sweat glands that could leave a scent and the characteristic scratch marks would serve to attract other dogs to the spot.

ABOVE A potentially aggressive encounter between two Border Collies usually ends without a serious fight. The subordinate dog, with tail down, tends to retreat.

Does the bark of dogs vary according to breed?

Barking is another means of communication available to the dog. There are considerable differences in the frequency of barking between breeds. Some dogs such as Grayhounds rarely bark while others, like the Chihuahua, can be extremely noisy. The Basenji is often said not to bark at all, but in reality these dogs are capable of making a noise despite the reduction in the size of their larynx. Dogs will bark for a variety of reasons, ranging from excitement to fear. The characteristic baying of hounds probably has a more specific function — it may serve to keep the members of a pack in contact with each other if they become split up. There is a clear aggressive warning in a growl, while whining usually indicates an attention-seeking mood on the part of an adult dog. This sound is rarely made in the company of other dogs, but puppies will use it to indicate that they are cold and distressed. The dog has an ability to hear sounds of a higher frequency than humans, and for this reason can detect the sound of dog whistles that are inaudible to the human ear.

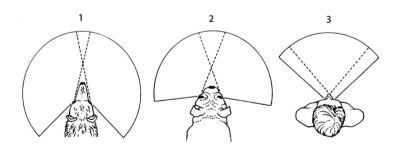

A DOG'S FIELD OF VISION

Dogs have a wide field of view because their eyes are located at the side of their heads. A dog with wide-set eyes can have as much as 270° (1), and a dog with more forward-pointing eyes normally covers some 200° (2) — still twice the angle achieved by the human physique (3).

The dog's sense of sight

It is of relatively little importance compared with the senses mentioned previously, and, indeed, the vision of a dog is not as good as that of a human in daylight. Their eyes are most responsive to moving objects, and their sight can be acute in this instance. It is said that dogs are capable of recognizing a fox over a kilometre away. They also have a broader field of vision than humans but a greatly reduced ability to distinguish between individual colors.

How to react if your pet is attacked by another dog

In most cases, the dogs will resolve the situation without direct conflict, but if you find that your dog becomes involved in a fight, try to walk on. Then call it. It will want to follow you and should make a rapid retreat. There is little point in trying to separate two determined combatants. You may simply worsen the situation. If all else fails, throw a bucket of water over them, if you are in a position to do so. The main danger lies in the fact that an aggressive animal may refuse to acknowledge the effective signs of surrender. This applies particularly in the case of breeds kept originally for fighting purposes. When you are out with your dog, be sure that it remains in close contact with you. By this means, you should be able to prevent a fight before it starts. Male dogs are usually the worst offenders when it comes to fighting, and a few individuals will attack other males at every opportunity despite all attempts to train them to the contrary. If you have the misfortune to own a dog like this, make sure it is kept away from others. The only effective means of overcoming the problem is to have the dog castrated, because the aggression is likely to be of hormonal origin.

ABOVE The responsive look on this dog gives some indication of dogs' superior sense of vision and hearing. Their eyes are extremely sensitive to movement and their ears are tuned to frequencies well above the human ear. Also, dog's eyes are specialized — with a greater proportion of rod receptacles on the retina — to operate well in low light conditions.

ABOVE A sign of subordination is displayed by the Boston Terrier rolling on its back, while playing with a Dalmatian. This kind of behavior can also be seen in a domestic situation when a dog has been scolded.

ABOVE The temperament of German Shepherd Dogs — highly intelligent and slightly aggressive combined with acute scenting abilities — make them perfect for training as guard dogs.

The causes of aggression

Obviously, a dog can become aggressive when protecting its own environment from strangers. This instinct is utilized in the training of guard dogs. The danger is always that an unsuspecting child may not appreciate a dog's warning signs. Similarly, a bitch with puppies will defend them if she feels they are threatened. Such aggression again stems from hormonal changes. This behavior may be unexpected, however, when the dog is

suffering from a phantom pregnancy. Items such as toys are seen as substitute puppies, and even a straightforward attempt to take such a toy in order to play with the dog may be met with an unexpected and uncharacteristic display of aggression. Pain may also result in an aggressive response, and other medical problems, including brain tumors, can cause the dog to turn savage, as can the dreaded viral disease, rabies, in its "furious" form.

Overcoming behavioral problems in your dog

This is a complex field of study and has been receiving increasing attention from animal psychologists in recent years. Many problems can be traced back to the owners themselves. A dog left on its own for long periods every day, for example, will get bored and in turn destructive. The remedy is obvious, but in practice it may not be possible to spend more time with the dog. Invariably the dog will either have to be moved to a new home or put to sleep. Indeed, major behavioral problems, ranging from aggression to soiling and destruction within the home, can often be traced back to poor training and a lack of interest on the part of the owner. In other instances, the dog may have achieved total dominance over its owner and the immediate family. Having bitten a member of the household, it may come to realize that it can retain this position by threatening to bite again. If you feel that you have a behavioral problem with your dog that you cannot overcome without help, refer first to your veterinarian. It may then be possible to consult an animal psychologist on recommendation from your veterinarian. You should probably find that you can claim a portion of the fees on your canine

LEFT Police dogs must learn behavior that human beings would find difficult and need specialized and patient training, the trainer having to assume the role of the pack leader.

ABOVE Destructiveness is an inherent feature of many dogs' temperaments but, in the same way as children, they can easily be trained to play with a stick or toy rather than devastating your home.

health insurance scheme if the veterinarian favors such treatment.

Stopping your dog from destroying your home when you are out

Once the permanent set of teeth have emerged (by seven months of age), the puppy's desire to chew is correspondingly reduced. It may be necessary to obtain a special spray in the interim to make furniture unpalatable to your dog. In an older individual, the destructive behavior may be a manifestation of the dog's worry about you leaving it or it could result from boredom or lack of exercise. It may also be a combination of these factors.

Try to accustom the dog to your absence for short periods, no longer than 10 minutes at a time, and give him a suitable chew toy before you leave. When you return and find the home undamaged, praise him. If he has reverted to his former habits, take no notice of him. Repeat the procedure at another time until the dog realizes what is expected of him and that you are not abandoning him when you leave him alone for short periods. Gradually, extend the time that you are away until he gradually becomes more used to his own company.

It may be that your dog also howls when you are out. Keep an ear open for such behavior as it can prove a source of valid complaints from near neighbors. While barking at the approach of strangers to the home can be beneficial, this activity should be controlled. Tell the dog to be quiet and praise it when it stops barking as requested. If it persists, it may need to be hit firmly but not hard to encourage him to desist. Electric-shock collars should not be used, even in countries where their sale is permitted, because the problem can be corrected by more humane means. Similarly, the cosmetic operation known as ventriculocordectomy, surgical muting of a dog, cannot be condoned.

PROBLEMS
Changing view of the dog

Nowadays, with so many distinctive breeds of domestic dog, it may be hard to imagine that, as selective breeding continues, they are still diverging further from their wild ancestor. Although breeding has already eliminated many undesirable traits that would have been apparent in the early days of domestication, such as restlessness and wariness of people, there have been distinct drawbacks, most notably in terms of the dog's physical soundness.

Physical problems

Problems such as hip dysplasia, in which the hip joints are weakened, and luxating patellas, a weakness which affects the kneecaps of smaller breeds especially, have become prominent in domestic dogs, whereas such afflictions are not encountered in the case of the wolf. Breeders are striving to eliminate such physical shortcomings from their bloodlines by careful monitoring of breeding stock.

Rage syndrome

Unexpected problems do crop up on occasions, however, and can relate to temperament as much as physical soundness. One of the most worrying examples of this type is the so-called "rage syndrome", which can be found in some normally placid breeds, such as cocker spaniels and labrador retrievers. Such dogs appear normal, but suffer from uncontrollable bouts of rage. They are highly unpredictable and will attack without the usual warning signals.

The only indicator of this problem may be a glazed expression. Research has shown that there are usually distinct genetic links in such cases. Once a problem of this type has been identified, suspect or affected bloodlines should not be used for breeding purposes, and dogs suffering from the condition should be destroyed to safeguard the community.

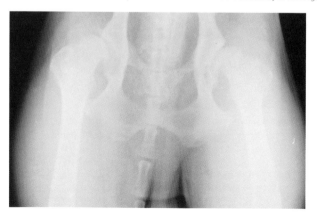

LEFT Weaknesses affecting the skeletal system such as hip dysplasia are fairly common in dogs, and can prove a severe handicap, especially if the dog is overweight. In this case the head of the femur does not sit snugly in the socket on the hip, failing to provide proper support.

Effects of dog shows

One of the positive aspects of the dog-show scene is that it has actually encouraged the development of those breeds with sound temperaments over the past century or so, ever since events of this type began to be held regularly. Judges will simply not give awards to dogs which show signs of aggression in the ring, either to other dogs or to people.

In fact, without the interest generated by dog shows such as Crufts and the Westminster Kennel Club Show held in New York, where a wide variety of breeds is put on view, it is possible that some might well have died out, or would have been greatly reduced in numbers.

Events where the dogs are judged to prescribed standards laid down for each breed, are different from field trials, which seek to assess the working abilities of individual dogs. They give an opportunity for dogs to work in close association with their handlers, which is a feature further developed in the various obedience and agility competitions, often held in conjunction with regular dog shows.

The type of dog is of no significance whatsoever at such events, and in fact, it is quite common to see both cross-bred and mongrel dogs taking part. These events can show just how the pack instinct present in wolves has been transformed into a very close bond between dog and handler.

ABOVE A judge checks a wire-haired dachshund for soundness. The requirements for such dogs and points for particular features are laid down in the official breed standard. This may also list faults in some cases.

ABOVE Show dogs have to learn to be tolerant of other dogs in close proximity to them, and to accept being handled by the judge, who is likely to be a stranger, without misbehaving in any way.

FEEDING
&
HEALTH

Dogs are highly adaptable in their feeding habits, and this characteristic underlies the wide range of the wolf, as well as helping to explain why dogs were so widely kept in primitive societies. While canids were instinctively carnivorous, they are not above scavenging, and when other food is in short supply they will consume almost anything edible, including insects, berries and even plants. Living in this way does take its toll however, with wolves having a much shorter life expectancy than their domesticated relatives. Great advances in the field of canine health care, particularly for older individuals, means that dogs are now living longer than at any stage in the past. Even the large breeds, which tend to have a shorter lifespan than their smaller relatives, are in many cases now living for more than a decade.

FEEDING
Food and diet

Dogs, like wolves, prefer to feed on meat but they will eat vegetables and there are even specially formulated vegetarian diets to keep them in good health. Feeding meat is not without its dangers because, whereas a wolf has access to the whole carcass, a domestic dog only receives selected parts, such as organ meat like spleen or the stomach (sold as tripe), which by themselves do not represent a balanced diet. These are low in calcium for example, and a dog fed in this fashion will soon start to suffer from nutritional deficiencies if its diet is not supplemented.

As a result, the availability of balanced foods has helped greatly to popularize the keeping of dogs. Containing all the essential ingredients to keep dogs in good health, these foods can be used straight from the can or packet.

Canned foods

Canned foods have proved popular for many years and tend to be preferred by dogs because their relatively high water content is similar to that of meat itself. Cans are heavy to carry in quantity, however, and any of their contents left uneaten will have to be stored in a refrigerator to prevent them deteriorating or attracting flies. Special plastic covers can be obtained for this purpose, which also prevent the odor of the food permeating into the surrounding air.

Dry foods

Dry foods for dogs are now very popular. They offer a more concentrated ration than canned food, and, because of their low water content, they do not require any special storage conditions, other than being kept dry. Take care to follow the instructions

Practical Pointer
When weighing your dog, lift it up and stand on the bathroom scales with it. Then subtract your own weight from the total to find the dog's weight.

LEFT The dog's level of activity will determine the type of food which it needs. Active dogs such as racing greyhounds require a different diet from that of a sedentary older pet. A growing range of prepared foods to meet the demands of dogs at all stages in their lives is now available.

regarding the amount of food required, however, because if you persist in offering an excess, your dog will soon show signs of obesity.

The use of dry foods can be especially recommended for breeds such as poodles, which may suffer badly from dental decay and gum disease, because such foods help to keep the teeth free from the tartar that predisposes to this type of problem. A dog fed on dry food, however, will drink more than if it were eating canned food, to make up for the relative deficiency of fluid in its food.

Semi-moist foods

The third type of food now available is semi-moist, although surprisingly, it has not proved especially popular with dog owners. It retains the moist characteristic of canned food combined with the convenience of a dry food. The addition of sugar as a preservative means that it is not recommended for dogs suffering from diabetes mellitus. Semi-moist foods are sold in packets which need to be kept sealed after opening

Obesity

One of the major problems in the dog world today is that an increasing number of dogs are suffering from obesity. This now affects roughly thirty percent of dogs. If you are concerned about your dog's weight, you can refer in the first instance to a book which contains the breed standard — this will provide you with an indication of the normal weight for the breed. Male dogs tend to be slightly larger and heavier than bitches. With a cross-bred dog, it is obviously harder to assess its ideal weight, but if you can no longer see or feel your pet's ribs, it is almost certainly overweight.

Obesity can have a number of adverse effects on a dog's health, and is a contributes to heart and joint disease. Neutering, by altering the hormonal balance in the body, can also predispose to obesity, to the

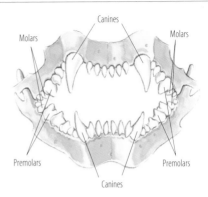

ABOVE The dentition of the dog. It shows the typical pattern of a carnivore, with the prominent canine teeth, used to kill prey, clearly visible at the corners of the mouth, with the incisors at the front often serving to seize prey in the first instance.

ABOVE A typical range of different types of prepared foods is shown here, as well as various types of chews and treats. Be careful not to overfeed your dog, as it can rapidly become obese.

extent that, after such surgery, the dog's food intake may need to be reduced significantly.

Special obesity diets are available to help in a dog's slimming program, but you should not rely on these alone. Increasing the amount of exercise will be just as significant in ensuring that your dog not only loses weight, but also stays fit. The domestic dog leads a very sedentary life compared with its ancestor, and will readily become obese as a result.

ABOVE Dogs will often prefer to drink from ponds and puddles rather than from a water bowl. They rarely fall ill as a result. Try to monitor how much they are drinking because this can be crucial to their health.

Water

A supply of fresh drinking water should always be available to dogs. A water container which will not be tipped over easily should be used for this purpose, because the dog may otherwise place its foot on the rim, tipping over the container and spilling its contents.

It is also important to wash the dog's water bowl thoroughly about twice a week. Bacteria can and do develop in stale water, and could cause a digestive disturbance. Nevertheless, dogs will often prefer to drink from standing sources of water, such as ponds or puddles, just like their wild ancestor. The reason for such behavior is unclear — perhaps it is partly to do with taste — but usually, no harm will result.

Drinking while out walking

There are potential risks when your dog is out for a walk, and becomes thirsty. It is then more likely to drink contaminated water than would otherwise be the case. Be particularly careful around any farm buildings, where there could be contaminated sources of water. It is always better to take a supply of drinking water for your dog if you are going on a relatively lengthy trek, especially if the weather is hot. Special water bottles for this purpose, which will also convert into drinkers, and can be easily carried on a shoulder strap, are now available.

The situation may be worse if you are on a beach, because without a drink, your dog may resort to drinking seawater, which, with its high salt content, will worsen its thirst and could make it seriously ill. In addition, dogs may encounter difficulties if they plunge into the water in search of a drink.

LEFT This convenient drinker means that you do not have to carry a separate water bottle and bowl when you go out with your dog. It comes complete with shoulder straps as seen here.

Monitoring water consumption

At home, always keep a close watch on the volume of water which your dog is drinking, particularly as it gets older. Increased water consumption may be indicative of kidney failure and a number of other ailments. Do not restrict your dog's water intake under these circumstances, as this is likely to have dire results. Obviously, drinking more will result in the production of more urine, so that your dog is more likely to soil in the house as well.

ABOVE Wolves and dogs drink in an identical fashion, lapping up water using their tongue, with the tip of the tongue expanding rather like a ladle for this purpose. Some water will inevitably be spilt, and so you should position your dog's water bowl on a non-absorbent surface. The bowl itself should also be designed so that it cannot be tipped over easily.

Practical Pointer

It is not a good idea to give dogs cow's milk to drink. Some dogs may not be able to digest it, and end up suffering from diarrhea. Stick to a dog-milk replacer, especially for puppies. This is available from pet stores and simply needs to be mixed with water.

FEEDING BEHAVIOR

Dogs can prove great scavangers and will also thieve food., intended for human consumption. A combination of firm training and thoughtfulness Will prevent conflict.

Dealing with fussy eaters

There is no convincing evidence to confirm that dogs get bored when given the same food every day. Provided they are receiving a balanced diet, there is no need to be concerned. By all means, vary the diet somewhat if you wish; offer cooked meat and corn meal occasionally instead of a convenience food. There is unlikely to be a link between the food you are offering and the dog's fussy eating habits. The root of the problem is almost certainly elsewhere. Do you feed a lot of tidbits between meals? This can depress appetite, particularly if the meal is less palatable than the snacks, although more nutritious. Do you get very concerned if your pet refuses to eat a meal? Some dogs soon come to realize that self-deprivation can bring rewards from their owners, either in the form of extra affection or more appealing food. Such behavior is most often seen in the toy (small) breeds.

Try to be firm. Cut out all additional food of any type offered between meals. Leave the dish of food available for an hour in the usual spot where the dog is fed, and then remove it even if none has been eaten. Repeat this procedure at the next meal time. The dog will soon come to recognize that it must eat what is being offered. It will not starve to death, even if it eats nothing for a couple of days. Do make sure that the food you are providing is as appealing as possible. You could add a little margarine over the surface of canned food, soak corn meal in warm gravy and make sure that the dog will not be disturbed more than necessary while the food is available. You

ABOVE Performing tricks such as standing on hind legs, in return for tidbits should be discouraged as food between meals may spoil your dog's appetite and may eventually lead to obesity.

want to encourage him to eat by offering food on your hand.

A number of medical reasons exist for loss of appetite. If the dog suddenly refuses to eat and shows other symptoms, such as a lack of interest in other activities like going out, then it is advisable to contact a veterinarian without delay. Or if your dog plays with the food, particularly corn meal, it may have a painful tooth or gum infection. Studies suggest that male dogs tend to be fussier about their food than bitches. This may be a throwback to their wild ancestry, when the dominant male in a pack had preference at the kill.

Dogs and chocolate

Chocolate is very palatable to dogs and can be given occasionally. It is available in the form of special treats at some pet stores. Do not give large quantities. This may affect the dog's appetite in the short-term and can result in other problems such as dental decay, obesity and possibly diabetes mellitus. Excessive amounts of chocolate can also give rise to diarrhoea, so always take care to place boxes of sweets well out of a dog's eager reach.

There are other, healthier tidbits that can be used as rewards during training and at other times. Raw carrots cut into small pieces appeal to many dogs to the extent in some cases that they may attempt to dig up carrots growing in a garden once they acquire a taste for them. Yeast tablets are also very palatable to dogs and provide a source of Vitamin B. Always restrict the amounts of such items that you give, so the dog does not come to view them as an extension to meals rather than a reward for good behavior.

Give a dog a bone?

From a strictly nutritional viewpoint, there is probably no need to provide bones, provided your dog is being fed correctly. Yet dogs certainly enjoy having bones to gnaw, and this activity may help to keep the teeth clean. There are potential dangers however; some dogs become extremely possessive about bones and need to be trained to relinquish them readily when told to do so. This can be carried out more easily with a young dog. Be careful when dealing with a strange dog as you cannot be sure how it will react. Provide only large marrow bones which cannot be accidentally swallowed causing a possible obstruction in the digestive tract. Chicken and rabbit bones, being light, are particularly dangerous; they splinter readily, often in the mouth where they can become embedded in the tissue. Larger bones such as those from chops may be inadvertently swallowed and become stuck in the throat. Try to be sure that the edge of the bones you provide are not rough, as fragments may break off and cause problems.

If, in the light of the above, you feel it is too risky to provide a bone for your dog to chew, consider one of the chew toys available at most pet shops.

LEFT Chewing bones is an enjoyable activity for dogs but, from a dietary standpoint, they are not strictly necessary, although they may help to keep a dog's teeth clean. Some dogs do get very possessive about bones, and so they must be trained from an early age to relinquish them on command. In warm weather bones attract flies, particularly if there is any flesh still adherent and so dog chews sold in pet stores are preferable.

How to prevent your dog from scavenging for food

Unfortunately, all dogs, to a greater or lesser extent, are scavengers by nature and will steal food if a suitable item presents itself. In certain instances, they may be driven by a medical reason. Pancreatic insufficiency, for example, often causes an increase in appetite; the dog will steal food at every opportunity while continuing to lose weight. Veterinary help must be obtained if a condition of this type is suspected. Otherwise, try to prevent a dog scavenging by placing food out of reach, and keep a close watch when you are out walking in case the dog finds the discarded remains of a picnic such as a chicken carcass. It is always possible that digestive troubles such as vomiting or diarrhoea or a combination of these symptoms will follow scavenging.

Dogs that eat grass

This behavior probably doesn't mean you have to change your dog's diet, but you could try increasing the level of fibre, especially if the dog is prone to constipation. Eating grass seems to be natural behavior; it is often followed by vomiting which presumably relieves some irritation. Puppies may vomit roundworms by this means. Check that your dog is not eating grass that has been treated with chemical sprays. Most dogs prefer thickish stems to ordinary lawn grass so this behavior is more likely to occur when you are walking close to an area of long grass.

A few dogs develop abnormal appetites for other more harmful things. If you take your dog to the beach, make sure as far as possible that it does not attempt to swallow pebbles. While the canine digestive tract is fairly tolerant of foreign bodies, pebbles can become stuck, causing more serious consequences.

How to tell if your dog has a food allergy

Such problems are not unknown, but relatively little study has been carried out in this area. Now that a link between hyperexcitability in children and certain ingredients in prepared foodstuffs has been found, similar links in dogs may be found in the future. It is important not to confuse an allergy with the virtually immediate reaction to eating indigestible food. In the case of a dog that cannot digest the lactose in milk, for example, the resulting diarrhoea does not come from an allergy to lactose,

BELOW A healthy dog, in this case a cross-bred Cavalier King Charles Spaniel, crossed with a Whippet, is totally dependent on his owner to provide food regularly which is of good nutritional quality, combined with plenty of exercise.

BELOW LEFT Eating grass is fairly common in dogs — it may act as a natural emetic or add fibre to the diet

but from the inability of the body to digest it. Skin rashes often result from an allergy. A wide range of foods may be implicated, and it can be a time-consuming task to track down the most likely cause. Various items have to be removed from the diet in a strict sequence, to see when the irritation disappears. An immediate improvement is unlikely to be apparent. It will probably take several days.

Obesity in dogs

It has been suggested that no less than about 30 percent of the dogs in the United States are obese, and this figure is mirrored in other countries such as the United Kingdom. Certain breeds are more likely to become overweight than others — Beagles and Labrador .Retrievers are especially susceptible. But the problem also affects small breeds such as the Dachshund. In this latter instance, obesity may well lead to intervertebral disc problems, to which Beagles can also be prone. Obesity more often affects bitches than male dogs, and neutered dogs are most at risk from becoming overweight. Obesity often becomes a problem in middle-age when a dog's level of activity declines.

Strategies for reducing the weight of your dog

First decide on the correct weight for your dog. If it is not a pedigreed animal, aim to reduce its weight to the level where its ribs can be clearly felt but not seen beneath the skin as a rough guide. Special obesity diets can be obtained from your veterinarian and should help to lower your dog's weight. Otherwise reduce the overall amount of food offered by about 40 percent. Keep a check on the dog's weight on a weekly basis. Weight loss in the smaller breeds should work out to about quarter of a pound (100 grams) weekly and will be about treble this figure in the case of big dogs.

ABOVE Obesity is more likely to affect middle-aged dogs and the risk of obesity increases with age, as the level of activity declines and food intake remains constant. The side effects are especially noticeable in warm weather, with the dog painting excessively, like this Labrador Retriever — a breed that is particularly prone to becoming overweight when kept in a domestic environment. Interestingly, studies have shown that the majority of obese dogs also have overweight owners.

The majority of obese dogs are overweight because they are being given too much food by their owners. It is vital to cut out all snacks while the dog is on its diet, and to make sure that no food is being scavenged from neighbors during this period. Studies suggest that dogs fed on home-prepared rations are most likely to become overweight. The dog is receiving surplus carbohydrates which is not being used on energy expenditure and is thus converted to fat. On a diet, part of the body's fat reserves are burned to meet the energy demands and are thus gradually reduced with a corresponding loss of weight.

Once you have succeeded in slimming your dog down to a better weight, try to ensure that it does not become fat again. Increase the amount of food offered by about 20 percent so it is receiving just 80 percent of its previous food intake. Obesity does not always result from excessive feeding, but hormonal changes with a similar effect are quite rare in dogs. In severe cases of obesity, a veterinarian may recommend hospitalization so the dog can be placed on a crash diet with only water being provided.

Providing adequate water for your dog to drink

Always make sure that your dog has a clean bowl of drinking water available; change the contents every day. There is no fixed amount that a dog will drink during a day. The quantity consumed will vary, depending on such factors as its diet, the temperature and the amount of exercise it receives. Typically, dogs fed on a dry diet will drink more to compensate for the relatively low amount of fluid in their food. And in hot weather and following exercise, the dog's thirst will be increased. You may not even know how much the dog is actually drinking since water bowls alone are not a reliable indicator. Unfortunately dogs will often drink from other sources such as puddles, when out for a walk, and toilet bowls at home. The latter is particularly dangerous, especially if there are chemicals such as bleach in the water. Keep the bathroom door closed and the lid of the toilet down at all times.

Measure the amount of fluid that your dog is drinking by filling the bowl with a fixed quantity and noting how much is left at the same time the following day. There are various medical problems which may encourage a dog to drink more than usual. If you are concerned, see your veterinarian. As a guide, a dog about the weight of a Cocker Spaniel should consume an average of two cups when kept on a canned diet. Never withhold water from your dog even if it is incontinent. This could be fatal because the dog needs to make up the excessive water loss from its body. The only circumstance in which it may be best to prevent your dog drinking water freely is when it is vomiting, as drinking water can precipitate further vomiting and further loss of vital body salts. Provide only a small quantity after vomiting appears to have ceased and seek veterinary advice. Conversely, there may be occasions when you need to encourage your dog to drink. This is usually when it has an infection of

ABOVE The water intake of dogs varies according to their diet and the prevailing environmental conditions. Excessive thirst however, can be indicative of certain diseases and is often linked with urinary incontinence.

the urinary tract, or has deposits such as bladder stones in the tract.

Your dog's water intake may be reduced if you are providing milk for it to drink. Remember that milk is not essential and cannot be digested properly by all dogs. Some individuals get a taste for tea, but this is probably because of its milk content and any sugar that may be present. Do not encourage your dog to drink any form of alcohol; this is potentially harmful, and dogs, like humans, can become addicted to alcohol, with similar consequences. If you are going to the beach for the day in the summer, take a supply of fresh water and a bowl for your dog. Otherwise, in hot weather especially, a dog may resort to drinking sea water, and this can prove fatal in any quantity because of salt-poisoning.

How to stop your dog eating its own faeces

Such behavior, known as coprophagia, is quite common in various mammals including not only dogs but also chimpanzees! Various reasons have been suggested for such behavior in dogs. It could be that the dog is suffering from a digestive problem, notably a deficiency of certain B vitamins or Vitamin K which are normally manufactured in the gut by bacteria. By consuming its faeces, it obtains these essential elements, which otherwise would be lost in large quantities from the body. It may be worth supplementing these vitamins to see if this overcomes the problem. Yet such behavior appears to be addictive and is often seen in dogs that have been kenneled under fairly unsanitary conditions for part of their life. A bitch will frequently eat the stools of her puppies, and they may consume hers early in life. It may be that this helps to establish the beneficial vitamin-producing bacteria in their intestinal tracts.

If a dog is suffering from a malabsorption disease, part of the food will pass through the digestive tract unaltered, and re-emerge in the faeces. These are attractive to dogs because of the undigested foodstuff present in them. A condition of this type requires veterinary attention; the behavior can be corrected by appropriate therapy for the original problem.

Nevertheless, in many cases there is no clear-cut explanation for coprophagia. Always try to clear up the faeces as soon as possible after they are expelled from the body so the dog has no opportunity to eat them. It is also possible to lace the stools with a foul-tasting substance such as curry powder. Other treatment involves the use of a drug called Cythiomate, normally used to control fleas, which will taint the faeces and cause then to taste bad when eaten. In severe cases, it may be necessary for apomorphine (which induces vomiting) to be administered as soon as possible after the dog eats its faeces.

Shortly afterward, the adverse effects of the drug will become apparent, and the dog will feel ill for a couple of hours or so. It then comes to associate the feeling of nausea with eating its own faeces and should then desist from this practice. Obviously such a drastic remedy must be discussed beforehand with your veterinarian.

Some dogs show no interest in their own excrement but are attracted to that of cattle and

ABOVE Dogs enjoy drinking water from alternative sources to their feeding bowls. They also have a tendency to roll around in mud as soon as possible after a bath, to restore their body scent

horses in particular. The dog may eat the faeces or (perhaps worse from the owner's viewpoint) roll in them, with cow pats being especially favored. While the eating of excrement is carried out for basically the same reasons as given previously, the deliberate soiling of the coat probably results from a totally different cause. Two schools of thought exist: one maintains that the scent from the herbivore's faeces disguises the strong canine odor and helps hunting dogs conceal their presence from potential prey; the other believes the smell may act to reinforce the dog's body odor.

The latter explanation seems more feasible in practice since dogs that have recently been washed often have the maddening habit of seeking out the excrement of herbivores to roll in at the first opportunity when out on a walk. Since a bath removes the usual canine odor, the dog may be seeking to reinforce its social status because it has been deprived of its natural means of doing so. Nevertheless, another bath will be necessary and the dog's access to such sources of faeces will have to be restricted as far as possible.

AILMENTS AND REMEDIES
Spotting problems early

By arranging for your dog to visit the veterinarian on a regular basis, you can be sure that any problems will be detected at an early stage, which in turn should make treatment more straightforward.

Blockage of the anal glands

One of the commonest problems that many dogs experience are those that affect the anal glands. These are a pair of small sacs that are located just inside the anus. These sacs have an important scent-marking function, producing a pungent liquid which is transferred to the feces as they are passed out of the body. This odor enables both wild and domestic dogs to recognize each other.

Unfortunately, in domestic dogs, these sacs often become blocked, which causes them to swell up and become very uncomfortable. The dog frequently tries to relieve the irritation by so-called "scooting" — dragging its hindquarters over the carpet indoors or an area of grass outdoors. It may also try to chew and bite this part of its body. Its efforts are likely to be in vain, however, with the result that abscesses may form in the sacs, making it very painful for the dog to defecate.

Your veterinarian will be able to free the blockage and empty these sacs, although if they are not treated and the secretions form into solid plugs, it may be necessary to anesthetize the dog and flush the sacs through to break down the blockage. Recurrences can be quite common, but adding bulk to the diet, in the form of bran available from pet, stores, may help to ensure that these sacs function properly in the future.

Heart malfunctions

More regular health checks, roughly every six months, may be recommended for older dogs. By

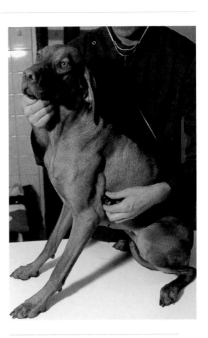

ABOVE Listening to the sounds of a dog's heart will alert a veterinarian to any potential problems. Dogs can be susceptible to heart disease, especially as they become older, with some heart defects afflicting puppies.

Practical Pointer

If your dog's breath is bad, arrange for a veterinary check-up. It may simply have a bad tooth or gum disease, although, alternatively, this can be a sign of kidney failure. Once diagnosed, this condition can now be controlled largely by careful dietary manipulation, at least for a time.

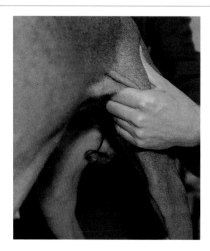

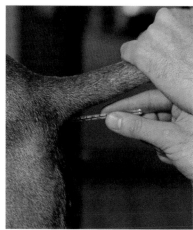

ABOVE Taking a dog's temperature will help give an indication of its overall state of health. This procedure needs to be undertaken carefully however, so as not to cause pain or injury. The dog will need to be restrained for this purpose.

ABOVE The easiest place to take a dog's pulse is as shown here, just inside the hind leg where the femoral artery runs. The pulse rate can be especially important after an injury. When trying to find your dog's pulse, do not press hard on the skin, as this tends to mask it.

listening to your dog's chest with a stethoscope, your veterinarian will be able to pick up any misfunctioning of the heart, which is relatively common at this stage in life. Dogs rarely suffer from coronary disease, however, unlike people, but they are more susceptible to valvular disorders.

Typical symptoms of valvular disease in dogs may be coughing and tiredness after a walk. This suggests that the mitral valve on the left side of the heart may have become thickened, and so is no longer working effectively. In contrast, when the failure involves the tricuspid valve on the right side, blood does not flow back as effectively as normal to the heart. This results in body organs, such as the liver, becoming swollen. In some cases, both valves may be affected, and the dog will then display a combination of these symptoms.

Effective treatment can be given to improve the dog's quality of life — digitalis, for example, helps to improve the contractibility of the heart muscle, making it work more effectively in spite of the valvular damage in the organ. Diuretic drugs will serve to remove excess fluid which builds up in the circulation as a result of the failing heart, so that the heart has to pump less hard, and can function more effectively. Once the initial course of drugs has been completed, the dose will have to be adapted down to a maintenance level, and continued throughout the rest of the dog's life, but this is not particularly expensive.

Practical Pointer

The heart itself is relatively easy to locate, being found opposite the point of the elbow on the left side of the dog's body.

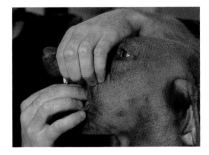

ABOVE Giving your dog a pill can be carried out quite easily by placing your left hand across the nose, with your finger and thumb on each side steadying the jaws.

ABOVE Use your right hand to pry down the lower jaw and slip the pill into the dog's mouth. (Reverse if you are left-handed). Keep the jaws upright to ensure the pill falls to the back of the mouth. Keep the jaws closed to encourage the dog to swallow the pill.

Administering medicines

It is no coincidence that dogs are now living longer than ever before. This is thanks in part to a better understanding of their veterinary needs, with some practices now even holding special clinics for older dogs. In contrast, wolves and other wild dogs will be lucky to survive in the wild for as long.

Giving pills

There are a number of very basic health-care procedures which owners of domestic dogs may have to carry out on occasions, and it is much easier to practice with a puppy. Giving a pill to a dog is a fairly simple task, but is one which some owners find quite difficult. It may be possible to hide the pill in your dog's food but this is impossible if you are using a dried food diet as the pill cannot be concealed.

In any event, it is important to train your dog to allow you to open up its mouth, to take a toy away for example, if the dog refuses to drop it. Follow the technique outlined on this page (right) and your dog should allow you to open its mouth and give it the pill it requires. If your dog is clearly reluctant to swallow its medication try stroking the dog under the throat which should help to make it swallow.

Giving liquid medication

Giving liquid medication is relatively straightforward as well, although it may help to lift the dog onto a bench, in a shed for example, rather than carrying out this task on the floor, where the dog will be more likely to struggle. By placing it on a bench, it should be less inclined to struggle. In the case of the larger breeds, be sure to bend your back so as not to injure yourself when lifting the dog. Place your left arm around its chest, and reach round its hind legs with your other hand, clasping the dog to your body when picking it up.

Avoid suddenly squirting the medication into the dog's mouth, as this could cause it to spit it out, or even choke. Instead, maintain a steady pressure on the syringe handle, trickling the medication into its mouth slowly. Insert the nozzle well back in the mouth, so that the liquid can run down the throat rather than out of the sides of the mouth.

Alternative health care

The growth of interest in alternative health care means there is a growing number of veterinary practices prepared to offer treatments based on herbalism or homeopathy. In the wild where dogs are reliant on their own abilities to treat themselves, they may eat coarse stems of grass for example, in order to vomit. This behavior is also often seen in domestic dogs, particularly when they are suffering from an accumulation of roundworms.

Herbalism

There is one essential difference between herbalism and homeopathy. Herbalism is more closely related to conventional medicine, but it relies entirely on plant extracts rather than on synthetic drugs. However, a number of conventional drugs were originally derived from herbs. The heart drug digitalis, for example, was originally derived from foxgloves.

Some herbal products such as raspberry-leaf tablets are recommended for preventive purposes. These are often used as a means of preventing whelping problems when a bitch is due to give birth. Seaweed powder is popular as a tonic, as it is a valuable source of iodine, which is used by the thyroid glands in the neck for the production of hormones which regulate the body's metabolism. Tea-tree extract has soothing antiseptic properties, and is valued for treating skin conditions.

Homeopathy

Homeopathy differs significantly, since its advocates believe in the principle that "like cures like". This means the treatment of a condition needs the use of a substance which will itself produce similar symptoms. The founding father of modern homeopathy was Samuel Hahnemann. Many of his treatments now in use derive from a wide range of sources, often coming from both animal and mineral origins rather than solely from plants.

Several different homeopathic remedies may be available to treat one particular condition. There is no single treatment. Homeopathic veterinarians

ABOVE A wide variety of alternative health treatments are now being applied in the veterinary field, as here, where this French bulldog is receiving acupuncture from its veterinarian. The costs of such treatments may still be covered by veterinary insurance.

much prefer to concentrate on the overall signs associated with the dog's illness, rather than on any specific symptoms. This holistic approach ensures that the remedy can be tailored specifically to meet the individual's needs.

Homeopathic treatments are available in a variety of forms, including tablets, powders, and liquids, so they are as easy to administer as conventional remedies. One aspect of homeopathy stressed by its practitioners, however, is the fact that there are no side-effects. It is even possible to give dogs specific vaccines made on homeopathic principles.

Other options

Other alternative health-care options which may sometimes be applied include acupuncture, which can be especially useful for the treatment of painful injuries. Bach Flower Therapy devotees also claim that this can have a calming effect on particularly nervous dogs.

LEFT An image of Samuel Hahnemann (1755-1843) regarded as the founder of modern homeopathy.

HEALTH

Disease threats

As the number of dogs has risen significantly, especially in urban areas, so has the potential for the spread of disease. Vaccinations will help to reduce the likelihood of infections, but because outbreaks of killer diseases, such as distemper, are relatively rare, epidemics do flare up when owners forget, or simply do not bother, to have their pets vaccinated.

Parvovirus

The age of the dog infected can have an impact on the course of the disease. Young puppies infected with parvovirus — a disease which became widespread from the late 1970s onward — are liable to suffer from heart disease as a result of the infection, while at a later stage in life, severe blood-stained diarrhea is more common, with corresponding damage to the intestinal lining being permanent.

Distemper, or hard pad

Other major viral diseases that dogs need to be protected against include distemper, also called hard pad. Once the virus has spread through the dog's body, typical symptoms are vomiting and diarrhea. Distemper also attacks the nervous system, where the effects are not often noticeable until many years later. A dog which suffers from occasional fits, along with twitching of the facial muscles, is likely to have been infected by distemper early in life.

Thickening of the pads on the feet is another long-standing sign, which is why this disease is also known as hard pad. In the case of infection in young puppies, their teeth can become brownish as a result of damage to the protective coat of enamel.

ABOVE Diseases can be easily spread from dog to dog by direct contact, which is why it is so important to ensure that vaccinations are kept up to date. Without this protection, dogs are at serious risk of falling ill.

RIGHT Stray dogs in an urban area can spread infections rapidly, with the dog's tendency to sniff leaving it exposed to infections transmitted via urine. Public places such as parks, where many dogs are exercised, can be especially dangerous for unvaccinated dogs.

Practical Pointer

Tell your veterinarian if you suspect that your bitch is pregnant when taking her for a vaccination. This will affect the type of vaccine which can be used.

Canine adenovirus

Canine adenovirus (CAV) type 1, which causes infectious hepatitis, affecting the dog's liver, is another serious disease. It is sometimes called "blue eye," because infected dogs which survive this disease often have a bluish haze over the surface of their eyes. They will remain infectious to other dogs for possibly six months, passing the virus in their urine. In contrast, CAV type 2 affects the respiratory tract, and is often implicated in cases of kennel cough (see page 169).

Leptospirosis

Another serious illness of dogs which can be prevented by vaccination is the bacterial illness known as leptospirosis. There are two forms of this disease, one of which is linked to rats. Those dogs that hunt rats, are especially vulnerable to it. The other form spreads via dog's urine, with the result that all dogs can be at risk at an outbreak.

BASIC INSTINCTS

Illness in wild dogs

One of the less obvious advantages of maintaining a territory is the fact that other dogs will not be inclined to enter the area, and so the likelihood of disease being spread is correspondingly reduced. Even so, wild dogs can succumb to diseases that are associated with their prey, such as anthrax, which will wipe out wildlife (and potentially people) quite indiscriminately when an outbreak occurs in an area.

LEFT A skin tumor on the leg of a bull terrier. In some cases, such growths may be caused by viruses and although they may be removed surgically, they will frequently recur in older individuals, whose immune system may be weakened. White dogs are especially vulnerable.

Rabies

This is the most dreaded disease that can afflict wild and domestic dogs, because it can be transmitted to humans. Once clinical signs develop, the outcome is invariably fatal. In several parts of the world, wild dogs are the main carriers of the disease, with domestic dogs being infected by a bite from an infected wild dog. In Europe, the red fox is the main carrier of rabies, while further east, in Asia, the remaining wolf population represents a major threat.

There have been major advances in the battle to control and ultimately eliminate this infection, although, at present, there are very few parts of the world which are free from rabies. These are essentially islands, such as Australia, the British Isles and Iceland. Rigorous quarantine measures are presently employed to reduce the likelihood of infection being introduced to these countries, although there are some moves to replace quarantine with a strict vaccination program.

Transmission of infection

Other animals apart from dogs can be infected with and transmit the rabies virus. In the United States, skunks and raccoons are the major wildlife carriers of the infection. Be especially suspicious of any wild animal which appears to be unusually friendly. It could suddenly respond by biting you, and so transmit the rabies virus.

It is not even necessary for the skin to be broken by the animal's teeth, since saliva containing the virus can enter via cuts on the hands. The length of time for symptoms to become apparent depends on the proximity of the bite to the central nervous system. The virus passes along the peripheral nervous system and ultimately reaches the brain, at which point its deadly effects will soon become apparent.

BELOW LEFT All warm-blooded animals are potentially vulnerable to the rabies virus which is spread via saliva. Dogs usually encounter the infection through being bitten. Within the pack, if one dog develops the virus, then it can be transmitted readily to the others, and will prove fatal.

BELOW International quarantine measures have been established to guard against the introduction of rabies to parts of the world where it does not occur in the native wildlife. Quarantine requirements vary from country to country, depending on the level of risk.

Symptoms

Rabies is especially alarming in dogs which develop "mad dog syndrome", in which their aggression becomes uncontrollable as the virus starts to exert its deadly effects. These rabid dogs find noises exceedingly disturbing — this is frequently one of the early signs of the clinical illness. They will then start to attack almost anything with which they come into contact — including inert objects, as well as any living creatures which cross their path. In contrast to the human manifestation of the disease, however, rabid dogs do not develop hydrophobia, or fear of water.

However, the paralytic form of the disease can be more dangerous as far as dog-owners are concerned. One of the earliest signs is a drooping of the lower jaw, which gives the dog the appearance of having an object stuck in its mouth. Examining the mouth at this stage is exceedingly dangerous, because of the risk of coming into contact with the virus. The dog will not usually attempt to bite — instead, the paralysis will spread through its body, resulting in its demise within hours of the initial signs becoming apparent.

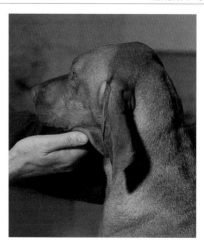

Practical Pointer

Vaccination for rabies is compulsory in many parts of the world where the virus is present, but the regulations do differ from country to country. Your veterinarian will be able to advise you accordingly.

BELOW A pack of gray wolves have long inspired fear among people, but they are not usually aggressive toward people. Most wolf attacks on humans can be linked to rabid animals which have lost their natural sense of caution, and they will then attack their victim in a frenzy.

External parasites

Both wild and domestic dogs are at risk from external parasites, which comprise various mites, lice, fleas, and ticks. In the case of wild dogs, such as foxes, the effects can be so debilitating that the animals move burrows to escape the worst of the infection. In animals already weakened by a lack of food, these parasitic infections, particularly mange, can ultimately prove to be fatal.

BASIC INSTINCTS

Under threat

Parasites can gain a hold on a weakened individual, and finally lead to its demise. Most wild dogs actually live for a much shorter period of time than their domestic relatives, because of the dangers and potential food shortages

The main external parasites
Fleas

Domestic dogs are most likely to suffer from fleas. These parasites have become a year-round problem in temperate areas, although they are still most prevalent in the summer.

Repeated scratching and itching, with the dog chewing its skin on occasions, are the common indicators of fleas. A special flea comb should be used, which will confirm the presence of these parasites. Groom the dog outdoors, so that any fleas which jump off will be less likely to cause problems. You are most likely to see tiny blackish specks among the fur, which are the droppings of the fleas. These contain traces of undigested blood sucked out from the dog's skin, and will leave reddish deposits if moistened on damp, white blotting paper. There are various ways of combating fleas. In the short term, a powder or spray is best. Special grooming combs with hollow teeth can be used to dispense flea powder deep within the fur.

In severe cases, you may be advised to bathe your dog using a special medicated wash. But this alone will not be enough — eggs laid on the dog by adult fleas will drop off, usually in or near the dog's bedding, and rapidly hatch into larvae. These pupate, and emerge as adult fleas.

It is therefore essential to wash all bedding thoroughly, and to vacuum in the vicinity of the dog's bed, particularly close to the walls, in order to reduce the likelihood of reinfection. There are now treatments that prevent the development of fleas or render them sterile. These are useful for preventing any build-up of these parasites, which may bite people as well.

Ticks

Ticks are far less of a problem on dogs, although they may be a nuisance, particularly if your dog is

LEFT This magnified picture of a tick shows it sticking closely to the dog's hair.

LEFT A larger than life-size picture of a flea, a parasite that can cause a dog much discomfort.

exercised on heathland. The tick will anchor itself onto the dog's skin with its strong mouthparts, and soon swells in size as it sucks the dog's body fluids. Do not pull off the parasite, because it could leave its head in the skin, creating an infection. Instead, smear its body with petroleum jelly, which will block its breathing holes, causing it to detach itself. Ticks can be carriers of Lyme disease, a serious illness causing fever and affecting the joints, as well as blood-borne, parasitic ailments.

Lice

Lice are rarely a problem with dogs, although they can sometimes be encountered in puppies reared under poor conditions. They stick to the hair, where nits will also be seen. Antiflea treatment will kill lice.

Mange

Mange, caused by microscopic mites is a problem to treat. The two types are demodectic and sarcoptic mange. Demodex mites are often associated with dachshund breeds, and live deep within the hair follicles, making treatment difficult. Sarcoptes mites are more superficial, and cause reddening of the bare skin on the underside of the thighs.

Internal parasites

The diet of carnivores such as dogs can leave them exposed to internal parasites, whose life cycles are closely linked with their prey. This link has largely been broken in the case of the domestic dog, however, which is fed in many cases on prepared foods, free from parasites, rather than on raw fish or meat. Even so, they can suffer badly from roundworms, which are transmitted directly from one dog to another.

Practical Pointer

Follow the deworming program as recommended by your veterinarian carefully, in order to prevent the likelihood of a build-up of these parasites.

BELOW Some parasites, notably tapeworms, may have a two stage or indirect life-cycle, which means they must pass through an intermediate host such as a flea or sheep before being able to infect a dog again.

The main internal parasites

As well as having serious effects on your dog, worms can also have quite serious effects on humans.

Roundworm

Puppies may even be born with roundworms, the result of an infection which they received from their mother before birth. The particular worry about the roundworm known as Toxocara canis arises from the fact that it can also infect people, particularly young children. The risk is greatest in places such as public parks, where dogs are frequently exercised, although such parasites can be equally deposited by foxes, or even wolves in some areas.

The key to curbing a roundworm risk is deworming, particularly of bitches prior to pregnancy. This will serve to minimize the risk of infection in the newly born puppies. The bitch may also infect her offspring directly after birth, by transferring larval worms to them in her milk. Once the worms have matured in the intestinal tract, the puppies themselves will then produce microscopic Toxocara eggs in their feces.

Children must always be taught to wash their hands after playing with a puppy, and always before eating, so that they do not ingest these eggs. Otherwise there is a minute risk of the larvae migrating around their body to the eye, where it could cause a cyst and, ultimately, blindness.

Tapeworms

Tapeworms can be quite easily distinguished from roundworms by their flattened shape. Dogs can be affected by a number of different types. One of the commonest forms is the dog tapeworm, Dipylidium caninum. It has a life cycle which involves the flea, so it is advisable to treat dogs which have had a problem with fleas with a tapeworm remedy afterward.

The tapeworm eggs pass out of the anus, and stick to the fur, where they are ingested by fleas. If the dog then catches and swallows a parasitized flea, the tapeworm is likely to develop in its body. Tablets are the usual treatment for tapeworms.

Heartworm

Depending on where you live in the world, other internal parasites may be of some concern, especially heartworm (Dirofilaria immitis), which is a potential problem in warmer countries. Biting insects, such as mosquitoes, spread the infection when they feed, by injecting the so-called microfilariae into the dog's body. These immature worms then develop in the circulatory system, localizing ultimately in the vicinity of the heart, with potentially dire consequences. Preventive treatment, which entails giving regular medication, is therefore advisable.

Hookworms

Hookworms can also have serious effects. These parasites tend to be found in damp surroundings, again often in warmer parts of the world. They are able to bore directly into the feet of dogs and other animals. They may then migrate to the intestines. Depending on the species of hookwork concerned they may cause severe anemia. Hookworms actually contributed directly to the decline of the red wolf in its last remaining stronghold (Texas), before the present reintroduction program was undertaken.

Practical Pointer

Clear up thoroughly after your dog, using a suitable tool. This will reduce the likelihood of adding to any existing contamination of the ground with Toxocara eggs, either at home or in public places. Eggs are not immediately infective. They take several days to mature outside the body, but can survive for years.

YOUR VET

It is not difficult to find a veterinarian in most areas, and soon after a new dog is acquired, it is a good idea to visit the local surgery, so inoculations can be given if necessary, and a check-up is carried out.

How to tell whether your dog is in need of medical attention

Key indicators are the dog's appetite and drinking habits, as well as its general alertness and desire to exercise. When you take your dog to a veterinarian, go with a written list of symptoms and the length of time they have lasted. The veterinarian may also want to know the date of the bitch's last heat or whether she has been neutered, how long you have had her, and if she has been inoculated. Some of this information may be available to the veterinarian if you have made previous visits, but have it on hand. Your veterinarian will probably ask you questions before carrying out an examination of the dog. This is sometimes referred to as "taking the history of the case". Be precise as far as possible. If your dog has been drinking more water, specify the amount. Keep a watch on your dog when it relieves itself. You will then be able to say whether or not it has any difficulty in urinating or defecating.

Does it matter whether I go to the same veterinarian every time?

In the larger cities, many veterinary practices are comprised of a group of veterinarians rather than

RIGHT The eyes, nose, mouth and ears are all good indicators of the overall state of health of your dog. The eyes should be clear and bright and the nose should also be free of any discharge or redness (top): a mucous discharge may be an early sign of any upper respiratory infection or even distemper. The mouth and gums should be pink (center): bad breath being a sign of tooth decay or gum disease. A dog with severe periodontal disease will be prone to dribble. Healthy ears (bottom) should be clean, free from any discharge and have no sign of unpleasant odour. A waxy discharge or an apparent irritation are signs of an ear infection.

a single one. There are obvious advantages to this system. Duty hours can be rotated, and veterinarians with particular interests can act as specialists in specific areas. It may even be possible to reduce costs, for a more efficient practice. Nevertheless, this does mean that you may not be able to see the same veterinarian on every visit. This is not crucial, however, because your dog's records will be on the premises and can be used by any member of the team.

This does not apply if you go from practice to practice. To change without notifying your existing veterinarian appears off-hand, and it also means that the dog's previous medical history and laboratory test results will not be available to the new veterinarian. This can make his or her work more difficult, and can be dangerous for your dog and more expensive for you. If you are unhappy with treatment you have received, you can transfer to another veterinary practice without any problem. Simply telephone and say you are changing to another veterinarian, or write if you prefer. This will also be necessary if you move out of the area, but your new veterinarian can refer back to previous treatment.

Is it possible for my veterinarian to give me advice over the telephone?

Most veterinary practices receive a large number of calls during the day. It is very difficult for a veterinarian to get a clear picture of a case without actually seeing the patient for an examination. You should, therefore, be prepared to take your dog to the office initially. Once treatment has begun, however, telephone for advice if you are concerned. A charge is made for telephone advice depending on the circumstances. Do not expect to be able to speak to your veterinarian automatically, especially if you have not called at a pre-arranged time. During the course of the day, the veterinarian may be tied up in a consultation or operating when you telephone. His staff will be able to deal with your query.

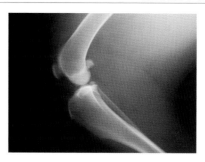

ABOVE X-rays have greatly simplified the diagnosis and treatment of limb fractures. They help in ascertaining the most suitable means of fixation of a broken limb and in checking progress toward healing

Home visits

The merits of a home visit from your veterinarian depend on individual circumstances. As a general rule, you should take your dog to the veterinarian's surgery where specialist help and equipment such as an X-ray machine are available. Home visits are extremely time-consuming, and the cost has to be passed on to the client. A veterinarian may call in an emergency situation, however, such as when a bitch encounters difficulties while giving birth. Most dogs tend to be easier to handle out of their own territory and this is another reason for taking your dog to the vet's surgery if possible.

Health checks for dogs

Provided your dog appears healthy, there is probably little point in visiting your veterinarian for a general check up. But be sure deworming and inoculations are kept up to date. This will probably involve a visit once or twice a year and your veterinarian can examine your dog then to check its state of health.

GENERAL NURSING

An owner can do much to assist the recovery of a dog if it becomes ill, or is injured in a domestic or road accident, although in the first instance, veterinary advice is likely to be re wired without delay.

Leaving your dog overnight at the veterinarian's when it needs to be anaesthetized

As a general rule, it is quite usual for a dog to be left at the veterinarian's when it has been anaesthetized, but it depends on individual circumstances. You will probably be asked to see that your dog receives nothing to eat or drink for a period beforehand. Under the effects of the anaesthetic, vomiting can occur and food or fluid can pass down into the lungs. Since the dog will not be able to cough as normal, this could have fatal consequences. A full stomach may also interfere with breathing when the dog is unconscious. If you suspect that your dog has scavenged something during the critical period beforehand, notify your veterinarian right away. It may be possible for him to attend to another patient and reschedule your dog's operation if necessary.

The risk of administering an anaesthetic to a dog is normally low. If the veterinarian is especially concerned, he will discuss the relevant factors with you. Obviously, old, obese dogs face a higher risk than young, healthy dogs. Complications are more likely to arise with certain breeds. In the case of the Grayhound, for example, there is little body fat to absorb the barbiturate anaesthetic administered by injection. It is quite usual for a veterinarian to keep the dog under close supervision until it has recovered from the immediate effects of the anaesthetic.

First hold your dog's muzzle with one hand and tilt her nose up a little; put your thumb in the space between the canine tooth and the first molar and press it against the roof of the mouth — this will force the dog to keep its mouth open.

Administering pills to your dog

The simplest method is to disguise the pills in food. The best way is to conceal the pill in a suitable piece of meat because dogs can readily detect the presence of an inedible object in their food.

It may be necessary in some cases to administer the pill directly (see page 152). This is not difficult with a dog that is used to being handled, but it can prove difficult in other cases. The key to success is to place the pill at the very back of the mouth so that the dog will swallow it almost automatically rather than attempting to spit it out. Grasp the upper jaw on either side with one hand, and raise, holding the lower jaw with the other hand and using your first finger and thumb to pop the pill onto the base of .the tongue. Hold the dog's mouth open; make sure the pill is on top of the tongue, not under it. Then hold the mouth closed and gently massage the throat until you feel the dog swallow the pill. For a right-handed person, the pill should be inserted with this hand. If you dislike placing your hand in the dog's mouth, use a pair of forceps for the purpose. There are also automatic dispensers that can be used. Try to give the pill on the first attempt. The dog is likely to become increasingly restless if the process proves protracted.

The medication may have a sugar or similar coating; it is vital that you do not break pills of this type because they may then have an extremely bitter and unpleasant taste. The dog will probably resent any future attempts to give it pills. If you need help to restrain the dog, get someone else to restrain the neck with an arm so that the dog cannot slip away from you. Initial dosing may lead to a noticeable improvement in the dog's condition, and it may appear healthy before the course of pills is completed. Nevertheless, always be sure to give all the pills prescribed by your veterinarian. Failure to give a full course of antibiotics may not only cause the condition to reappear but can also lead to bacterial resistance to further treatment by the drug concerned. Antibiotics have altered the face of veterinary medicine, but not in every instance.

Administering liquid medicine to your dog

The easiest means of giving liquid to a dog is with a syringe. The required quantity can be measured precisely, and then the syringe can be placed at the back of the dog's mouth from the right side, and its contents emptied with steady pressure from the right hand. The left hand is used to open the mouth sufficiently to allow the syringe to be placed within the dog's mouth while restraining both jaws. It is helpful to have someone else available to restrain the dog for you. If you run the medicine in slowly, the dog should not attempt to choke. If it does, let the head down without relinquishing your grip. The head needs to be positioned at an angle of about 45° from the horizontal. Do not tilt it too far back as this will lead to coughing as fluid enters the larynx.

It is much harder to administer liquid medicine to a dog by means of a spoon. Dosing will be easier to carry out if the dog is at a reasonable height off the ground — stand it on a table, for example, but protect the surface, both from the dog's claws and any spilled medicine.

Afterward, wash the syringe or spoon thoroughly and do not forget to show affection to the dog. It is a useful idea to open a puppy's mouth regularly, so that in later life, it will let you administer treatments via the mouth when required.

For further advice on administering liquid medicine, see page 152.

Dosage directions for your dog's medicine

You should always try to follow directions as closely as possible. Some drugs, such as tetracyclines, are not absorbed well from the intestinal tract in the presence of food; calcium combines with this group of antibiotics leaving lower quantities to be absorbed. Its effectiveness in fighting infection is reduced. This will ensure that a therapeutically active level of the drug is retained within the body at all times. For drugs such as tetracycline and ampicillin, the dose for a 25-pound dog should be 250 milligrams per day. The precise time is not as important as the time interval during which the level of the drug in the body is declining. In order to be effective, they must he administered regularly for at least five days. In circumstances, as with eye infections where the tear fluid is constantly washing the medication away, more treatments will be needed.

Keeping a sick dog warm

An infrared heater is probably most satisfactory. A heating pad can be used in the basket, and a hot water bottle is also suitable, as long as the dog cannot burn itself accidentally. This applies especially in the case of a dog which is in a semi-comatose state. The most important factor is to use warm water, as boiling water can burn the skin. Wrap the hot water bottle in a thick towel as a precaution. Rubber bottles are preferable to those of stone which are uncomfortable for the dog to lie on, and make sure the top is fitted properly and that the rubber is in good condition because otherwise water will saturate the dog's bed rapidly.

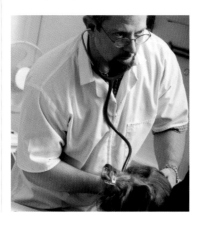

Finding your dog's heartbeat in an emergency

Flex the elbow joint on the left-side of the body to its maximum extent. This will give you the approximate position of the heart. It should be possible to feel the heartbeat, particularly after exercise as long as the dog is not excessively overweight

There are various places on a dog's body to take its pulse, but the femoral artery, running down each hind limb is probably the easiest site. Do not press too hard when taking a pulse, or the sensation will be dulled.

Caring for a paraplegic dog

A dog which is unable to walk (usually because of spinal injury) needs considerable care. If it lies in the same position over a long period, it may develop pressure sores, particularly on bony parts of the body. Bigger, heavier dogs run the greatest risk. Pressure sores should not be confused with the thickening skin commonly seen on the elbows of healthy dogs of the large breeds although the case is similar.

Caring for a paraplegic dog is a considerable undertaking. It can be made easier by making a foam bed with removable covers, or by encouraging the dog to lie on a bean-bag. Do not allow the dog to remain in the same position for more than a couple of hours, and if any sores appear and form ulcers, contact your veterinarian.

Giving your dog an injection

The only circumstances in which you are likely to have to administer injections to your dog is if it becomes diabetic. Your veterinarian will show you how to carry out the necessary injections of insulin, and you can practise using an orange as a substitute for the skin. The insulin will have to be administered subcutaneously (under the skin) rather than into a vein, which makes the process easier. Having filled the syringe, scruff the loose skin on the back of the dog's neck and insert the needle through the skin.

ABOVE The position of the heart is most easily found by flexing the elbow joint against the body on the left-hand side. The tip of the joint provides the approximate position where the heartbeat can be detected, using a finger gently applied between the ribs. In this case (right) a veterinarian is using a stethoscope to amplify the heartbeat.

Draw back slightly to ensure that no blood appears in the syringe and if all is well, push the plunger firmly and then withdraw the needle. It is important to use a new needle each time. Dog's skin is surprisingly tough, and a blunt needle makes the process more difficult. Dispose of your old needles carefully by placing the protective covers back on them and returning them to your veterinarian.

A dog's wet nose

This is generally accepted as a sign of good health; the moisture is produced in the lateral nasal glands in the nose. Dogs that are dehydrated but otherwise healthy will have dry noses because the body responds by reducing fluid output via urine and even in the nasal glands. A dog that has been sitting in a warm spot may also have a temporarily dry nose. A dog that has recovered from distemper at an early age may be left with a permanently dry nose.

How to tell if a health problem is an emergency that requires immediate veterinary treatment

Conditions which require rapid veterinary attention are normally those of sudden onset. If your dog collapses, appears unable to breath, loses consciousness or starts having convulsions, then you must contact you veterinarian without delay. Injuries from accidents can also be life-threatening. In addition to giving first-aid on the spot, you should contact a veterinarian at once. Serious haemorrhaging, an obvious fracture, poisoning, drowning or scalding are cases in point. Any problems during whelping are likely to require urgent veterinary attention.

LEFT A dog's wet nose is quite a reliable indication of good health.

When to contact your veterinarian

Some cases are less urgent than others, but if it is no emergency, arrange an appointment at a convenient time. A veterinarian will always see a genuine emergency at any time, but will not welcome being called if the dog has been ill for two weeks and you have done nothing until late on a Sunday night.

Taking a temperature

Raise the tail with the left hand and insert the thermometer — which should be lubricated with petroleum jelly — with the other hand, into the anus. The thermometer should be held in place for about three minutes. Take care to restrain the dog while doing this. Normal temperature is about 101.5°F (38.5°C) but a slight rise after exercise is normal.

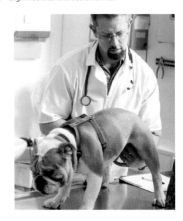

BOARDING KENNELS
Vacation and quarantine boarding

There are likely to be times when you may need to use the services of a boarding kennel for your dog. If you do not know the kennels in your area, ask dog-owning friends for their advice, or arrange to visit several kennels to see the facilities on offer, before confirming a booking. Those in your area can be found in the telephone book.

Choosing and booking kennels

The kennels should be clean, with secure runs and heated sleeping quarters if the weather is likely to be cold. Do not be influenced just by the premises — the attitude of the staff is also important, to ensure that your dog settles well into strange surroundings. Ask what you should bring with you. A familiar blanket, containing the scent of home, may provide reassurance for your pet during your absence, as may a toy.

Always check out boarding kennels in advance if you have not used them for your pet before. Cleanliness is obviously very important, and particular attention must be paid to the space available for exercise, so your dog does not become bored in its surroundings.

Practical Pointer

Should you be unable to find your pet's vaccination certificate, your veterinarian may well be prepared to issue you with a duplicate from the practice records, although you may have to pay a fee for the extra paperwork.

You should also leave details of your veterinarian, so that the kennels will be able to contact the practice in the event of any emergency. It will also help if you can give them a contact number where you can be reached while you are away. Be sure to discuss any particular requirements of your dog in advance as well, and if you have a bitch which could come into season while you are likely to be away, arrange with your veterinarian to postpone this heat by means of an injection. Having a bitch on heat is likely to be especially disrupting within the confines of a kennels housing many dogs.

How will your dog settle into kennels?

Most dogs will actually settle very rapidly into such surroundings, although the change in environment can be stressful. Sharing the same air space with other dogs means that the risk of infections spreading is much higher than at home. This is why responsible kennels will always insist that all the dogs brought to them must have been currently vaccinated, and you will need to take a certificate to this effect with you when you check in your dog for its stay there.

Dogs will often bark for long periods in kennels, because of the sounds of other dogs around them. The close proximity to other dogs means that respiratory illnesses can spread easily, which is why it may be worthwhile having your pet vaccinated for kennel cough before you go away, although this is not compulsory at all kennels.

Kennel cough

There is no single cause of kennel cough but canine adenovirus type 2 and a bacterium, Bordetella bronchoseptica, are often involved.

The vaccine will therefore not cover all the causes, but it will give a high degree of protection.

This is especially valuable for older dogs, which are more likely to succumb to the infection. In most cases, an affected dog develops a distinctive cough which can be triggered easily if you place your hand on the underside of the throat. It should clear up spontaneously within about three weeks of the infection first becoming apparent, but in older individuals, it can develop into pneumonia.

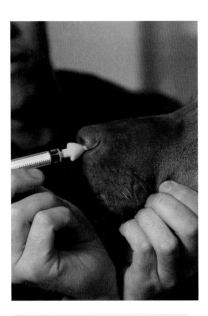

ABOVE Prior to going into kennels, it may be recommended that your dog is protected against kennel cough. This vaccine is administered by being squirted up the nasal passage as shown.

Practical Pointer

Show dogs are regularly vaccinated against kennel cough. The spread of this infection is virtually impossible to prevent in areas where dogs are being brought together and housed indoors.

THE TRAVELING DOG

At some point or another, a dog will have to be transported by car and will probably adapt fairly well to this experience.

The best way to carry a large dog

Probably by grasping it with your right arm around the back of the hind legs and your left arm extending under the neck. Smaller dogs may be supported under the chest. If you ever have to handle a nervous dog though, it is probably safer to dispense with the arm around the hindquarters and support this area with your elbow using your arm to grasp behind the forelegs. Your other hand can hold the dog's scruff so that it is unable to turn round and bite you.

Overcoming the problem of travel sickness in your dog

Actually it is best to take your puppy out in the car several times, not just to the veterinarian's, in the early weeks. In this way, he will become accustomed to traveling by this means and should not associate it with a probably distressing visit to the veterinarian's office. Perhaps surprisingly, it is usually young adult dogs rather than puppies that suffer from car sickness. A conflict arises between the senses of vision and balance, and this triggers the vomiting response. In order to minimize the effects, do not feed your dog for four hours or so before you travel. Be sure that ventilation within the car is good, and do not get angry at the dog if it vomits. This is a reaction over which it has no control. Try to avoid long journeys at first, and stick to local trips. In this way, the dog will get used to the car, and the risk of car sickness is reduced. Be careful if your dog likes to stick his head out of the window while the car is moving. This can be dangerous as he may get something in his eye or even try to jump out.

Carrying a dog

Whenever a dog is carried, it must be well supported — small dogs present fewer problems than their bigger counterparts. The chest provides a convenient means of support; never lift a small dog simply by its neck, leaving the remainder of the body dangling.

Using a sedative to calm a dog while traveling

Just as a veterinarian may prescribe treatment for chronic car sickness, so may he give a sedative to control a badly behaved dog in a car, but this is really only a last resort. Many dogs look forward to going out in a car and get into a state of great excitement because it means they will be having a walk. If your dog persists in leaping about and barking in the back of the car, tell him firmly to be quiet. Then park the car and disappear from sight for a few moments. Ignore your dog at this stage — if you make a fuss over him, he will think that you want to encourage this behavior. The delay in reaching the site for the walk means that the dog will not have achieved his aim. It is important for the dog to realize that not every trip in the car will end in a walk and run, particularly if the owner travels a lot with the dog.

A word of caution about leaving dogs in cars. The heat in the interior of a car builds up frighteningly fast. Never leave your dog alone in a car with the windows closed, especially during the summer months. In an emergency, try to park in a covered or underground parking lot, out of the direct rays of the sun. It is no exaggeration to say that dogs can die within minutes from the effects of heatstroke.

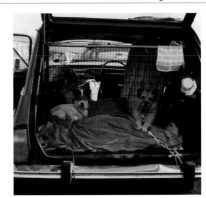

Dog guards alleviate the possibility of traveling dogs distracting or impairing the visibility of the driver. Try to accustom and familiarize your dog to traveling from an early age.

Like babies, dogs prefer to be held firmly and securely, in close contact with their owners and with plenty of body support.

BREEDING PROBLEMS

Pseudopregnancies

Wild dogs, such as wolves, have only one period of heat during the year, and within the pack it is usually only the dominant female which becomes pregnant. Even so, the other females in the pack usually become involved in rearing her young and become "pseudopregnant," which means that they have milk available. Thus, should any disaster befall the breeding female, her cubs can still be reared successfully by other pack members — otherwise they would inevitably die.

LEFT Pseudopregnancies may recur throughout the bitch's life if the animal is not neutered.

Pseudopregnancy in dogs

The situation in the case of the bitch, however, is slightly different. Pseudopregnancy, also known as phantom pregnancy, arises when the hormones in the bitch's body tell her that she is pregnant, although she has not actually mated. It occurs because, at the points where her eggs leave the ovary, structures called corpora lutea form. These are vital for a successful pregnancy, releasing the hormone called progesterone.

This normally allows the developing eggs to implant in the bitch's uterus, where they start developing into puppies. If mating has not actually taken place, these corpora lutea soon cease to produce this hormone, and so the signs of pregnancy do not usually become apparent.

Where the case of a pseudopregnancy is concerned, however, the output of the hormone progesterone continues. This has widespread effects on the body, creating the impression that the bitch is really pregnant. Her uterus grows in size, causing her abdomen to enlarge as a result. The output of progesterone may even be sufficient to cause the bitch's mammary glands to swell and she may actually start to produce milk. Treatment of pseudopregnancy

A bitch suffering from a pseudopregnancy is liable to regard toys or other objects, such as shoes, as her puppies, and will be very protective

Practical Pointer

Do not feel inclined to allow a bitch to have a litter of puppies at her next heat, as this will not prevent pseudopregnancies at subsequent heats. You will also face the additional problem of finding good homes for the puppies, which can be difficult, and if you have to keep some of them yourself, will also be costly.

toward them, snapping fiercely if you try to take them away from her. Your veterinarian will prescribe medication, possibly in the form of tranquilizers, and also hormonal treatment, which should help her over this period quite quickly, and will also dry up any milk. Otherwise, if it is left unchecked, the progesterone output can continue for up to three months in total.

Once the symptoms disappear, they are very unlikely to resurface until after the next heat, but it is often better to have the bitch neutered beforehand. This is partly because pseudopregnancies tend to recur at each season, and also because the effects often become more severe. It is also possible that bitches which suffer from pseudopregnancies could be at greater risk of developing an infection of the uterus, called pyometra, in the future. This can be potentially life threatening.

Practical Pointer

If your bitch starts to drink considerably more, this may be an early indication of a pyometra. Seek veterinary advice without delay. There may be a discharge from her vagina, but in other cases — a closed pyometra — the pus simply accumulates in the uterus.

BASIC INSTINCTS

Pack support

Death of the cubs could, in time, affect the hunting ability of the pack as a whole, causing its break-up. This applies particularly in some parts of the wolf's range, such as the far north, where large and potentially dangerous animals, such as moose, have to be overpowered by the wolves. A small pack is less likely to be able to obtain sufficient food, while the individual members run a greater risk of being killed or injured when hunting such quarry. There is real strength in numbers in this case, with pseudopregnancy providing useful support !

GROOMING
&
CARE

The amount of grooming required will depend very much on your choice of dog. Gray wolves have coats of variable length, depending largely on their area of origin. Those from the cold north tend to have longer coats than those occurring further south. Selective breeding has led to an increase in the coat length of many breeds, and if you opt for a long-haired dog of any type, you will need to be prepared to groom your pet on a daily basis. Greater emphasis on grooming is particularly important when the dog is molting: Otherwise, its coat is likely to become knotted, and the matted areas of fur will have to be cut away.

Different breeds require different levels of care to their ears and eyes, as well as to their teeth and nails. For example, Pekingese with their prominent eyes are quite vulnerable to problems and injuries to their eyes.

GROOMING
Brushing, washing and shampooing

Regular grooming to remove the loose hairs in your dog's coat will not only make it feel more comfortable, but should also ensure that there are less hairs shed around the home. The amount of hair shed tends to increase during spring, particularly in the case of those breeds, such as the German shepherd dog, which have dense winter coats. These are then replaced with less profuse coats for the warmer part of the year. The second major period of molting takes place in the fall, to complete the molting cycle.

There is not necessarily any need to throw away your dog's molted hair. Some owners collect it so that they can spin it and ultimately make small garments from it. The amount of grooming needed will depend on the breed concerned, with long-haired dogs, such as the Afghan hound, requiring more grooming than the sleek-coated pharaoh hound. A variety of suitable tools may be purchased for grooming purposes. They range from simple brushes and combs to grooming mitts, which are rather like a glove and can be used to give a good gloss to the coat of sleek-coated breeds. Regular daily grooming is essential in the case of long-haired dogs, otherwise their hair is likely to become matted. It will then be impossible to break down these chunks of fur, so they will have to be cut out which will spoil the dog's appearance until the fur in these areas has regrown.

Inspecting the coat

Regular grooming also gives you the opportunity to check on the condition of your dog's coat, and to

Practical Pointer
A recent grooming advance in the battle against fleas is a special comb that gives off a low electrical charge when operating. This will knock out any flea with which it comes into contact, and the motor cuts out to alert you to this fact. You can then locate and remove the flea easily without having to resort to chemical methods of control.

BELOW Removing loose hair from the coat with a special grooming tool will prevent its accumulating on carpeting around the home, with daily grooming being recommended. Hair will be shed almost constantly, but in greater quantities when the dog is molting in the spring particularly, losing its thicker winter coat.

check on any problems, such as fleas, which may be lurking there, although to trap these parasites, you will need to use a special, fine-toothed flea comb.

Always keep a close watch for the appearance of any bald areas on your pet's coat, particularly if it has been near any farms. Hair loss in a characteristically circular pattern is the main indicator of ringworm, which, in spite of its name, is caused by a fungus rather than a parasite. This is a particular problem in young cattle, and the spores will remain in an area for a long time, on fence posts for example, where the cattle have rubbed themselves.

Once ringworm has been diagnosed, specific antifungal treatment will be required, and the grooming equipment will have to be disposed of or disinfected, because the spores can linger on it and

BASIC INSTINCTS

Thick coats

As with wolves, it is no coincidence that dog breeds which originated in areas where the weather is cold in the winter tend to have more profuse coats than those found further south, in the Mediterranean region, for example. The insulating down hairs close to the body help to trap warm air close to the skin, providing an insulating barrier against the cold. The actual markings of the dog will be consistent throughout its life, irrespective of when it molts.

will reinfect the dog. The main danger, however, is that members of the household could also acquire this infection. In people, it gives rise to reddish circular patches, often on exposed parts of the skin, such as the forearms. Seek medical advice if you suspect that you may have contracted this disease.

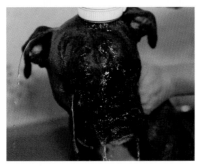

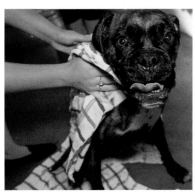

ABOVE Dogs may become frightened by being placed in a bath, so it is a good idea to accustom them to this experience from an early age. Always wet the head last, as this is the part which often proves to be most distressing for them, and then rinse the shampoo out of the coat thoroughly.

Washing your dog

Most dogs will enter water readily, and they can swim if necessary, using their legs to provide the propulsive thrust under the water, while their tail serves to act as a rudder. As domestication has proceeded, so some dogs have been developed for retrieving game in marshland areas, and similar localities where swimming may be necessary. Such dogs have a dense, water-resistant coat, and they may also have webbed toes, to give greater power when swimming.

Where to wash your dog

When it comes to bathing, most dogs will benefit from a bath every three months or so, to remove any trace of that distinctive doggy odor which can linger in the home or coat, particularly if your pet has been outdoors and ended up slightly damp. It is not a good idea to use your own bath when washing your pet, first because this is not very hygienic, and second because there is also the distinct likelihood that the dog will scratch and damage the base of the bath with its claws.

It is much better to wash your dog outdoors on a fine day. If you have a small dog, you can use a suitable baby-bath as a container. In the case of a much larger animal, you will need to rely on a basic shower attachment which, for example, can be easily fitted onto the kitchen faucets and run out of a convenient window.

Special shampoos for dogs are available from pet stores. You will also need a jug, so that you can bale water over your dog. Start by filling the bath with tepid water and then lift the dog into it. Most dogs will stand quite happily in a bath with a non-

Practical Pointer

Do not forget to clean the underside of your dog's ear flaps when giving it a bath, but be sure that water does not run down the ear canal, while you are doing this.

slippery base, provided that the water is reasonably shallow and does not extend above chest level.

How to wash your dog

Using the jug, gently pour the water over the dog's hindquarters first, to wet the fur, and then apply the shampoo to create a good lather. Leave the head until last as washing this particular area is most likely to upset your pet.

Take particular care to avoid any shampoo entering the dog's eyes. It may be best to use an old cloth when cleaning here.

After washing the coat thoroughly, you can then rinse out the shampoo. This is when the shower attachment, or even a garden hose, can be very useful, but you should aim to use tepid water for this purpose. Finally, lift the dog out of the bath or allow it to jump out on its own. Once out of the water, your dog will almost certainly shake itself vigorously to remove the remaining water from its coat, so stand

ABOVE Dogs will regularly clean their own coats by licking them. This is fine, but if your pet has any potentially harmful substances on its coat, such as oil, the affected area must be cleaned immediately, to prevent the contaminant being ingested.

back for a moment. You can then start to dry the dog with a large towel.

Do not allow your dog to stay outside while its coat is still wet, especially when the weather is cold, as deprived of the natural insulation of its coat, the dog is likely to catch a chill. Indoors, a hairdryer can be used to speed the drying process, provided that the noise does not disturb your pet. You should also check that it is on a relatively low heat setting, to avoid any risk of burning the dog.

Practical Pointer

For the first few days after its bath, keep your dog away from areas where cattle may have grazed recently. This is because, when deprived of their natural scent, some dogs will run off and roll in manure to regain a distinctive body odor.

ABOVE Some dogs react better to being groomed in strange surroundings, where they will be less inclined to treat the procedure as a game. It is important to position the dog at a comfortable height and in a good light.

Professional grooming

There are a number of breeds which do not molt their coats in a regular fashion. These include various terriers, such as the Bedlington, as well as the poodle breeds. If these dogs are not being kept for show purposes, their coats will require clipping every six weeks or so. Wire-coated dogs also require more grooming than usual, and need to have the dead hair stripped out of their coats in the spring and autumn. Professional grooming parlors will undertake these tasks for you, and will even bathe your pet if required.

When choosing where to take your dog to be groomed, you can seek recommendations from the breeder who supplied your pet, or your veterinarian may also feel able to advise you. Alternatively, you can simply resort to the telephone book, but bear in mind that dog-groomers are rather like hairdressers

— not all are necessarily equally talented or as well trained, so it can be reassuring to go to someone with qualifications in this field.

Poodles

Although not everyone likes the appearance of breeds such as poodles, with their highly manicured coats, it is often forgotten that the appearance of these dogs today is actually a direct reflection of their working ancestry. They were formerly used as retrievers of waterfowl and so were often required to swim in what could frequently be very cold water.

While a thick, heavy coat would protect the dog against the cold, it would also tend to drag it down

ABOVE There are some breeds, such as poodles, which are best groomed professionally. For poodles there are various types of trim, depending on whether you intend to show your dog or not.

Practical Pointer
You can find out about dog-grooming courses through advertisements in the dog press, or your local library may be able to advise you.

when soaked. A compromise was therefore reached whereby the fur on the muscular parts of the body was trimmed short, while the joints were left with a good covering of fur to protect the dog when it was in water close to freezing.

There are a number of different grooming styles available for poodles today. Puppies are traditionally given the so-called "lamb clip", in which the coat is trimmed to an even length over the entire head and body. This is the simplest style, and there is no reason why adult dogs being kept as pets cannot have their coats kept in this fashion.

Much more elaborate and costly is the so-called "lion clip", which is the style often favored for show purposes. Not surprisingly, a number of breeders and exhibitors are also groomers, having learnt the craft so they can groom their own dogs effectively.

RIGHT These two photographs reveal just how the appearance of this golden retriever has been improved by bathing and grooming. Having been bathed however, beware that your dog does not go off and roll in the dirt to enhance its scent. Bathing every two months or so is usually recommended to curb the characteristic "doggy" odor.

BELOW A selection of grooming tools that can be purchased from most pet stores.

Dogs outdoors

Dogs are relatively hardy, although those without fur will be most susceptible to the weather. When a dog goes for a walk on a wet day, equip it with a jacket. Apart from the Mexican hairless, other breeds are likely to feel the cold more than others.

Weather protection

These include grayhounds and whippets, which have little body fat beneath the skin, and a thin, short covering of hair. Elderly dogs will also benefit from the protection of a jacket when the weather is bad. The distance from the back of the neck to the base of the tail is the significant measurement when choosing a dog jacket.

The actual design is not necessarily important, but check the way in which the jacket is tied around the dog's body. This should be by means of a secure tie that is actually attached to the jacket, rather than simply looping around it. Otherwise the jacket can be more easily lost when the dog is out walking,

ABOVE Clothing for dogs now extends well beyond a simple coat, and can be used to protect most of the body from becoming muddy. This will also serve to keep a dog warm after it has been in water.

by getting caught up on undergrowth and being pulled off as your pet struggles to free itself.

A button is a far less reliable means of attachment than a buckle.

Dealing with a muddy dog

When exercising your dog, it is inevitable, especially if you are walking off the grass in woodland, that your dog will end up with muddy paws. The mud may often extend up the legs as well, particularly in the case of breeds such as setters, which have longer hair, described as feathering, at the back of their legs.

It is useful to keep an old towel in the car with which you can dry your dog's feet before allowing it back into the vehicle. Removing mud from the legs is difficult, however, apart from by washing the dog, which should not be carried out too often. The best solution is to wait until the mud dries, when it can be groomed out of the coat easily with a brush.

BELOW Dogs appreciate the comfort of having their own bed for sleeping purposes, which should be lined with a blanket which can be washed as necessary.

RIGHT A beach can pose a number of hazards for dogs if they are left to roam here unsupervised. This dog became immersed in wet mud, and might have become trapped. It will now need to be bathed and groomed.

Foot problems

Other, more serious grooming problems may arise following a walk, particularly in the late summer. Always check your dog's feet at the end of the walk, particularly in the case of a long-haired breed, for any signs of grass seeds sticking to the coat, or between the pads.

If left, especially under the feet, the sharp end of the seed may penetrate the skin between the pads and work its way into the foot as the dog walks. Grass seeds can move up the legs, and cause great pain and discomfort.

A frequent early indication is when the dog repeatedly chews and nibbles at a foot, and is reluctant to place its weight on it. This apparent lameness helps to distinguish between the likely presence of a grass seed and an infestation of harvest mite (*Trombicula autumnalis*) in the foot. The free-living form of this parasite resembles a tiny red spider, and the larvae themselves congregate on the underside of the foot, causing a severe irritation between the toes.

BASIC INSTINCTS

Sleeping out

Dogs are generally hardy, with wolves and foxes being found in areas of the world where the temperature regularly falls below freezing. Their dense coats help to conserve body heat, along with their habit of curling into a ball, as shown by this red fox. As they become warmer, so they will stretch out and lie on their side.

CARE

Dogs show considerable variation in the appearance of their eyes and ears. In some breeds, such as the Pekingese, the eyes have become especially prominent, while in the case of the basset hound, the ear flaps, compared with those of wolves, have become greatly enlarged and are no longer held vertically.

Care of the ears

It is thought that many hounds have pendulous ears to protect the inner ear canal from being damaged by vegetation as they move through undergrowth. Pendulous ears, however, have the potential to favor the development of infections, especially when they are heavy and covered in long hair. Spaniels often suffer from ear infections, which can be caused by a combination of various bacteria, fungi and ear mites. This is why it is important for the ears to be examined by your veterinarian, so that the most appropriate treatment can be given.

Unfortunately, relapses are not uncommon, and before long, your dog may be pawing at its ears again, in obvious pain. Early treatment will give the greatest likelihood of success and you should follow the instructions for the use of the medication carefully, in the hope that the problem will not recur.

Be sure to finish the course of treatment — some owners do not bother once their pet appears to have

LEFT The bloodhound makes an affectionate companion and is good with children. It needs a lot of regular exercise and is best suited to a rural environment. The bloodhound should be groomed daily.

recovered, and this can lead to a rapid recurrence of the problem. In the worst cases, where there has been a chronic inflammation in the ears for a long period of time, the only solution will be surgery. Known as an aural resection, this entails opening the ear canal so that it can be properly cleaned and will subsequently remain open. This causes the dog no apparent discomfort once the wound has healed. Nor is it very disfiguring, because, in the case of breeds with pendulous ears, it is generally hidden by the ear flap.

Care of the eyes

Dogs with prominent eyes are most vulnerable to eye injury, while their shortened face makes them prone to tear-staining, because of the compression of the nasolachrymal glands on the lower eyelid. The accumulation of dirt around the lower part of the eye should be gently bathed with some absorbent cotton as necessary, to wipe away the tear-staining.

If the eyes need to be treated with drops, be sure to hold your dog's head securely so that it cannot twist away, causing the drops of medication

ABOVE Ear cleaning should always be carried out gently and carefully using soft absorbent cotton lightly dipped in hand warm water. For any other treatment, consult your veterinarian and follow his or her instructions.

EARS

BUTTON

The ear flap folding forward and the tip lying close to the skull, covering the orifice and pointing toward the eye (Irish terrier).

HOUND

Triangular and rounded, the ear flap falling forward and lying close to the head (Beagle).

PRICKED

Standing erect and generally pointed at the tips (German shepherd dog).

ROSE

A small drop ear that folds over and back so as to reveal the burr (Pug).

EYES

GLOBULAR

Appearing to protrude, but in fact not bulging when viewed in profile (Chihuahua). ALMOND Almond-shaped (German shepherd dog).

ALMOND

Almond-shaped (German shepherd dog).

HAW

The term used for the third membrane in the inside of the eye. Its appearance is a fault in some breeds (Bloodhound).

CIRCULAR

As round as possible (Smooth-haired fox terrier).

to miss their target. If this does happen, or your dog blinks at the vital moment, you will need to repeat the treatment.

In order to maintain a therapeutic dose of the drug, you may have to treat an infected eye about four times a day. This is because, unfortunately, the fluid in the eye will wash it away, diluting its effectiveness. However, eye ailments can respond very rapidly to treatment.

If you are prescribed ointment to treat your dog's eyes, squeeze this out gently from the bottom of the tube, applying it in a horizontal line across the eye if possible. Again, as with all medication, it is important to complete the treatment, even if your dog appears to have recovered fully beforehand.

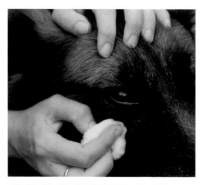

ABOVE Wipe away any tear-staining using absorbent cotton dampened with a little water. Use gentle strokes away from the eyes until the staining is removed.

Teeth and claws

Domestic dogs, which tend to enjoy a more leisured life style today compared with their ancestors, are more vulnerable to dental disease, as well as to overgrown claws. Too many treats and soft food, and less time spent gnawing on bones, have left dogs' teeth more vulnerable at a time when they are living longer than ever before. Meanwhile, lack of exercise has ensured that the claws do not receive as much wear as they would in the wild.

Care of the teeth

Having accustomed your puppy to having its mouth opened on a regular basis, you can start to brush its teeth every week or so. This will help to prevent the accumulation of plaque, which is likely to lead on to gum disease and weaken the roots of the teeth. Special toothbrushes and paste are available for cleaning dogs' teeth. Ordinary toothpaste is not suitable — dogs dislike its taste. Do not brush the teeth hard, or cause the gums to bleed, but remember

Practical Pointer

A long-haired dog which dribbles because of bad teeth may be suffering from an infection of the outer lips. Trimming back the hair around the mouth may be advisable under these circumstances.

it is at the junction between the teeth and the gums where problems are most likely to arise.

It is also possible to help the teeth to stay in good condition by providing chews and offering your dog dried food on occasions. Dogs' teeth do not develop dental cavities like ours. If necessary, your veterinarian will clean your dog's teeth under anesthetic, removing any heavy accumulations of tartar. Bad breath, coupled with a tendency to dribble, are typical indicators of serious dental disease in dogs.

Clipping the claws

A dog's dew claws are the claws which are most likely to become overgrown, simply because they are not in contact with the ground and will continue

BELOW Dental care begun early in life should help to save your dog from discomfort with its teeth when it is older. There are special toothbrush and paste kits which you can obtain for dogs, and if used regularly, they should help to prevent a build up of tartar which is likely to be very damaging.

BELOW Some dogs will allow their teeth to be cleaned more directly with a finger brush. This can be especially useful to prevent accumulations of food and tartar building up at the margin of the gums and teeth.

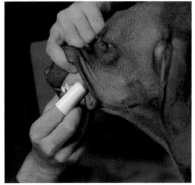

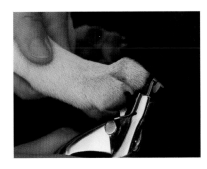

ABOVE Puppies in particular often have sharp tips to their claws, and it can be helpful to trim the ends off with special clippers, to prevent any risk of the dog becoming caught up on bedding. Always check for the blood supply first, to prevent any bleeding.

growing. If they were not removed early in life, they will need to be trimmed back, before they can curve around into the pad behind. Alternatively, it is possible to remove the dew claws but this is a more major operation in an older dog.

When it comes to clipping these or other claws, you can either arrange for your veterinarian to undertake this task, or do it yourself. For this purpose, you will need a suitably stout pair of clippers, which can be obtained from most pet stores. Choose those of the guillotine type, with a sliding blade, as they are easier to use with precision, and you are less likely to cut the claws too short and cause them to bleed.

Start by placing the dog at a convenient height, on a table or bench in a good light, so that you can have a clear view of the claws. You should start by locating the blood supply, which extends a short distance down each claw as a pinkish streak. It is then a matter of cutting the claw some distance below the point where this streak disappears.

The claws of some dogs are blackish, which can make it extremely difficult to determine the extent of the blood supply. Under these circumstances, cutting needs to be carried out with some caution,

and it may actually be advisable to seek veterinary advice rather than risk hurting your pet.

Gauging accurately where the cut should be made is largely a matter of experience. If you do have the misfortune to clip a claw too short, pressing on the cut end for a few moments with damp absorbent cotton should stimulate the clotting process. Applying a styptic pencil, as used for shaving nicks, may also be helpful.

Most dogs do not resent having their nails clipped, although it helps if they have been trained since puppyhood to be accustomed to having their feet picked up. Although nail-clipping itself should be painless if carried out correctly, some dogs dislike being restrained for this purpose. When clipping the front claws, it may help if someone else picks up and holds the dog. You will then be able to reach these claws easily, and the dog will be less inclined to struggle under these circumstances because he or she will feel secure and will not be so afraid of falling.

RIGHT These guillotine-type clippers provide a simple and safe means of trimming claws.

Practical Pointer

Never be tempted to use scissors to try to cut a dog's claws. They are unlikely to be strong enough to cut though the nail cleanly, and may well cause it to split

DIRECTORY OF
DOG BREEDS

This directory looks at the six main dog breeds: Non-sporting breeds, Working breeds, Herding breeds, Gundogs, Hounds, and Terriers. Each dog is accompanied by a full-color photograph for ease of reference, and at-a-glance symbols, which give tips on care.

BREED CLASSIFICATION

Dog breeds are divided into groups and these are of considerable help and importance not only in categorising the breeds for exhibition purposes, but also in aiding the purchaser to select the breed best suited to his needs.

NON-SPORTING BREEDS
May have performed tasks in the past, but they are now companions, like the Chow Chow.

HERDING BREEDS
Originally bred to herd, they are also extremely adaptable. The German Shepherd, for example, is a well-known police dog.

WORKING BREEDS
Traditional guards and workers — rescue, sled and armed services dogs such as the Rottweiler.

GUNDOGS
Used variously to detect, flush out and retrieve game. Usually good natured, like the Golden Retriever.

HOUNDS

Divided into those that hunt by scent, the Beagle for instance, and those that rely on good eyesight, such as the Grayhound.

TERRIERS

Bred to go to ground, hunting vermin and bolting foxes from their lair. Terriers are affectionate by nature, like the Yorkshire Terrier.

TOY BREEDS

Many toy breeds are splendid guards, keenly intelligent and affectionate like the Pomeranian.

Caring for your dog

The key boxes in each entry provide at a glance the basic requirements of each breed. One is the least needed; four the greatest required.

 Exercise

 Food

 Grooming

 House Space

DOG
BREEDS

BOSTON TERRIER

The Boston Terrier is a compactly built, well-balanced dog with a rather short body. It is a good companion, nevertheless it is determined and self willed. The breed takes its name from the city where it was developed as a crossbred Bulldog/Terrier.

Origin USA.
Height 15-17 in (38-43 cm).
Weight 15-25 lb (7-11 kg).
Coat Short and smooth.
Color Brindle with white markings.
Longevity 10-12 years.
Character Lively, intelligent, loving family pet.

BULLDOG

Despite its fearsome appearance the Bulldog adores children and makes a delightful pet. Sadly, it has quite a short life span and only has a walking capacity of about half a mile. Care must be taken to avoid overexertion in hot weather.

Origin Great Britain.
Height 12-14 in (30-36 cm).
Weight 40-55 lb (18-25 kg).
Coat Short, smooth, finely textured.
Color Tan, brindle, piebald.
Longevity 9-10 years.
Character Gentle and good natured.

FRENCH BULLDOG

Also known as the 'Frenchie', this breed usually gets on well with children and other pets. Owners must become accustomed to its gentle snuffling and occasional sulks. As with all flat-nosed breeds, exercise in hot weather should be avoided.

Origin France.
Height 12 in (30 cm).
Weight 24-28 lb (11-13 kg).
Coat Short, smooth, finely textured.
Color Brindle, pied or fawn.
Longevity 11-12 years.
Character Good natured, affectionate, courageous.

DALMATIAN

A friendly and outgoing carriage dog capable of great speed, the Dalmatian should be free of any aggression or nervousness. It requires plenty of exercise and is highly intelligent. However, deafness in this breed is quite common.

Origin Dalmatia (Croatia).
Height 19-23 in (48-59 cm).
Weight 50-55 lb (23-25 kg).
Coat Short, dense, sleek and glossy.
Color White with black/brown spots.
Longevity 12-14 years.
Character Affectionate and energetic.

GIANT SCHNAUZER

The Giant Schnauzer, a German breed, was used in the UK for herding cattle, and they have also been used as police dogs. These dogs are pure black in color, but may also be seen in shades of pepper and salt.

Origin Germany.
Height At shoulders: 25½-27¼ in (63-67 cm)
Weight 73-77 lb (34 kg)
Coat Harsh, hard, and wiry.
Color Pure black, or pepper and salt.
Longevity 10 to 12 years.
Character Reliable, good-natured companion.

SCHNAUZER

There are three varieties, the Standard, the Giant and the Miniature. They were originally used as all-purpose farm dogs and made good rafters.

Origin Germany.
Height Standard 17-19 in (44-49 cm).
Giant 23-27 in (60-70 cm).
Miniature 12-14 in (30-31 cm).
Weight Standard 33 lb (15 kg).
Giant 73-77 lb (33-35 kg).
Miniature 13-15 lb (6-7 kg).
Coat Harsh and wiry, soft undercoat.
Color Pure black, or pepper and salt.
Longevity 12-14 years.
Character Robust, attractive, playful.

CHOW CHOW

The Chow Chow has always had a reputation for ferocity but, although a formidable opponent, it is unlikely to attack unless provoked. It makes a good pet but requires considerable grooming daily with a wire brush.

Origin China.
Height 18-22 in (46-56 cm).
Weight 45-70 lb (20-32 kg).
Coat Abundant, dense, coarse.
Color Solid black, red, blue, fawn and cream.
Longevity 11-12 years.
Character Faithful, but strong minded.

LHASA APSO

The Lhasa Apso is a small indoor watchdog originally kept in the temples and palaces of Ancient Tibet. It is a firm family favorite and makes an excellent pet, despite having thick a coat that requires a great deal of grooming and care.

Origin Tibet.
Height 10 in (26 cm) .
Weight 13-15 lb (6-7 kg).
Coat Long, heavy, straight top coat.
Color Golden, smoke, black particolor.
Longevity 13-14 years.
Character Happy and adaptable.

SHIH TZU

The Shih Tzu whose Chinese name means 'lion dog' originates from Western China. It could be the result of crossbreeding between the Pekingese and the Lhasa Apso with which it is sometimes confused.

Origin China.
Height 10-11 in (23-27 cm).
Weight 9-18 lb (4-8 kg).
Coat Long, dense.
Color All colors permissible.
Longevity 13-14 years.
Character Courageous and elegant.

SHAR-PEI

An unusual and attractive breed, the Shar-Pei was used to herd flocks and hunt wild boar in China. It was also matched against other dogs in trials of strength. No longer the 'rarest dog in the world', it is affectionate, calm and independent

Origin China.
Height 18-20 in (46-51 cm).
Weight 40-55 lb (18-25 kg).
Coat Short, bristly.
Color Solid black, red, fawn, cream.
Longevity 12-14 years.
Character Alert and active.

POODLE

The Poodle's intelligence makes it popular at obedience trials as well as being a good family pet and show dog. It comes in three size varieties: the Standard Poodle, Miniature Poodle and Toy Poodle.

Origin Germany.
Height Standard 14-15 in (37-38 cm). Miniature 11-15 in (28-38 cm). Toy 10-11 in (25-28 cm).
Weight Standard 45-70 lb (20-32 kg). Miniature 26-30 lb (12-14 kg). Toy 14-16 lb (6.5-7.5 kg).
Coat Profuse, dense, harsh texture.
Color All solid colors.
Longevity 11-15 years.
Character Dependable, happy.

TOY POODLE

The Toy version of the Poodle is recognized as a separate breed. Poodles were originally used to guard sheep, and, being descended from the Irish Water Spaniel, would also readily enter water as retrievers.

Origin Germany.
Height At shoulders: 10 in (25 cm)
Weight 15 lb (7 kg)
Coat Profuse and dense; harsh texture.
Color All solid colors; clear colors are preferred.
Longevity Many live well into the teens.
Character Happy, hardy and devoted.

BICHON FRISE

'Bichon' is French for lap dog. Similar in appearance to the Miniature Poodle the Bichon has always been bred as a pet and is recognised as a Franco Belgian breed. It requires extensive regular grooming.

Origin Canary Islands.
Height 9-11 in (23-30 cm).
Weight 7-12 lb (3-6 kg).
Coat Long fine and corkscrew curls.
Color White cream or apricot.
Longevity 14 years.
Character Friendly, lively, easily trained.

FINNISH SPITZ

While still a favorite with hunters in Scandinavia, the Finnish Spitz is kept almost entirely as a companion and show dog elsewhere. It is good with children and adept at guarding. It requires plenty of brushing and daily exercise.

Origin Finland.
Height 15-20 in (39-50 cm).
Weight 25-35 lb (11-16 kg).
Coat Short on head, longer on body.
Color Reddish gold.
Longevity 12-14 years.
Character Faithful and home-loving.

JAPANESE SPITZ

The Japanese Spitz and its close relative the Nordic or Norbotten Spitz, have the same origins.
They derived from Finnish Spitz or Norwegian Buhund ancestry and the Japanese Spitz was developed as a separate breed in Japan, and is not unlike the Pomeranian (another Spitz variety) but in a larger frame.

Origin Japan
Height At shoulders: 12-14 in (30-36 cm)
Weight 13 lb (6 kg)
Coat Straight, dense, stand-off outer coat; thick, short, dense undercoat.
Color Pure white.
Longevity 11 to 13 years.
Character Alert, intelligent, bold, wary of strangers.

KEESHOND

Like other spitz breeds, the Keeshond (pronounced "kayshond") is believed to derive from an Arctic breed. It became popular in Holland as the companion of barge-dwellers and as a watchdog.

Origin Arctic.
Height At shoulders: 18 in (45 cm)
Weight 55-66 lb (25-30 kg)
Coat Long and straight with the hairs standing out; a dense ruff over the neck.
Color A mixture of gray, black, and cream; undercoat pale.
Longevity 12 to 15 years.
Character Good natured and devoted.

BOXER

The Boxer is a vibrant dog and takes a long time to grow up. They enjoy long country walks but should avoid the heat of the day in summer. The Boxer is loyal, obedient and they make good guard dogs.

Origin Germany.
Height 21-25 in (53-63 cm).
Weight 55-70 lb (25-32 kg).
Coat Short, glossy, smooth.
Color Fawn or brindle with white markings.
Longevity 12 years.
Character Fun loving, affectionate, gentle.

ROTTWEILER

The Rottweiler has been known since the Middle Ages when it was used for boar hunting, later as a cattle drover. They are excellent guard dogs in the hands of experienced owners but caution is urged around children, as normally docile dogs can become uncharacteristically aggressive.

Origin Germany.
Height 22-27 in (55-69 cm).
Weight 90-110 lb (41-49 kg).
Coat Flat and coarse, medium length.
Color Black with tan or deep brown.
Longevity 11-12 years.
Character Courageous companion-guard.

DOBERMAN

The Doberman was developed as a guard dog in the 1880s in Germany for its stamina, courage, intelligence and tracking ability. It is now used for guarding by police forces worldwide.

Origin Germany.
Height 24-28 in (60-70 cm).
Weight 66-88 lb (30-40 kg).
Coat Smooth, thick, short and close.
Color Solid black, brown, fawn or blue with rust markings.
Longevity 12 years.
Character Intelligent, loyal and obedient.

GREAT DANE

One of the tallest dogs in the world, a gentle giant, originally used as a wild boar hunter and bodyguard. They are easy to train and enjoy being treated as one of the family. Require regular exercise on hard ground.

Origin Germany.
Height 28-30 in (71-76 cm).
Weight 100-120 lb (46-54 kg).
Coat Sleek, short and dense.
Color Brindle, fawn, blue, black or white with black/blue ragged patches.
Character Friendly, good natured and easy to train.

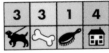

BERNESE MOUNTAIN DOG

Originally developed as a herder and guard, it is still used to pull milk carts in its native Switzerland. Popular as a show dog and a family pet needing plenty of exercise and grooming.

Origin Switzerland.
Height 23-28 in (58-70 cm).
Weight 88 lb (40 kg).
Coat Thick, long, wavy, soft, shiny.
Color Jet black with reddish and white markings.
Longevity 10-12 years.
Character Good natured, good with children and easy to train.

3	3	2	3

JAPANESE AKITA

The largest of the Japanese breeds, originally bred as a deer/boar hunter. It is equally happy in water or deep snow as it has webbed feet. It is revered in Japan where at one time it could only be owned by the nobility.

Origin Japan.
Height 24-28 in (61-71 cm).
Weight 75-101 lb (34-49 kg).
Coat Coarse straight outer coat, soft dense undercoat.
Color Any color including white brindle or pinto.
Longevity 10-12 years.
Character Loyal, alert hunter, energetic.

3	2	2	3

PYRENEAN MOUNTAIN DOG

Sometimes known as the Great Pyrenees, these dogs have been used for centuries to guard flocks in the Pyrenean mountains bordering France and Spain. The dogs need plenty of exercise, grooming and must be well trained.

Origin Asia/Europe.
Height 26-32 in (65-81 cm).
Weight 99-132 lb (45-60 kg).
Coat Profuse, coarse wavy outer coat, soft thick undercoat.
Color White, with or without patches of gray.
Longevity 11-12 years.
Character Gentle, faithful, protector.

ST. BERNARD

Descended from mastiffs and famous for rescuing climbers in the Swiss Alps, the St. Bernard has been revitalised by the introduction of Newfoundland blood. They require space, lots of food and gentle exercise.

Origin Switzerland.
Height 24-28 in (61-71 cm).
Weight 110-200 lb (50-91 kg).
Coat Both long and short haired breeds.
Color Orange, mahogany-brindle, red-brindle or white.
Longevity 11 years.
Character Gentle with children, very loyal.

SAMOYED

Named after the Siberian tribe of Samoyeds, they have great endurance abilities having been taken on expeditions to the North Pole. They have also been used for hunting reindeer and as guard dogs.

Origin Siberia.
Height 18-22 in (46-56 cm).
Weight 50-66 lb (23-30 kg).
Coat Thick water resistant with a soft short undercoat.
Color Pure white, cream; outer coat   silver tipped.
Longevity 12 years.
Character Devoted, obedient.

SIBERIAN HUSKY

Developed by the Chukchi nomads of North-East Asia to pull sleds and herd reindeer, they became famous in the gold rush era of Alaska, as sled racing dogs. Since the Second World War, they have been used as search and rescue dogs.

Origin Siberia
Height 20-24 in (51-60 cm).
Weight 30-60 lb (16-27 kg).
Coat Straight, medium length, soft, dense undercoat.
Color All colors and markings.
Character Intelligent, friendly, hard working.

MASTIFF

One of the most ancient breeds of dog, it has been used as a formidable guard dog and as a hunter. St. Bernard blood was introduced in the 19th century. They are large dogs which are expensive to feed and require regular walking to build up their muscles.

Origin Turkey.
Height 27-30 in (70-76 cm).
Weight 190-220 lb (86-100 kg).
Coat Short, smooth, dense.
Color Fawn, brindle or red.
Longevity 7-10 years.
Character Loyal, good-natured.

BULLMASTIFF

The result of a cross between the Mastiff 60% and the British Bulldog 40%, 200-300 years ago. Powerful animals, they have a large appetite, require regular exercise and need grooming every few days. Dependable with children.

Origin Great Britain.
Height 25-27 in (64-69 cm).
Weight 90-130 lb (41-59 kg) .
Coat Short smooth and dense.
Color Any shade of brindle, fawn or red; black muzzle.
Longevity 10-12 years.
Character Loyal, playful, excellent guard.

NEAPOLITAN MASTIFF

The origins of this Italian dog stretch right back to the fierce Molossus dogs of ancient Rome. These Mastiffs have particularly large heads, supported by equally powerful bodies.

Origin Italy.
Height 24-31 in (60-78 cm).
Weight 165 lb (74 kg).
Coat Dense and smooth.
Color Shades of gray and black.
Longevity 10 to 11 years.
Character Fierce and territorial. Not suitable for children or first time owners.

ANATOLIAN SHEPHERD DOG

The Anatolian Shepherd Dog, previously known as the Anatolian Karabash, has existed for centuries, from the Anatolian plateau of Turkey right across Afghanistan. Such powerful dogs were once used as war dogs and to hunt big game.

Origin Turkey.
Height At shoulders: 29-32 in (72-80 cm).
Weight 110-141 lb (50-70 kg)
Coat Short, dense, with a thick undercoat
Color Best is solid cream to fawn with black mask and ears.
Longevity 12 to 15 years.
Character Strong willed and independent, loyal and loving. Makes an excellent guard dog.

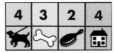

ESTRELA MOUNTAIN DOG

The Estrela Mountain Dog, also known as the Portuguese Mountain Dog, originated centuries ago in central Portugal. Bred as a herding dog, it bears some resemblance to the Mastiff and the Saint Bernard.

Origin Portugal.
Height At withers: 26-29 in (65-72 cm).
Weight 90-120 lb (40-50 kg).
Coat Strong, slightly thick, not too harsh.
Color Fawn, wolfgray, and yellow; white markings permitted.
Longevity 9 to 14 years.
Character Alert, dignified. Distrustful of strangers.

WELSH CORGI PEMBROKE

Two distinct breeds of Corgi are recognized. The Pembroke is of slighter build and has a less bushy tail than the Cardigan Corgi. The Welsh Corgi Pembroke is a favorite with British royalty, and it may be descended from the Swedish Vallhund or from Flemish stock.

Origin Great Britain
Height At shoulders: about 10-12 in (25-30 cm)
Weight 27 lb (15 kg)
Coat Medium length and straight, with a dense undercoat.
Color Red, sable, fawn, or black and tan, with or without white markings on legs, brisket, and neck.
Longevity 12 to 14 years.
Character Devoted companion, tireless worker and fine guard.

SMOOTH COLLIE

Collies were another of the herding dogs originally bred in Scotland. They first attracted attention when Queen Victoria brought some of these dogs back to her kennels after a visit to Scotland in 1860. The Rough Collie has since become by far the most popular of the two forms.

Origin Great Britain.
Height At shoulders: 22-26 in (55-65 cm).
Weight 45-75 lb (20-35 kg)
Coat Short, harsh, and smooth, with a dense undercoat.
Color Sable and white, tricolor, blue merle
Longevity 10 to 14 years.
Character tenacious sheepdog of great tractability.

BORDER COLLIE

Descended from the working collies on the borders of Scotland and England. Naturally good at herding with stamina and intelligence, they are used all over the world as sheepdogs.

Origin Great Britain.
Height 18-21 in (46-54 cm).
Weight 30-49 lb (14-22 kg).
Coat Smooth or long, both are thick and straight.
Color Variety of color but white should not predominate.
Longevity 12-14 years.
Character Loyal, obedient, intelligent.

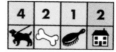

ROUGH COLLIE

Recognised as the star of the 'Lassie' films. They have been used as sheepdogs in the Scottish Highlands for centuries. They are intelligent and need lots of exercise. There is an identical Smooth-haired variety.

Origin Iceland.
Height 20-26 in (51-65 cm).
Weight 40-75 lb (18-34 kg).
Coat Dense harsh outer coat.
Color Sable and white, tricolor.
Longevity 12-13 years.
Character Loyal, affectionate, excellent guard dog.

BEARDED COLLIE

One of the oldest herding dogs in Scotland, descended from three Polish Lowland Sheepdogs in 1514. Nearly extinct in the 1940s, today's dogs are the descendants of a pair bred in Ayrshire, Scotland by Mrs G. Wilson.

Origin Poland.
Height 20-22 in (51-56 cm).
Weight 40-60 lb (18-27 kg).
Coat Flat, harsh, shaggy and slightly wavy.
Color Slate gray, reddish fawn with or without white markings.
Longevity 12-13 years.
Character Alert, active, good natured.

JAPANESE AKITA

The largest and best known of the Japanese breeds, the Akita originated in the Polar regions and has a history that can be traced back more than 300 years. It is swift, can work in deep snow, and is a strong swimmer.

Origin Japan.
Height At withers: 26-28 in (65-70 cm)
Weight 75-101 lb (35-60 kg)
Coat Outer coat coarse, straight, and stand-off; soft, dense undercoat.
Color Any, including white, brindle, and pinto, with or without mask.
Longevity 11 to 15 years.
Character A versatile hunter and retriever, and a first-class guard dog, it is being kept widely as a pet. Can be formidable and needs obedience classes.

SHETLAND SHEEPDOG

Originally from the Shetland Islands off the North coast of Scotland where it is known as the 'Sheltie'. Believed to be descended from working collies which arrived at the islands on whaling ships.

Origin Great Britain.
Height 14-15 in (35-37 cm).
Weight 14-16 lb (6-7 kg).
Coat Long harsh outercoat, soft close undercoat.
Color Sable, tricolor, blue, black, tan and white.
Longevity 12-14 years.
Character Sensitive, intelligent, good show dog.

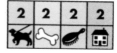

OLD ENGLISH SHEEPDOG

Believed to have developed from a cross of a Briard and the Russian Owtcharka, they have been used as a drover's dog. Their docked tails were an identification mark in the 18th century when drover's dogs were exempt from taxes and they acquired the nickname of 'Bobtail'.

Origin Great Britain.
Height 21-22 in (53-56 cm).
Weight 66 lb (30 kg).
Coat Profuse, shaggy, good texture.
Color Shades of gray, grizzle or blue.
Longevity 12-13 years.
Character Good temperament, exuberant, thrives on affection.

NEWFOUNDLAND

Believed to be descended from the Tibetan Mastiff, the Newfoundland has adapted to the conditions in Eastern Canada by developing webbed feet and an oily coat. This allows it to remain in water for long periods and helps its strong rescue instinct.

Origin Canada.
Height 26-28 in (66-71 cm).
Weight 110-50 lb (50-68 kg).
Coat Double coat, dense, coarse and oily.
Color Black brown, gray or Landseer.
Longevity 12 years.
Character Docile, patient, very gentle.

AUSTRALIAN CATTLE DOG

A superb worker which drives herds by nipping at the cattle's heels. The breed traces vack to the now-extinct Black Bobtail.

Origin Australia.
Height At withers: 18-20 in (45-50 cm).
Weight 34-45 lb (15-20 kg)
Coat Smooth, hard, straight, and water-resistant top coat and short, normally dense undercoat.
Color Blue, blue mottled, or blue speckled with or without black; or red speckled with or without darker red markings on head.
Longevity 11-15 years.
Character Intelligent and good tempered.

BRIARD

One of France's most popular companion dogs. Best known as a sheepdog, having been introduced to Europe with other sheepdogs from Hungary and Russia.

Origin Asia.
Height 22-27 in (55-68 cm).
Weight 75 lb (34 kg).
Coat Long and wavy, dense undercoat.
Color Solid black, fawn.
Longevity 11-13 years.
Character Gentle, intelligent, very

GERMAN SHEPHERD DOG

Believed to be descended from the Bronze Age wolf, they are extremely intelligent and trainable. They make excellent guide dogs for the blind as well as police dogs. They need plenty of exercise and a job to do so they do not get bored.

Origin Germany.
Height 22-26 in (55-66 cm).
Weight 75-95 lb (34-43 kg).
Coat Medium length, straight.
Color Solid black or gray, with tan or gray markings.
Longevity 12-13 years.
Character Very intelligent, trainable and good guard dog.

BELGIAN SHEPHERD DOG

There are four varieties: the Groenendael (pictured), the Tervueren, the Malinois and the Laekenois. All were developed from sheepdogs of different colors and sizes in Belgium at the end of the 19th century.

Origin Belgium.
Height 22-26 in (56-66 cm).
Weight 62 lb (28 kg).
Coat Either long straight or short harsh.
Color Black, gray, red, fawn.
Longevity 12-14 years.
Character Strong herding and guarding instincts.

PICARDY SHEPHERD DOG

This breed is said to be the oldest French herding dog and is unsurpassed at guarding both flocks of sheep and herds of cattle. Trustworthy with children, they superbly combine the role of a working dog and affectionate family pet.

Origin France.
Height 22-26 in (256-66 cm).
Weight 50-70 lb (22-32 kg).
Coat Hard, long with a heavy undercoat.
Color All shades of gray and fawn.
Longevity 10-12 years.
Character Energetic, affectionate, trustworthy.

HUNGARIAN PULI

The best known of the Hungarian sheepdogs introduced by the Magyars over 1000 years ago. They have been used for herding sheep for centuries and recently for police work. Their corded coat, requires special care and attention.

Origin Hungary.
Height 14-18 in (37-44 cm).
Weight 22-33 lb (10-15 kg).
Coat Dense, corded.
Color Black, white or gray and apricot.
Longevity 12-13 years.
Character Loyal, devoted, intelligent.

LABRADOR RETRIEVER

Introduced to Great Britain by Newfoundland fishermen who used the dogs to help land the fishing nets. Black was their usual color although today yellow labradors are much more popular and are used as guide dogs.

Origin Canada.
Height 21-25 in (54-61 cm).
Weight 55-75 lb (25-34 kg).
Coat Short, dense, weather resistant.
Color Solid black, yellow or liver/chocolate.
Longevity 12-14 years.
Character Easy to train, good with children, loves the water.

GOLDEN RETRIEVER

Popular as a show and working dog, they were originally bred for finding, picking up and carrying hares or birds. They have developed from a combination of yellow flat coated dogs with Tweed Water Spaniels. Ideal as guide dogs for the blind.

Origin Great Britain.
Height 20-24 in (51-61 cm).
Weight 55-75 lb (25-34 kg).
Coat Flat or wavy with good feathering.
Color Any shade of gold or cream.
Longevity 13-15 years.
Character Friendly, good family pet, sound temperament.

FLAT COATED RETRIEVER

Originally called the Wavy-coat Retriever, this breed is not so well known although they were very popular with gamekeepers at the turn of the century. Excellent retrievers both on land and water.

Origin Great Britain.
Height 22-24 in (56-61 cm).
Weight 55-80 lb (25-35 kg).
Coat Dense, medium length, lying flat.
Color Solid black or solid liver.
Longevity 12-14 years.
Character Intelligent, good temperament, hardy, happiest at work.

IRISH WATER SPANIEL

An enchanting-looking animal, the Irish Water Spaniel is a first class water dog, skilled at wild fowling and trainable as an all round sporting dog. It is the tallest of the spaniels and there is a smaller American variety.

Origin Ireland.
Height 20-24 in (51-60 cm).
Weight 45-65 lb (20-30 kg).
Coat Tight dense ringlets.
Color Dark liver with purplish tint.
Longevity 12-14 years.
Character Devoted, affectionate, boisterous.

AMERICAN COCKER SPANIEL

The breed originates from a British bitch brought back to America in the 1880s. They are the smallest of the American gundogs and until recently were shown exclusively in the ring. Latterly field trials have been reintroduced.

Origin USA.
Height 13-15 in (34-39 cm).
Weight 24-28 lb (11-12 kg).
Coat Short on head, medium on body.
Color Black, black/brown and tan, tricolors.
Longevity 13-14 years.
Character Gundog, show dog, good with children.

CLUMBER SPANIEL

The heaviest of the spaniels, the Clumber is a slow-but-sure dog, common in the country where it excels at flushing out gameover rough ground. Brought to Britain from France prior to the Revolution, to stay at Clumber Park from where they get their name.

Origin France.
Height 17-20 in (42-50 cm).
Weight 55-70 lb (25-38 kg).
Coat Abundant and silky.
Color White with orange/lemon markings.
Longevity 12-13 years.
Character Good temperament, good family dog.

ENGLISH COCKER SPANIEL

Originally from Spain, the Cocker is the smallest of the spaniel gundogs and gets its name from being used at flushing out woodcocks. They are first class gundogs, as well as gentle pets. Special care should be given to their distinctive long ears.

Origin Spain.
Height 15-17 in (38-43 cm).
Weight 28-32 lb (13-15 kg).
Coat Flat and silky texture.
Color Various and pure colors.
Longevity 13-14 years.
Character Gentle, first-class gundog, popular pet.

ENGLISH SPRINGER SPANIEL

Once known as the Norfolk Spaniel, the breed were used for springing or flushing out game prior to shotguns being used. They are popular gundogs with unlimited stamina and love water.

Origin Great Britain.
Height 19-20 in (48-51 cm).
Weight 49-55 lb (22-25 kg).
Coat Close and straight.
Color Liver/white, black/white, with tan.
Longevity 12-14 years.
Character Intelligent, reliable, good with children

WELSH SPRINGER SPANIEL

Smaller than the English Spaniel, the Welsh Spaniels are excellent retrievers with lots of stamina and are superb working dogs. They have a distinctive rich, red and white coat which distinguishes them from other spaniels.

Origin Great Britain.
Height 17-19 in (42-48 cm).
Weight 35-45 lb (16-20 kg).
Coat Straight and flat, silky.
Color Rich red and white only.
Longevity 12-14 years.
Character Hardworking, affectionate.

3	2	2	2

IRISH SETTER

The breed was developed through crossing the Irish Water Spaniel, the Spanish Pointer and English and Gordon Setters. It is ideally suited for work as a gundog in the open countryside. It is famed for its classic, poised stance.

Origin Ireland.
Height 25-27 in (63-69 cm).
Weight 60-70 lb (27-32 kg).
Coat Short head and legs; moderately long body.
Color Rich chestnut.
Longevity 13 years.
Character Good family pet, boundless energy.

3	2	1	3

IRISH RED AND WHITE SETTER

They are said to be evolved from red and white spaniels brought to Ireland from France and crossed with Pointers. Combination of sportsman's dog and family pet.

Origin Ireland.
Height 23-27 in (59-67 cm).
Weight 40-70 lb (18-32 kg).
Coat Flat, straight with good feathering.
Color Particolored, white base with red patches.
Longevity 13 years.
Character Good natured, affectionate.

GORDON SETTER

Scotland's only native gundog, formerly known as the Gordon Castle Setter. The largest of the setters is at its best when hunting game birds particularly grouse. They are able to work without water for longer periods than most other setters.

Origin Great Britain.
Height 23-26 in (57-70 cm).
Weight 45-80 lb (20-36 kg).
Coat Short on head/legs; long on body.
Color Deep, shining coal-black with tan markings.
Longevity 13 years.
Character Tireless gundog, pet and watchdog.

ENGLISH SETTER

The oldest of the setters, they were developed to hunt in open country. Beautiful and affectionate, the breed successfully combines the role of family pet and sportsman's dog.

Origin Great Britain.
Height 24-27 in (60-68 cm).
Weight 40-70 lb (18-32 kg).
Coat Long, straight and dense.
Color Black/white, orange/white liver/white.
Longevity 14 years.
Character Good natured, friendly, loyal and affectionate.

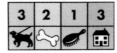

POINTER

Thought to have originated in Spain, the Pointer is famed for its classic stance. They are popular as show dogs but were originally used as gundogs, when they would 'point' to where game was lurking. Good with children.

Origin Spain.
Height 23-28 in (57-70 cm).
Weight 45-75 lb (20-34 kg).
Coat Short, dense and smooth.
Color Orange/white, liver/white, black/white.
Longevity 13-14 years.
Character Affectionate, easy to train.

MÖNSTERLÄNDER (Large and Small)

The breed combines the best qualities of the setter and the spaniel and has been established as a gundog in Germany since the 18th century. The Small Munsterlander is the result of crossbreeding the Brittany and German Long-haired Pointer.

Origin Germany.
Height Large 23-24 in (58-61 cm). Small 19-22 in (47-55 cm).
Weight Large 55-65 lb (25-29 kg). Small 33 lb (15 kg).
Coat Long, dense with feathering.
Color Black head, body white or blue roan.
Longevity 12-13 years.
Character Loyal, friendly, trustworthy.

WEIMARANER

They are believed to have developed from the crossing of Bloodhounds with local pointers and hunting dogs. Once used against big game, they are now popular as police dogs where their intelligence and agility are put to good use.

Origin Germany.
Height 22-27 in (56-69 cm).
Weight 70-85 lb (32-38 kg).
Coat Short, smooth and sleek.
Color Metallic silver gray.
Longevity 12-13 years.
Character Intelligent. Makes a good pet if given enough exercise.

HUNGARIAN VIZSLA

This is another of the ancient Hungarian breeds and from this base contemporary bloodlines have evolved. The name `Vizsla', translates as `responsive and alert'. These characteristics were essential attributes for a gundog to working in hot conditions, performing effectively as both pointers and retrievers.

Origin Hungary
Height At withers: 23-24 in (58-61 cm).
Weight 55-65 lb (25-29 kg)
Coat Short, dense, and straight; tightly fitting.
Color Russet gold; small white marks on chest and feet are acceptable.
Longevity 14 to 15 years..
Character Versatile, easily trained gundog which makes a first-class pet and is good with children.

SAINT GERMAIN SETTER

A refined and stylish dog, the Saint Germain Setter is said to have derived from a 19th century mating between an English Pointer and a French Setter. It is an attractive gundog, resembling the English Pointer, but not as heavily boned.

Origin France
Height 20-25 in (50-63 cm).
Weight 40-57 lb (25-30 kg).
Coat Short and soft.
Color White with orange markings.
Longevity 12 to 13 years.
Character A strong hunting dog. Affectionate, gentle, and intelligent, but can be stubborn.

BOURBONNAIS SETTER

Associated with central France, the Bourbonnais Setter derives from the Pyrenees. The Bourbonnais, described as the short-tailed setter tail, has a striking Dalmatian-like coat pattern on a distinctly thickset body.

Origin France.
Height Average height: 21 in (53 cm)
Weight 40-57 lb (25-30 kg)
Coat Short
Color White and light brown
Longevity 12 to 15 years.
Character A good-natured sporting and family dog; easy to train.

CHESAPEAKE BAY RETRIEVER

The Chesapeake Bay Retriever probably descended from a Newfoundland which mated with various working breeds in the Chesapeake Bay area. Combining the superb swimming ability of the Newfoundland and the duck-retrieving abilities of local dogs, the Chesapeake Bay Retriever was kept strictly as a sporting dog until fairly recently. However, it is now finding its way into the family home and the show ring.

Origin Canada.
Height 23-26 in (58-65 cm)
Weight dogs 65-80 lb (40-60 kg)
Coat Thick and reasonably short (not over 1 in long), with harsh outercoat and dense undercoat.
Color Dead grass (straw to bracken), sedge (red-gold), brown; white spots on chest, toes, and belly.
Longevity 9 to 15 years.
Character A good-natured pet.

AFGHAN HOUND

They are an ancient breed of dog and a member of the grayhound family. Their long shaggy coat was developed to withstand the harsh climate of Afghanistan. Its speed and stamina were used to hunt leopards, wolves and jackals.

Origin Afghanistan.
Height 25-27 in (63-68 cm).
Weight 50-60 lb (23-27 kg).
Coat Long and fine.
Color All colors acceptable.
Longevity 12-14 years.
Character Elegant, beautiful, affectionate but Slightly aloof.

BASENJI

The breed comes from Central Africa where they were used as a hunting dog They are famed for the fact that they do not bark but instead give out a kind of yodel. The Basenji wash themselves like a cat and have no doggie smell.

Origin Central Africa.
Height 16-17 in (40-43 cm).
Weight 22-24 lb (10-11 kg).
Coat Short, sleek, close and fine.
Color Black, red, or black and tan; white chest, feet and tail tips.
Longevity 12 years.
Character Intelligent, playful, dislikes wet weather.

BLOODHOUND

They are one of the oldest hound breeds, said to have been brought to Britain by William the Conqueror in 1066. The Bloodhound has the keenest sense of smell of any domestic animal and are used to track lost people and animals.

Origin France.
Height 23-27 in (58-67 cm).
Weight 80-100 lb (36-45 kg).
Coat Smooth, short and weatherproof.
Color Black and tan, liver and tan or red.
Longevity 10-12 years.
Character Affectionate, good with children.

4	3	1	3

BORZOI

This breed was used in Russia for wolf hunting and coursing. The dog tracked the wolf, grabbing it by the neck and throwing it so that it could be finished off by a blow from a dagger. Its in-built hunting instincts mean that it is not good with children.

Origin Russia.
Height 27-29 in (68-74 cm).
Weight 60-105 lb (27-48 kg).
Coat Silky, flat and wavy or curly.
Color Any color acceptable.
Longevity 11-13 years.
Character Elegant, intelligent.

3	3	1	4

BASSET HOUND

The Basset was bred from the French Basset Artésien Normand and crossed with the Bloodhound, to produce a slow-but sure dog used to track rabbits and hare. Now, kept as a companion, pet or show dog. It needs a lot of exercise.

Origin France.
Height 13-14 in (33-35 cm).
Weight 40-60 lb (18-27 kg).
Coat Hard, smooth, short and dense.
Color Black, white/tan, lemon/ white.
Longevity 12 years.
Character Lovable, gets on well with children.

BEAGLE

The smallest of the hounds, the Beagle has been used for hunting hare and wild rabbit, and can be trained to seek out and retrieve. It is a fine show dog and needs only an over age amount of exercise

Origin Great Britain.
Height US 13-15 in (33-37 cm). UK 13-16 in (33-40 cm).
Weight 18-30 lb (8-14 kg).
Coat Short, dense and weatherproof.
Color Any recognized hound color.
Longevity 13 years.
Character Friendly, fine show dog.

AMERICAN FOXHOUND

A highly valued hunting dog, the American Foxhound is a descendant of English Foxhounds taken to Maryland, United States, in 1650. George Washington is also known to have imported Foxhounds from England.

Origin United States of America.
Height 22-25 in (55-63 cm)
Weight 66-75 lb (29-34 kg).
Coat Hard and close.
Color All colors acceptable.
Longevity 10 to 13 years.
Character Good natured, can become less attentive and more wilful as it grows older.

ENGLISH FOXHOUND

The breed is descended from St. Hubert Hounds and the Talbot and their prime function is to hunt foxes alongside mounted huntsmen. They are able to work for long periods without a break. They cannot be kept as pets in Britain but are the property of the hunting packs.

Origin Great Britain.
Height 21-25 in (50-62 cm).
Weight 65-70 lb (29-31 kg).
Coat Short and hard.
Color Black, white and tan, or tan and white.
Longevity 11 years.
Character Intelligent, working dog.

DACHSHUND

There are six breeds of Dachshund: Smooth-haired, Long-haired and Wire-haired each occurring as both Standard and Miniature. They are derived from the oldest breeds of German hunting dogs and were bred to go to ground.

Origin Germany.
Height 5-10 in (13-25 cm).
Weight Standard UK 20-26 lb (9-12 kg); US 16-32 lb (7-14 kg). Miniature UK 10 lb (4.5 kg); US 11 lb (5 kg).
Coat Smooth, long hair. Dense and short.
Color Any color but white permissible.
Character Devoted pet, good watchdog.

GRAYHOUND

The breed has altered little from dogs depicted on the tombs of the pharaohs and is mentioned in the Holy Bible. They were a favorite with the nobility as they were highly valued as a courser. More recently they have competed on the greyhound racing tracks.

Origin Egypt.
Height 27-30 in (68-76 cm).
Weight 60-70 lb (27-32 kg).
Coat Fine and close.
Color Black, white, red, blue, and fallow brindle.
Longevity 10-12 years.
Character Gentle, good with children, faithful.

WHIPPET

Resembling a small grayhound, the Whippet was bred expressly as a racing dog and is the fastest breed in the world. Adaptable to domestic life, the Whippet needs plenty of exercise.

Origin Great Britain.
Height 17.5-20 in (44-51 cm).
Weight 28 lb (12.5 kg).
Coat Short, fine and close.
Color Any color or mixture of colors.
Longevity 13-14 years.
Character Good with children, a fine watchdog

IRISH WOLFHOUND

The tallest dog in the world, and the national dog of Ireland. Bred to kill wolves, they became highly prized dogs and were exported to Europe. Needs no more than average exercise.

Origin Ireland.
Height 30-34 in (75-85 cm).
Weight 105-120 lb (48-55 kg).
Coat Rough and harsh.
Color Gray, brindle, red, black, white, fawn or wheaten.
Longevity 11 years.
Character Calm temperament, popular show dog.

PHARAOH HOUND

The Phoenicians are believed to have brought these hounds to the islands of Malta and Gozo over 5,000 years ago, and, since then, the breed has developed largely in isolation. They are popular here for hunting rabbits and, although sight hounds, they can also track their quarry by scent.

Origin Great Britain.
Height At withers: 22-25 in (55-63 cm)
Weight 28 lb (12.5 kg).
Coat Short, fine and close.
Color Any color or mixture of colors.
Longevity 12 to 14 years.
Character has a happy, confident personality, likes children and makes a good family pet.

BASSET GRIFFON VENDÉEN

This breed comes in three sizes, Grand, Bassett or Petit. They are French sporting dogs. The Grand was originally used to hunt wolves and wild boar and other varieties hunt hare and rabbit.

Height Grand 24-26 in (61-66 cm). Basset 15-17 in (38-43 cm). Petit 13-15 in (34-38 cm).
Weight Grand 66-77 lb (30-35 kg). Basset 40-44 lb (18-20 kg). Petit 25-35 lb (11-16 kg).
Coat Rough, long and harsh.
Color Solid fawn or hare.
Longevity 12 years.
Character Intelligent, hunters.

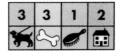

ANGLO-FRENCH HOUNDS

As its name suggests, the Anglo-French came about through crossings between French medium-size hounds and English hounds. The Anglo-French Tricolor is one of the most popular hounds in France. They are usually kept in packs, and used to hunt large and small game.

Origin France.

Height 20 in (50 cm).

Weight 49-55 lb (23-25 kg).

Coat Short and smooth.

Color Tricolor black, white, and orange: white and black; white and orange.

Longevity 10 to 12 years.

Character Good-natured pack hounds.

POITEVIN

The Poitevin was developed in the late 1600s in south-west France as a wolf hunter, possessing great speed, courage, and scenting ability.

Origin France.

Height At shoulders: 24-28 in (60-70 cm).

Weight 66 lb (30 kg).

Coat Short and glossy.

Color Tricolor with black saddle; tricolor with large black patches; sometimes orange and white or badger-pied.

Longevity 11 to 12 years.

Character Large, distinguished hound, swift and intelligent, but timid and reserved. Happiest to move in a pack.

ARIEGEOIS

The Ariégeois, originating in the Ariége, a French province on the Spanish border, is the result of a crossing between the native medium-size hounds, the Gascon Saintongeois and the Gascony Blue.

Origin France.
Height At shoulders: 22-24 in (55-60 cm).
Weight 66 lb (30 kg).
Coat Fine and close.
Color White with black markings and small tan spots; rich tan should not be normally encouraged.
Longevity Teens.
Character Finely built with a calm disposition and friendly expression. A most pleasant animal.

BILLY

The Billy was devised in south-west France, for the express purpose of hunting wild boar and deer. Selective breeding commenced in 1888, using the wolf-hunter, the Poitevin, the Céris, a hunter of both wolf and hare, and the Montemboeuf, a large, noble hand that would follow only those animals selected as quarry.

Origin France.
Height At shoulders: 24-26 in (61-66 cm).
Weight 55-66 lb (21-30 kg).
Coat Short and hard to the touch.
Color White or "café au lait"; white with orange or lemon blanket, or mottling.
Longevity 12 to 13 years.
Character Intelligent, with exceptional hunting and scenting abilities. It is known to be somewhat argumentative with its fellows. Kept in a pack.

BULL TERRIER

The Bull Terrier began life as a fighting dog, the result of crossing an Old English Bulldog with a terrier and is described as 'the gladiator of the canine race'. Despite its fierce appearance, it makes a faithful and devoted pet. The bitch is utterly reliable with children.

Origin Great Britain.
Height 21-22 in (52-55 cm).
Weight 52-62 lb (23-28 kg).
Coat Short and flat.
Color White, brindle.
Longevity 11-13 years.
Character Faithful and devoted.

STAFFORDSHIRE BULL TERRIER

Not to be confused with the American Staffordshire Terrier or Pit Bull. Derived from a crossing of an Old English Bulldog and a terrier at a time when dog fighting and bull-baiting were popular sports. A popular pet and show dog, it adores children but does enjoy a scrap with other dogs.

Origin Great Britain.
Height 14-16 in (33-40 cm).
Weight 24-38 lb (11-17 kg).
Coat Short, smooth and dense.
Color Red, fawn, white, black, brindle.
Longevity 11-12 years.
Character Courageous, intelligent.

AIREDALE TERRIER

The king of the terriers and the largest member of the terrier group. An expert ratter and duck-catcher, they can be trained to the gun and make good guard dogs.

Origin Great Britain.
Height 22-24 in (56-61 cm).
Weight 44 lb (20 kg).
Coat Hard, dense and wiry.
Color Black or grizzle with tan legs and head.
Longevity 13 years.
Character Good family pet, loyal.

FOX TERRIER

Originally used as a stable dog hunting out vermin, they are great rabbiters and will pursue foxes as their names suggest. There are two types: smooth- and wire-haired. Needs regular grooming.

Origin Great Britain.
Height 15 in (38-39 cm).
Weight 16-18 lb (7-8 kg).
Coat Smooth. Straight, flat and smooth; Wire. Dense and very wiry.
Color Smooth. White with tan/black.
Character Affectionate, trainable.

KERRY BLUE TERRIER

An excellent sporting dog and fine swimmer, the Kerry Blue was used to hunt badgers, foxes and otters. They are now mainly kept as pets. It has a fierce temper with other dogs or pets but is good with children.

Origin Ireland.
Height 17-20 in (44-49 cm).
Weight 33-40 lb (15-18 kg).
Coat Soft, spiky, wavy and plentiful.
Color Blue, with or without black points.
Longevity 14 years.
Character Good guard dog.

PARSON JACK RUSSELL TERRIER

Named after the Parson who developed this strain of terrier from early types of wire-haired fox terriers. The intention was to produce a dog which would run with hounds and bolt the fox.

Origin Great Britain.
Height 12-14 in (30-35 cm).
Weight 10 lb (4.5 kg).
Coat Smooth, or rough and broken.
Color Entirely white or with tan, lemon or black markings.
Character Good working dog, popular pet.

BORDER TERRIER

This dog originates from the Borders region between England and Scotland and was bred to run with hounds and to bolt the fox from its lair. The smallest of the working terriers, they make first class pets and love children.

Origin Great Britain.
Height 10 in (25 cm).
Weight 10-15 lb (5-7 kg).
Coat Harsh and dense, close undercoat.
Color Red, wheaten, grizzle and tan, blue and tan.
Longevity 13-14 years.
Character Able to walk owners off their feet, good watchdog qualities.

CAIRN TERRIER

Popular Scottish terriers used to catch vermin, they are named after the cairns of stones where their prey hid. Originated in the West Highlands, the Cairn is a predominantly working dog.

Origin Great Britain.
Height 9-12 in (24-30 cm).
Weight 13-16 lb (6-7 kg).
Coat Profuse, harsh.
Color Cream, wheaten, red, gray or nearly black.
Longevity 14 years.
Character Affectionate, lively, adaptable, minimum grooming required.

NORFOLK TERRIER

Once classified as the Norwich Terrier, the Norfolk Terrier is distinguished by its ears which drop forward. The breed is probably a mixture of Cairn, Border and Irish terriers and they are among the smallest of the terriers.

Origin Great Britain.
Height 10 in (25.5 cm).
Weight 11-12 lb (5-5.5 kg).
Coat Hard, wiry and straight.
Color Red, wheaten, black and tan, or grizzle.
Longevity 14 years.
Character Sociable, hardy, alert, fearless, good temperament.

NORWICH TERRIER

The breed is named after the city of Norwich and appears to have originated in East Anglia. At one time they were classified together with the Norfolk Terrier but the breeds were separated in 1979, the Norwich having prick-up ears, the Norfolk having flat ears.

Origin Great Britain.
Height 10 in (25.5 cm).
Weight 10-12 lb (4.5-5.5 kg).
Coat Hard, wiry and straight.
Color Red, wheaten, black and tan.
Longevity 14 years.
Character Hardy, adaptable.

SCOTTISH TERRIER

Once known as the Aberdeen Terrier, the breed was developed to dispel vermin and has taken many forms over the centuries. They have erect ears and prominent eyebrows on a long face which give the 'Scottie' a somewhat stern appearance.

Origin Great Britain.
Height 11 in (25-28 cm).
Weight 19-23 lb (8-11 kg).
Coat Sharp, dense and wiry.
Color Black, wheaten or brindle.
Longevity 13-14 years.
Character Reliable temperament, very loyal.

WEST HIGHLAND WHITE TERRIER

Like other small working Scottish terriers, the 'Westie' was bred to hunt vermin. Their name has evolved over the years as their classification has changed. They need regular grooming to keep their coat in shape and are good with children.

Origin Great Britain.
Height 11 in (25-27 cm).
Weight 15-22 lb (7-10 kg).
Coat Harsh, and free from curl.
Color White.
Longevity 14 years.
Character Easy to train.

SKYE TERRIER

The breed was developed from small dogs kept to go to ground after badgers, fox, otter and rabbit. Believed to originate from the Isle of Skye, and at one time thought to be the same breed as the Cairn Terrier. Its magnificent coat requires regular grooming.

Origin Great Britain.
Height 9-10 in (24-25 cm).
Weight 25 lb (11 kg).
Coat Long hard straight, flat and free from curl, with **close** woolly undercoat.
Color Black, dark or light gray, fawn.
Longevity 13 years.
Character Suspicious of people

MANCHESTER TERRIER

Once known as the Black and Tan Terrier, the Manchester Terriers have been long established as sporting terriers. The introduction of other blood such as the Doberman and the Italian Grayhound account for its smooth coat and slightly arched back.

Origin Great Britain.
Height 15-16 in (38-40 cm).
Weight 12-22 lb (5-10 kg).
Coat Close, smooth, short and glossy.
Color Jet black and rich tan.
Longevity 13-14 years.
Character A one person animal.

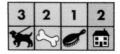

DANDI DINMONT TERRIER

Believed to be a relative of the Skye Terrier, they were originally bred to hunt badgers and foxes. Believed to be named after a character in a Walter Scott novel, as the author kept these dogs himself. Enjoys exercise and is good with children.

Origin Great Britain.
Height 8-11 in (20-27 cm).
Weight 18-24 lb (8-11 kg).
Coat Soft, linty undercoat.
Color Pepper or mustard
Longevity 13-14 years.
Character Enjoys being sole family pet.

SEALYHAM TERRIER

The breed has been traced back to the 15th century and were used to dig badgers and hunt with hounds. The name comes from the village of Sealyham in Wales where they were bred.

Origin Great Britain.
Height 12 in (31 cm).
Weight 18-20 lb (8-9 kg).
Coat Long, hard and wiry.
Color White with lemon, brown, blue markings.
Longevity 14 years.
Character A fine show dog and family pet.

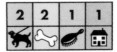

MALTESE

A member of the Bichon family, the Maltese is one of the oldest European breeds of lap dog. They have been painted by many famous artists such as Goya and Rubens. They are a long lived little dog and require daily grooming.

Origin Great Britain.
Height 10 in (25.5 cm).
Weight 4-7 lb (2-3 kg).
Coat Long, straight silky coat.
Color White with lemon markings.
Longevity 14- 15 years.
Character Happy, lovable, adaptable.

BRUSSELS GRIFFON (and PETIT BRABANCON)

Bred to kill vermin in stables, the rough coated Brussels Griffon became a companion dog because of its appealing character. The Petit Brabancon is believed to have had Pug, Yorkshire and Irish Terrier blood introduced into the breed which has produced a smooth coat.

Origin Belgium.
Height 7-8 in (18-20 cm) .
Weight 5-10 lb (2-5 kg).
Coat Brussels Griffon. Harsh and wiry. Petit Brabancon. Soft and smooth.
Color Red, black or black and rich tan with white markings.
Longevity 12-14 years.
Character Intelligent, cheerful.

YORKSHIRE TERRIER

Developed through a crossing of the Skye and extinct Black and Tan Terriers. The 'Yorkie' is now one of the most popular toy breeds in the world. They are suited to town or country living and are utterly fearless. They are first class show dogs for those with time for intricate grooming.

Origin Great Britain.
Height 9 in (22 cm).
Weight 7 lb (3 kg).
Coat Glossy, fine and silky.
Color Dark steel blue with rich tan.
Longevity 14 years.
Character Affectionate, bossy, lively.

PUG

It is believed to have originated in China and may be a relative of the Tibetan Mastiff. The Pug was introduced into Holland from trading ships and subsequently brought into Britain by William of Orange. They are sturdy dogs despite their small size.

Origin China.
Height 10-12 in (25-27 cm).
Weight 14-18 lb (6-8 kg).
Coat Fine, smooth, short, glossy.
Color Silver, apricot, fawn or black.
Longevity 13-15 years.
Character Intelligent, happy.

PAPILLON

The Papillon is named after the French for butterfly and comes from the breed's erect ears. It is also known as the Continental Toy Spaniel and is often mistaken for the Long-coated Chihuahua, a variety it helped to produce.

Origin Spain.
Height 8-11 in (20-28 cm).
Weight 9-10 lb (4-4.5 kg).
Coat Long, abundant, silky.
Color White with patches of any color except liver.
Longevity 13-15 years.
Character Intelligent, obedient.

POMERANIAN

A member of the Spitz family, the Pomeranian originates from White Spitz, in Pomerania, Northern Germany, which were much larger dogs. They were bred down after being introduced to Britain about 100 years ago.

Origin Germany.
Height 11 in (27.5 cm).
Weight 3-7 lb (1-3 kg).
Coat Long, straight and harsh.
Color All colors permissible.
Longevity 15 years.
Character Robust, lively, affectionate.

PEKINGESE

Believed to be a relative of the Lhasa Apso and the Shih Tzu, the Pekingese were kept in their thousands in privileged circumstances by the Chinese Imperial court. Five of these dogs were brought to Britain following the Boxer Rebellion in 1860.

Origin China.
Height 6-9 in (15-23 cm).
Weight 11-12 lb (5-5.5 kg).
Coat Long, straight, coarse, profuse.
Color All colors permissible.
Longevity 15 years.
Character Dignified, intelligent, fearless.

CHIHUAHUA

The Chihuahua is the smallest dog in the world, and derives its name from the state of Chihuahua, in Mexico. There are two varieties, the Long-coated (pictured) and Smooth-coated. The practice of interbreeding is no longer allowed.

Origin Mexico.
Height 6-8 in (16-20 cm).
Weight Up to 6 lb (3 kg).
Coat Long coat. Long, soft.
Smooth coat. Short, dense soft.
Color All colors permissible.
Longevity 12-14 years.
Character Intelligent, affectionate, possessive.

ENGLISH TOY TERRIER

Bred from the Manchester Terrier with blood from the Italian Grayhound and possibly the Whippet, the English Toy terrier has gone through several name changes. They too are excellent ratters like the Manchester Terrier.

Origin Great Britain.
Height 10-12 in (25-30 cm).
Weight 6-9 lb (2-4 kg).
Coat Thick, close and glossy.
Color Black and tan.
Longevity 12-13 years.
Character Intelligent, affectionate, one person dog.

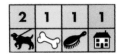

KING CHARLES SPANIEL

Smaller than the Cavalier King Charles, the King Charles Spaniel became popular when the fashion for short nosed dogs came about. There is still a law prevalent in England which enables a King Charles Spaniel "to go anywhere".

Origin Japan.
Height 10 in (25 cm).
Weight 8-14 lb (3-7 kg).
Coat Long, silky straight coat.
Color Black and tan, ruby, Blenheim, tricolor.
Longevity 12 years.
Character Full of fun, delightful pet, adaptable.

ITALIAN GRAYHOUND

An obvious descendant of the Grayhound, the little Italian has been around for a very long time. It is a house-loving family pet which enjoys plenty of exercise. It feels the cold and always needs a coat in chill weather.

Origin Italy.
Height 12-15 in (32-38 cm).
Weight 5-10 lb (2-5 kg).
Coat Short, fine and glossy.
Color Solid black, blue, cream, fawn, red or white.
Longevity 13-14 years.
Character Delightful, affectionate, sensitive.

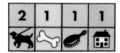

MINIATURE PINSCHER

The 'Min Pin' is a delightful high stepping natural showman and a joy to watch. It is descended from the German Pinscher with Italian Grayhound. However, this dog has got a mind of its own and is inclined to yap if unchecked.

Origin Germany.
Height 10-12 in (25-30 cm) .
Weight 10 lb (4.5 kg).
Coat Hard, smooth, short coat.
Color Black, blue or chocolate with tan.
Longevity 13-14 years.
Character Fearless, self possessed, intelligent.

TIBETAN SPANIEL

Despite its name, this breed is not related to the spaniels and is not known to have been used as a hunting companion or gundog. The origin of the Tibetan Spaniel is obscure. The first Tibetan Spaniel was recorded in the UK in 1905, but it seems to have been the late 1940s before the breed made any impact there.

Origin China
Height 10 in (25 cm).
Weight 10 lb (4.5 kg).
Coat Moderately long and silky in texture.
Color All solid colors and mixtures.
Longevity 12 to 15 years.
Character Charming, independent, self confident, energetic, intelligent and good with children.

CAVALIER KING CHARLES SPANIEL

A larger toy breed, the Cavalier is immensely popular because of its good temperament and attractive appearance. It is a faithful, loving companion, reliable with children, and draws enormous entries in dog show classes.

Origin Great Britain.
Height 10 in (25 cm).
Weight 12-18 lb (5-8 kg).
Coat Long and silky, free from curl.
Color Black and tan, ruby, Blenheim, tricolor.
Longevity 10 to 11 years.
Character Sporting, affectionate and fearless. Ideal pet, good with children.

GLOSSARY

Apple-headed The high, domed shape of the skull, notably associated with Chihuahuas.

Apron The longer hair which forms a frill at the base of the neck in certain breeds such as Rough Collies.

Bat ears Broad ears, with rounded appearance like those of a bat. A feature of the French Bulldog.

Beard Thick, long hair on the lower jaw of dogs such as the Brussels Griffon.

Benched The term used to describe a show dog in its official resting area.

Bite The relative positions of the upper and lower jaws when the mouth is closed.

Blaze Thin white stripe on the forehead, typically dividing the eyes.

Bloom The gloss on the coat of a healthy dog.

Blue merle A mix of blue and gray hairs in a black coat, resembling marble in overall color.

Bobtail A dog typically lacking a tail. Associated with the Old English Sheepdog.

Bone The appearance of the legs. A well-boned dog has a sound and powerful gait.

Bossy Excessively muscular shoulders, typically associated with the French Bulldog.

Brindle A coat with dark and light hairs, such as black and brown.

Brisket The underpart of the chest beneath the forelegs.

Broken Irregular patterning.

Brood bitch Breeding female.

Brush Thick tail, resembling that of a fox.

Burr Inner part of the ear.

Butterfly nose Blackish nose, with pinkish areas.

Button ears Vertical ears that fall forward at their tips.

Canid Belonging to the genus Canis. Includes domestic dogs.

Canines Sharp and long teeth situated at the corners of both jaws.

Castration neutering of a male dog.

China eye A clear blue eye.

Check chain A chain which when fitted correctly should assist with training, discouraging the dog from pulling ahead or lagging behind when walking on a leash (also referred to as a choke chain).

Chops The folds of skin or jowls on the upper jaw, which are especially pronounced in some breeds, such as the Bulldog.

Clip The trimming of the coat, especially significant in poodles.

Coarse A dog with poor show potential.

Cobby Short and thick-set appearance.

Collar A means of controlling a dog, or, white markings also around the neck.

Couplings The part of the body extending from the last rib to the hip on each side, which can be variable in length.

Coursing The hunting of game by sight hounds. Can be organized as hare coursing.

Crank tail Low carriage of the tail.

Crest The highest part of the neck. Also specifically, the area of hair present on the head of a Chinese Crested Dog.

Cropping A surgical procedure which keeps the ears erect in dogs such as Boxers. It is said to create a more fearsome appearance but is outlawed in many areas.

Cross-bred Essentially a first-generation cross, between two pure, yet different breeds.

Croup The rear end of the body.

Crown The highest point of the skull.

Cryptorchidism Absence of one or both testicles from the scrotal sac, being described as unilateral or bilateral respectively.

Culotte The longer hair on the back of thighs of breeds such as the Pomeranian.

Cur Mongrel.

Cushion A thickening of the upper lips, seen in breeds such as Bulldogs.

Dam Female parent.

Dapple Mottling No single dominant color in the coat.

Dew claw Vestigial digits terminating in claws, found on the inside of the legs, slightly off the ground. Often removed by surgery to prevent injury.

Dewlap Pendulous skin beneath the throat.

Dock Remove all or part of a young puppy's tail. Dog Notably the male.

Drop ears Pendulous ears which lay close to the head.

Ectropion Eyelids directed abnormally away from the eye.

Entropion Eyelids directed abnormally inwards towards the eye.

Expression The facial appearance.

Eye teeth Canines in the upper jaw.

Fall Hair obscuring the facial features.

Feathering The fine long areas of hair, at the back of the legs and ears, especially apparent in Setters.

Flag A long tail or flowing hair around the tail. Flanks Sides of the body from the end of the ribs to the hips.

Flews Pendulous top lips.

Furrow Area Runs from the centre of the skull to the top of the nose.

Grizzled Bluish-gray coloration.

Guard hairs Longer hairs hiding a shorter undercoat.

Gun-barrel front Very straight forelegs.

Hackles The hairs on the neck and back that are raised when the dog is under threat.

Hard-mouthed A Retriever which marks game with its teeth.

Harlequin Dark patches, normally blue or` black, offset against white areas, typically associated with the Great Dane.

Harsh coat Wiry, or possibly in poor condition.

Heat The bitch's period of reproductive activity.

Hocks Heel joints, between stifle and pastern joints.

Inbreeding The mating of very closely-related stock, such as sire to daughter.

Incisors The teeth between the canines at the front of the mouth.

Jowls The pronounced fleshy area of the lips associated with some breeds such as the Bulldog.

Kiss marks Small spotted areas on the face, usually brownish in color.

Leathers The ear flaps.

Line-breeding Mating of more distantly-related stock than is seen with inbreeding.

Litter The puppies born in a single whelping. Liver Dark reddish-brown.

Milk teeth The first, decidious set of teeth.

Muzzle The area below the eyes on the face. Also a means of restraining a dog so that it cannot bite.

Occiput The rear high point of the skull.

Outcross The use of a totally unrelated dog or bitch for breeding purposes within a stud.

Overshot Protruding upper jaw, causing upper incisors to extend past the lower ones.

Pads Tough yet vascular areas on the feet which are devoid of hair.

Particolored Two colors with even distribution in the coat.

Pastern Foreleg extending between the carpus and digits.

Pedigree The ancestry of a pure bred dog over several generations.

Points The color on the extremities of the body.

Prefix The kennel name which precedes the dog's individual name for the purpose of its official pedigreed name.

Premolars Teeth between the molars and canines.

Pricked ears Carried erect, but can show pointed tips.

Roached back A curved back, as seen in the Whippet.

Roan White and colored hairs mixed together, as is seen in Cocker Spaniels.

Rose ear A small ear which is folded to reveal the inner surface or burr.

Ruff The characteristic area of long hair around the neck of the Chow.

Sable Typically gold mixed with dark black hair, as in the Shetland Sheepdog.

Saddle Black marking extending over the back. Screw tail Short and twisted tail.

Season The active reproductive phase of the bitch's cycle.

Self-colored Single-colored.

Spay Surgical neutering of a bitch.

Splay foot Toes kept wide apart.

Standard The features of the various breeds, as laid down by the governing authority concerned.

Staring coat A sign of poor condition.

Stern Tail of a hound or other sporting dog.

Stifle Hindlimb joint between upper and lower thighs.

Stop The slight indentation where the nasal bones fuse with the skull.

Top knot The tuft of hair at the top of the skull.

Tricolor Three colors, normally black, tan and white in approximately equal proportions on the coat.

Tuckup Sharp curvature in the stomach region, associated with Grayhounds and similar broad-chested breeds.

Undershot Lower jaw and incisor teeth protrude past the upper when the jaws are closed.

Wall eye Iris is whitish or bluish in coloration. Only one eye may be affected.

Whelping Giving birth.

Wire-haired Rough-coated.

Withers Highest point of the shoulders, from where the dog's height is measured.

INDEX